MARESSA MORTIMER

Downstream

First published by Good Hope Publishing 2024

Copyright © 2024 by Maressa Mortimer

All rights reserved. No part of this publication may be reproduced, stored or transmitted in any form or by any means, electronic, mechanical, photocopying, recording, scanning, or otherwise without written permission from the publisher. It is illegal to copy this book, post it to a website, or distribute it by any other means without permission.

This novel is entirely a work of fiction. The names, characters and incidents portrayed in it are the work of the author's imagination. Any resemblance to actual persons, living or dead, events or localities is entirely coincidental.

I used the KJV for Bible quotes, paraphrasing where fitting verses into conversation.

First edition

ISBN: 978-1-8383134-9-4

This book was professionally typeset on Reedsy. Find out more at reedsy.com

Can a woman forget her sucking child, that she should not have compassion on the son of her womb? yea, they may forget, yet will I not forget thee. Behold, I have graven thee upon the palms of my hands; thy walls are continually before me.

Isaiah 49: 15-16

Main characters and places

Main characters
 Gax *(with guttural G as in Loch)*
 Macia *(Mat-sia)*
 Caecilia
 Riu *(Ree-you) friend in Colchuyni*
 Amara *Macia's mother*
 Brutus *Macia's father*
 Halit *Macia's brother*
 Felix *General Manager of Downstream*

Main places:
 Mataiox *(Ma-ta-yoks) City where Gax and the girls are living after escaping Elabi (See Walled City and Beyond the Hills)*
 Aniquist *Large town from where to cross to Colchuyni, miles from Mataiox*
 Colchuyni *Hillside village on the edge of the jungle*

Groups in the jungle:
 Levato *Riu's group*
 Scitabi *Group of mainly young people from the jungle village*
 Elutera *Group hiding in the jungle causing trouble*

Chapter 1

"Radio chatter? What do you mean by that? And you are prepared to change your life again?" Gax's mum looks at Macia and Macia can feel her face warming up.

Caecilia swallows and stirs her potatoes around her plate in small circles. She had expected as much from Gax's parents.

Macia lays down her fork, "Linu from Gax's Mission School picked up radio chatter. You know, when you're on a frequency and you can hear voices." She swallows and looks at Gax, "Gax said Linu told him it sounded like the Elabi lilting voices. It might not lead to anything, I was simply saying that the news shocked me."

That's an understatement and makes Caecilia snort. "It did shock me, as well," and she smiles at Gax, "but we have to trust that all things will work for our good, even this news. Gax," Caecilia swallows, her face warm as she glances at his mother, "Gax told us and it brought back a lot of memories."

Feelings too, but she doesn't want to say that. She glances at Gax, takes a deep breath and looks at his mother. "We're on kitchen duty tomorrow morning, and this gravy is wonderful. Is it hard to make?" She points at her plate with her fork, "The food at the shelter can be dry and having gravy will make it taste and look better."

Gax's mother sighs, opens her mouth, then nods. "It is easy to make, you get it from a tub," she says. "You add hot water, and that's your gravy, although I add some of the juices from the meat as well to make it richer."

After the meal, the girls lean back in Gax's parents' lounge chairs, the tension still with them. They don't want to appear in a rush, and spending time with Gax is precious. "We will have to go soon," Caecilia says in the end and Macia nods, unusually quiet. "Kitchen duty is early and I have some reading to do."

Macia grins, and Caecilia elbows her. "Not just the book I borrowed," she says, "one of my assignments for my course is due soon."

Gax's father nods, "You girls have worked hard, and you have come a long way. Not just in distance, but from where you started when you left Elabi all those months ago." He looks at Macia especially, "Your arm has healed well and Gax says you might have a space on the course you wanted, to train others?"

Macia nods and smiles, "Yes, the course will be just right, and I have already started helping the coaches at the shelter to get more experience."

She hides her hands behind her back, making tight fists, as she knows what Gax's father is driving at. And Gax talked about her to his parents? The warmth on her face is nothing to do with his father's stern look this time. "I'm grateful for those that have helped us, and like we said," she ignores Caecilia's small noise, "nothing has changed. It's just something Linu mentioned, that's all. I only mentioned it for your prayers, as you know where we have come from and have been so good to us." She manages to make her smile warm.

Gax opens the door of his old car. Macia smiles at him, and looks away as Caecilia gets in after her. "Thank you Gax, it is kind of you to drop us at the house," Caecilia gushes. "It's been lovely to spend time with your parents; your mum is a wonderful cook. I'm always glad when it's her turn to help at the Meeting House dinners."

Gax smiles in the rearview mirror at Caecilia. "Me too," he rolls his

CHAPTER 1

eyes, "some months the dinners can be hard work."

Macia laughs, "Last time it was great. I needed to spend an hour extra in the gym every day to make up for it," she smiles at Caecilia, then looks out of the window, watching the houses fly past. The car drive still amazes her, even after being in Mataiox for months. She swallows as she looks at Gax. "It's been great living in Mataiox, so different from what I expected. It means a lot to have you and your parents supporting us. I hope I didn't upset anyone."

"Maybe we need to speak to Linu first," Caecilia says, not looking at the two others. "It's better to know more about it, as it feels too… too emotional. I still don't understand exactly what she meant with radio chatter and why she feels it's to do with Elabi."

Gax doesn't say much until they arrive at the terraced house where Macia and Caecilia have a room each, sharing the house with two other girls. "I will ask Linu if she knows more and maybe we can see her? I don't know if there is anything that you can do about it. I thought it was more to let you know…" His voice trails off as he realises he doesn't know what his thoughts had been. Should he have kept Linu's information to himself? His mother will be asking a lot of questions once he gets back. He sighs, but grins at the girls. "I will let you know as soon as I can," and he gives a cheery wave from his car as he pulls away from the curb, then releases a noisy breath.

"Why would you even think about it? Looking back at where you came from? Who would want to go back to that?" Sonja rolls her eyes and shares a laugh with Greta, the other girl. Then she sobers up again, "Look, you've both changed a lot since we met you and you moved into the house. You're still, well, not like others, but that's probably to do with the Book you're reading a lot. But look at the difference to where you came from, you know," she waves her hand, the glitter on her fingernails catching the sunshine, "that place along the river, wasn't it? From what you mentioned, it wasn't great and they didn't particularly want you there either." Sonja and Greta laugh again.

Macia swallows, "We left Elabi, but we still have family there," she hopes, "and this friend says she heard voices on the radio. I think it was to do with different wavelengths?" Greta nods but Sonja shrugs, and Macia continues, "Nothing might come of it, but that's what Caecilia and I were talking about."

Sonja smiles as Caecilia changes the subject by complimenting her bright coloured nails. "I love these. And it's why I get Greta or you girls to clean the kitchen," Sonja laughs, and Caecilia chuckles, as it's true. "As we're handing out compliments, I like your shoes," she points at Caecilia's new shoes. "I don't think they'll be good for long walks, so don't go back to wherever it was along the river," and she laughs with Greta, before waving at the girls, "I better go. We're off to watch something with friends."

The house feels silent as the two girls leave and Macia releases her breath. "They're friendly," she says, making it sound like a question, "but they never ask us to do something with them and they're always commenting on our past." She glances towards the kitchen, clean, thanks to Caecilia's effort earlier.

Caecilia nods. "Greta is quieter, but I like Sonja more." She looks at her shoes and smiles a little. "Glad she actually liked my shoes. It must be the first time ever she has liked anything we were wearing." Sadly, Gax hasn't noticed the new shoes.

Life has changed for the girls. What they wear, read, say, and do is a world apart from the controlled society of Elabi. Macia rubs her arm, "My arm says it's going to be wet later," she grins, sure that the healed break can predict the weather. "I better go for a run now, before we have to help in the shelter." She smooths out one of her nails, and continues slowly, "I hope Gax will know more soon." She swallows, "It's made me struggle to sleep at night, and I have had to write my imaginary diary again," she laughs as she gets up to get ready for her

CHAPTER 1

run.

Caecilia goes up to her room, not wanting to stay in the shared lounge by herself. She lowers herself on her bed, thinking. "Dearest friend," she whispers, thinking of Macia and her diary, "maybe I should have a dearest friend as well, as my head is spinning. I wanted to forget Elabi, but it's there and my parents and my family," she wipes tears away that have suddenly splashed on her cheeks. She can't remember ever crying in Elabi, but since arriving in Mataiox nearly a year ago, she has changed. Even Macia, who has not even been a year, has changed. "Anyway, dearest friend," Caecilia forces her mind back to the diary in her head, "I am confused. I would love to leave it all behind, but the mention of Elabi has stirred something in me. I should pray about it, but I don't know how to, as I can't work out what I want."

Working in the Shelter is a good diversion, both girls agree. The Shelter provides sleeping spaces and meals for homeless people. "That's the sad side of Mataiox," Caecilia says to Macia as they're stirring large pots and pans, filled with wholesome food. "It's free, or less controlled, but it comes with many problems. Sometimes I wonder if the freedom is worth it for many people, until we're back at the Meeting House, then I am glad!"

"I like the freedom," Macia says, "freedom to wear what you want," and she looks down at her new jeans, and grins at Caecilia, "Well, I like them," she says, lifting her chin, "They are comfortable and everyone wears them." Caecilia shrugs but Macia carries on, "And there are other freedoms I like. It might come at a price, but in Elabi, there is a price too. Think of Downstream, and beyond the hills. Here, people can change, like some of the people visiting the Shelter. They might visit the Shelter for a while, but some of them do get back on their feet." She stirs a little slower, "Maybe not many, and definitely not all, but there is a way back from their struggles. People are around to help the homeless people. Downstream is final and the hills are often final."

Gax is waiting for the girls as they finish cleaning up the kitchen. The Shelter is quiet now, leftover food is boxed up and put away, and most of the staff has gone home. Gax watches the girls, and as Caecilia smiles at him, he says, "I talked to Linu today, after my morning Ethics class." Both girls stop what they're doing and Gax shrugs. "There isn't much more I can tell you, but maybe we could go for a quick walk along the beach?"

Macia is glad of her new jeans when they get out of Gax's car. The wind is sharp and she tugs her coat tighter. Caecilia shivers, but keeps her smile in place. She clutches her new handbag, hoping Gax will notice. It's similar to the bag his sister has. Gax smiles at her, causing a warm glow inside her and the three walk onto the soft sand, Gax in the middle.

Macia is the first to break the uneasy silence by taking a deep breath through her nose. "I love the smell of the sea," she says, "it reminds me of my paddleboarding lessons." Her mind wanders back, thinking of the woman who helped her and even provided the board that brought her to freedom. It always fills her heart with gratitude as well as worry for the woman's safety.

Caecilia nods, "It reminds me of my father's lighthouse," she says softly, hugging her large bag a little tighter, forcing her voice to stay light.

Gax smiles at her. "That lighthouse is special," he grins, "it was the first thing I saw, getting into Elabi, and in a way the last thing as well." He looks away. "Linu says the chatter isn't from Elabi itself." The girls nod, as Gax had shared that part already. "She tried to get more information, and says the main word she managed to unscramble was," he hesitates, "...was Requipacem."

Both girls gasp and Caecilia takes a step away from Gax whilst Macia stares out over sea. Requipacem. The word indicating the

CHAPTER 1

ending of someone's life in Elabi. Macia keeps her back towards Gax, but manages to ask, "Why would that be part of a radio conversation?"

Gax looks at his shoes, not wanting to look at the girls. "Linu thinks the chatter isn't from Elabi or from beyond the hills. She isn't sure where exactly it is from, although she has managed to narrow it down. We think… we think it might be from Downstream."

Macia spins round, opens her mouth, closes it and turns back to watch the gentle waves hugging the yellow sand, leaving darker lines. She doesn't move as Caecilia asks, "Does she know whereabouts Downstream is in that case? And would it matter at all?"

Macia spins round at that. "I agree. What difference would it make? People go Downstream for Requipacem, I'm sure. There is nothing down there. There can't be anything." She chews her nail, "There has never been anyone returning, otherwise, if they could they would. She would." She gives a small gasp as the last couple of words escape her mouth. She blinks, sniffs then continues, her voice no longer fierce. "She would have returned for us, if there was a way back. Once my little brother had gone, she would have returned, I'm sure."

Caecilia touches Macia's arm with her fingertips. "She wouldn't have been received well, and she would have known that. Maybe she could have found a way back, but it wouldn't have been worth it. Your father wouldn't have received her back with open arms, would he? And the city leaders wouldn't have accepted her back either, as every parent of sick and imperfect children would have followed her example."

Macia gives a small sob and whispers, "What if she stayed there then? What if she is alive and living Downstream? Maybe she is still there."

Chapter 2

The only noise heard is the water touching the sand and Gax hesitates to break the silence. "We know nothing of what Downstream looks like," he says softly. "Linu says there is no direct access, and it will be hard to reach it. I wanted you to know what Linu had found."

Caecilia nods and tightening her hand around her bag strap says, "We'll just have to pray about it," and Macia manages to cover the snort into a cough and a shiver.

"I'm cold," she says, looking at Gax, "and Caecilia is right. We will need time to think and maybe talk to Linu? I would love to see what she says about it." She turns back towards the car. "Thank you for letting us know," she manages to make her mouth smile at Gax and he grins back.

"Thanks for bringing us to the beach, Gax," Caecilia says, although her teeth are chattering, "It's good to be outside after the hot Shelter kitchen and its smells of burnt oil," her voice a little too loud and high pitched, making her face warm up. She avoids looking at Macia, wishing they were home already.

Gax's beaten up car feels warmer than they thought possible. "I can't wait for Spring," Gax says as he cranks up the heat as far as it will go. "When even my car feels warm, it's not good news!" He waves a free hand around the frosty car park, "It does make parking near

CHAPTER 2

the beach easier though," and Caecilia laughs a little too much. Macia stays quiet, licking a speck of blood where she has bitten her nail.

"Dearest friend," Caecilia mutters that evening, staring at the ceiling, hardly visible in her dark room. "Dearest friend, I need help for my other friend. I haven't seen Macia this quiet for a long time, not even when she first arrived and was so ill. We have been welcomed here and we have so many good things going on. Our help at the Shelter is needed and people at the Meeting House have been helpful to us, and there are our courses and plans... There's Gax." She swallows tears that blur her vision. "We have lost so much already, and we have been through too much. There is nothing we can do to change the Downstream facility. Why would we travel there, risking everything? But Macia..." She hesitates. She can't lie to her inward diary, can she? Macia hasn't said anything about Gax's news and Caecilia has no idea what her friend is thinking. "Anyway," she whispers, "I just hope and pray Macia will recover from this without too much damage."

Would she want to go Downstream if her mother had left like Macia's? Caecilia's grandparents went Downstream, but they were both old and struggling. She is well aware that they won't be alive anymore. She doesn't know anyone that went Downstream whilst still able to contribute to society. It's different for Macia. What would she do in her friend's circumstances? She sighs, "What could happen? Even if she got there and saw the mother, would her mother want to leave with Macia?"

Sonja harps on in the same vein the next day. "What will you do when you get there? If you ever get there? You said you'd just been accepted onto the course that you wanted? What will you say to them?"

Macia shrugs, "I know. Nothing is decided, and I don't know enough. But wouldn't you want to find your mother?"

"Only if she gave me money for hair implants," says Sonja and with

Greta she shrieks with laughter. After a while she says, "I know what you mean, but I wouldn't give anything up for my mother. I wouldn't mind travelling or anything, but not if it meant missing out on opportunities myself. I don't think my mother would want me too, either. Once I turned eighteen, she expected me to make my own way, and she supports me. I love my mother, but I wouldn't stop life for her. Or anyone else, for that matter. Where even is this place?"

"We don't know yet," Caecilia says, pulling her mouth in a smile. She can see Macia's face and she quickly adds, "We should hear soon, and that will help. It's hard, because we left so many people behind. There isn't really a way back, but we're praying for the right decision." She keeps the smile in place even as she can see Sonja and Greta looking at each other.

"Well, I'm sure your God will build a special path for you," Greta giggles, and Sonja snorts, but doesn't say anything. "Not my idea of a good life, but it seems to work for some. Personally, I think love is overrated, whether it's from parents or some spiritual being, I think it's loving yourself that makes for the best life. It's the kind of love that can be easily adjusted as well. Like loving yourself with chocolate or loving yourself with the gym, it's all love. Or just loving yourself with going places, rather than wait for others to shower the right kind of love on you." She takes a deep breath, and looks at her expensive watch. "We better go," she says to Sonja, "we need to love ourselves with that shopping trip," she laughs, and leaves the room.

Sonja looks at the girls, "I haven't heard that many words from Greta for a while," she shrugs, "but she has a point. Love yourself, rather than try to buy your mother's love or even your God's love by doing all the right things." She follows Greta out, leaving Macia and Caecilia in silence.

"I'm going for a run," Macia says, her voice strained as she gets up quickly.

CHAPTER 2

Caecilia leans back, the comfortable sofa feeling safe and welcoming. "Dearest friend," she breathes once the room is empty, "I don't know what to say to Macia. I don't agree with the other girls, but to go back? So many people need help in this place and the people coming to the Meeting House seem so few. Your love has given us hard days already, wasn't that enough? Shouldn't living in your love mean good days now, sharing that love?"

Linu smiles at them as they join her in her large office at the Mission School. Macia is grateful for her two friends, protesting that she didn't mind going by herself, but glad when Caecilia assured her she'd never let her do something like that by herself. Gax nods towards Linu's desk. "Is that the map?"

Linu points at the large map spread out on her desk. "This is where the chatter was from," she says. "As you can see, there isn't much filled in that way. Maps are still limited, although our government is working on it.We're relying on some old maps that say there's a river or estuary. Elabi is there," and they follow her hand waving towards another part of the map. "The Hills are there, and the chatter didn't come from either of those two areas. We are sure it came from there," and they're back staring at the first place.

"Can you get there at all?" Macia asks, her voice higher than usual. She peers at the map, her eyes exploring all around the area, noticing the nearby coast.

Linu nods, "Yes and no. It's a hard area to reach. There isn't a safe way to get to Downstream head on, using the river, provided you could find the entrance. You would have to get past Elabi, and we don't know what else is along the river or how far it is." She shrugs at their faces, "There is a way, I think, but you would have to come from this side," and she points behind where DS is marked on the map in pencil. She taps the map, "This area is jungle, and we don't know how safe it is to cross. At the other side of the jungle, there is a small village.

A very closed community, as they can only be reached once a year."

Macia frowns and points at the water beyond the village, but Linu shakes her head. "We once looked at it as a Mission School, but it didn't work out, as you would have to commit for a longer time. A year to be exact. No boats are allowed, not even a coracle," she grins at Gax, referring to his mode of transport in and out of Elabi. "Once a year, the water becomes a mudflat that can be crossed if you're with a guide. It's a long walk. You have to wait till the following year before you can go back. We don't know much about the village. They're mostly self-sufficient, farming on the hillside, that kind of thing."

They all stare at the map in silence, thoughts spinning. "Look, we don't know about your mother," Linu says, her voice soft. "There isn't very much chance you will find her, but I still wanted you to know. Like I said, it's not impossible to get there, just very hard. You will need to book the guide, and you need to stay in the village for a year. I have no idea about crossing the jungle, or what you would find the other side. You will need to think and pray about it."

Macia nods, looking at the map, her fingers tracing the jungle, the water, the pencilled in DS. Will her mother be there? Will her mother even want to see her? The old photograph, hidden in her bedroom in Elabi comes to mind. Her mother's sweet face, and she remembers the moments with her, all those years ago, and the anguish when she left, all the emotions that had to be tamed, and dealt with. Surely her mother would have felt the same, even if she had to go with her sick little boy?

She looks up, avoiding her friends, "What is the town called?"

Linu points at the map, "The one where you need to get a guide? Aniquist. It's not a large town, but it's a good place to start. You would need some time there, as it's very high, and your body needs to acclimatise. They will also sell seeds and necessities to take with you to the village. The village is called Colchuyni."

CHAPTER 2

Macia nods, although the words hardly register. Her heart is beating wildly, as she tries to weigh up options, plans, ideas. Linu's voice breaks through eventually. "You will need to think about it," she smiles at Macia. "Check what you need, what options you have for your room here and your residential status, and whether it's worth trying. You could wait a few years…" She sighs, "We might hear more, or there might be new students at the Mission School or something might change. As I said, nothing is known about the area, and we wouldn't be able to help you if something happened."

Macia is glad to leave the building, and breathes deeply from the cold air. She tries to smile as Gax ask if she's alright. "It's great to see it on the map," he enthuses, "and I'm sure Linu will try to find out more as well."

Macia swallows and forces her voice to sound even, "I wonder when the Mission School thought about sending students. Mind you, there isn't just the village to reach, there's also Downstream. Maybe they will reconsider this time?"

She glances over her shoulder at Caecilia, who looks up, "It's a lot to take in," Caecilia says softly. "It made me think of my grandparents. I wonder what it's like Downstream. It looks so isolated, even more than Elabi."

Macia nods. Would a year be long enough to get through the jungle and to her mother, back through the jungle, ready to cross the mudflat again? And what if her mother is thrilled to have her again, and won't leave her? Will she come with Macia to Mataiox? Her thoughts drift off, and she is hardly aware of Gax holding the door of his car. They ride home in silence.

Caecilia glances at Gax and back at Macia, her heart beating too fast. She frowns, watching the houses glide past. She swallows. Will Macia give all this up to go Downstream? She hides her shaking hands in the folds of her woollen skirt, and turns to Gax. "I'm glad your parents asked us for another meal tomorrow between meetings," she smiles, "it makes the day even better when spent with others."

Gax smiles back, after a quick glance in the rearview mirror. Caecilia notices his look, and chews her lip.

When they get to the girls' house, Gax opens the car doors for them. "I will have to get the handles fixed one day," he laughs, and looks at Macia. "I will ask at the Mission School," he says softly, "you might be right about sending students, knowing there are more people."

Macia nods, and looking over Gax's shoulder at Caecilia opening their front door says softly, "People at the end of their lives might be more open to the Message of the Book." She avoids his eyes as she adds, "There might be some who will remember, like the woman at the fountain you told us about. It could be a good opportunity for… for someone able to understand their Elabi mindset."

She smiles, thanks him for the lift and quickly follows Caecilia before Gax can notice her face warming up. The thought of getting to Aniquist, then the village for a year by herself fills her with dread. If only Gax would come along…

It takes Macia several days to get the information she needs. "I will be able to keep my residential status in certain circumstances," she tells Gax as they walk along the beach again. Caecilia walks a little ahead, as Macia stops to show Gax a special shell. "And the landlord says I can keep my room, just put my things in storage for a year, as he often has short term lets. My sports course says they will let me start the following year as well, so I could go if I wanted to."

Together, they look across the sea, smooth and cold. "It sounds like it's not impossible, but still a large commitment," Gax says softly.

"I know," Macia says, "but it also means there is an opportunity to reach those people of Colchuyni as well as the Elabi people Downstream. I know the Message didn't reach many people in Elabi as you had to be careful, but imagine what the opportunities Downstream

CHAPTER 2

could be? There won't be that many guards as it's smaller, and they might not care anyway, as people are about to die. It could be what you prayed for in Elabi, but maybe it was meant for Downstream." She makes sure to keep her voice down, and her eyes averted. She didn't want to tell Gax that the only way to keep her residential status is if she travels with a citizen from Mataiox.

Gax sighs. "I did feel I failed in Elabi," he says and smiles as Caecilia joins them. "I had such hopes when I landed, but then…" His voice trails off and he looks at Macia. "Of course, you are both here, so I haven't failed, but it can feel like that when I think of all the other people in Elabi. I like what you said," he adds softly and Macia nods.

Caecilia bites her lip as she walks on with Macia and Gax, the sand soft and difficult to walk on, but she's hardly aware. Macia seems to be considering going Downstream. She knows she's been making calls to find out about her status as well as her room, and Caecilia blinks away tears. "Dearest friend," she thinks, "I don't know what to do. What will it be like to be in Mataiox alone, without Macia in the house?"

Of course, she was alone before Macia arrived, although Gax's parents had put her up for several weeks, but that was different. She is used to being with Macia now and the thought of being alone once more brings tears to her eyes. She looks up at the dark night sky, noticing the stars, and thin moon.

And what had Macia said to Gax? She can feel her heart racing as she wonders if Macia is persuading Gax… but surely, he won't leave Mataiox again?

Chapter 3

Macia smiles softly, "It will only be for a year, then Gax and I will be back."

Caecilia swallows, fighting to keep the shock from showing. "Gax? A year? But…" So many questions flood her mind. Will the Meeting House allow it? And the Mission School? And what about Gax's parents? She knew Gax had talked about it with Macia, she had seen them talking softly together on the beach, but resentment had made her stay away each time, rather than interrupt. But the unease had been growing inside her, waking her in the middle of the night. She stifles a yawn as she hides her shock at Macia's statement, making herself look at Macia as her friend carries on.

"We might be taking one of the younger students from the Mission School with us. She's quiet, but she knows Gax. I think they went to the same school in Mataiox and have known each other for a long time." She looks away, not wanting Caecilia to know what she thinks about the arrangement. She understands why they will need to have someone with them; that doesn't mean she has to like it. The girl doesn't seem to like Macia very much, or maybe it is because Macia feels the girl is difficult?

Caecilia takes a deep breath, her mind spinning but the way ahead is clear. She has no other choice. "I have been thinking about it," she says, "and although I like it here and I love the life we have here, I

CHAPTER 3

do want to see Downstream. And I want to learn what happened to my grandparents. Also, like you said to Gax the other day," her voice wobbles a little, as she thinks of the many conversation snippets she has overheard, "about reaching people from Elabi at the end of their lives and how the Message might be able to reach them, I feel that is important too." She avoids looking at Macia, and is careful to keep Gax out of her statement.

Macia feels her face warm up. Caecilia won't have missed the conversations she's had with Gax over the last weeks. Macia sticks her chin out a little. It wasn't just to her advantage that Gax is coming along. Yes, she might have been rather persistent, but Gax has made that choice himself. Leaving Mataiox with Gax, with Caecilia staying behind would have been hard.

"And I have looked at Aniquist and Colchuyni," Caecilia says quickly, and she dashes to her room and is soon back with papers and a library book. Macia grins as Caecilia spreads the papers out on the coffee table, trying to hide her shaking hands. "I wanted to know what we would be facing," Caecilia says, "so I looked into it and made lists."

The girls both laugh and Macia leans over the papers, smiling at Caecilia's neat writing. "Yes, we will need special shoes for walking across the mudflat," she points, "and they will probably be ruined by the time we're across."

There is a knock and Macia beams at Gax as he enters the lounge. "Good timing," she says, and smiles at Caecilia.

Gax's face glows with pleasure as Caecilia tells him she will be joining them. "I'm so pleased," he says, and then pulls a face. "My parents aren't as pleased, but they do try to understand. I think there's something special about the three of us going. Better than Nora, the girl who was talking about coming along. She doesn't know Elabi."

He looks at the papers and the book about Aniquist. Soon, the three are busy planning and making more notes and lists. "We will need suitable clothing," Caecilia points out. "It's higher than Mataiox, so the nights will be cold, but days can be hot, and the sun bright. The jungle will be warm and humid, and long sleeves will give better protection."

"We will be limited in what we can carry," Gax explains, and he opens his bag, "so I bought these." He pulls out wipeable sheets. "You write on them with these pens, and then reuse them. We won't be able to carry enough paper for a year."

The girls nod, and Caecilia ticks it off on one of the many lists. "We will need seeds for vegetables," she says, "as Colchuyni is self sufficient. We might be able to buy seeds to plant, but it's better if we bring most of it with us." Her voice wobbles a little, "I hope we will find somewhere to live for the time we need to stay in the village?"

Macia frowns, "Can't we go Downstream at once? And stay near there?"

Caecilia shakes her head, sitting taller. "The jungle is dangerous for some of the year. It's passable, but unwise to do so. We will need to stay in the village for most of the year," she says, tapping the book. "We will need to think about a house to stay. I don't know if there are empty houses in the village." He frowns, "We might end up having to stay with people."

Caecilia shudders. The thought of staying with strangers for nearly a year doesn't sound inviting.

Macia nods. "We will have to pray about accommodation," she says, not looking at the others. She leans over the lists and books, not seeing Caecilia's frown.

"Of course, we need to pray about it," Caecilia says, "and you're right about trusting, like the book you let me borrow, Gax," and she smiles brightly, pushing worries away from her thoughts.

Macia frowns and fidgets, tapping the description of the jungle. "If they say it's passable…" Her voice trails off as she glances at Gax and Caecilia. Maybe she shouldn't push them right now, with the worry

CHAPTER 3

of accommodation, and leave the timing of getting through the jungle up to God as well. She can feel her face warming up. Of course, she has prayed about it and although she might have talked to Gax about it a lot, she has left it with God, hasn't she? She mumbles something about the bathroom as she quickly leaves the room. Has she trusted God with the entire trip? She chews a loose nail. God would have closed the door, surely, if He didn't want them to go? She brightens up, determined that having Gax as well as Caecilia coming along must be a sign of God's blessing.

Back in the lounge she smiles at she watches the list growing. "I am taking my course book," Caecilia says, "and the new copy of the Book Gax's parents gave us." She smiles at Gax, then looks away before he can see the tears in her eyes. They're leaving everything and everyone behind again. Just for one year, she tells herself, but can they be sure?

The next few days sees the lists grow and change. "I found a book on growing food as we might be dependent on other people," Caecilia says, and waves a second book at Macia standing in Caecilia's bedroom doorway, "and this one is about jungle vegetation. I don't know how long the trek through the jungle will be, but we might have to live off food we find."

Macia nods, stretching, ready for another run, "Don't forget to work on your shoulders," she says, smiling, to take off the edges, "Your rucksack will be heavy and the walk across the mudflat won't be easy without some training."

Caecilia waves as Macia leaves the house. She went to the gym a few days ago, and her shoulders are still aching, but she's sure she'll manage. There is still time. Now, mosquito repellent for the jungle, her utility knife, microfiber towel… she swipes at her eyes, and decides to try out the special paper.

As she writes her list, she begins to feel overwhelmed by fears. "Is it bad to feel? To feel a lot?" she wonders. She puts the pen down and tries to peel back her thoughts to find the reason or her unease. The way she feels towards Macia every time her friend mentions Gax. Then longing for the special times she and Gax shared in Elabi. Suddenly, Caecilia finds her face wet with tears, missing Elabi with all her heart, the feeling squeezing her heart tight, making it hard to breathe. She burrows her face into her pillow and sobs for all the losses of the past year. Her nighttime meetings, the lighthouse, her family, Gax's special attention…

Gax's parents aren't pleased. "I still don't know why you are going along," the girls can hear Gax's mother's voice in the kitchen, where Gax is helping her clean up after the meal. "Those girls know their people, they know enough about the Message to share it, or the Mission School could help them with that. What will you do when you get to those dying people? They won't welcome you, especially as you're an outsider. You have just returned, gotten your life back on track, and now you're throwing everything away. You've had your mission trip, like other young people. Yes, I know you feel it didn't go as well as you'd hoped. Yes, I know, Gax." The girls look at each other, wondering if they should…

Gax's voice isn't audible, but his mother is clearly disagreeing. "None of the other young people go twice. There is one trip, and it doesn't have to be as successful as the others. It's not about numbers. But here you go again. And jungles can be difficult to cross. You know hardly anything about where you're going, and it's not like Elabi where you could leave whenever you needed to. And where will you stay when you get to the village?" There's the rattling of crockery, Gax's mumbling voice, then his mother again, "Yes, of course your father and I trust God with the outcome, but that doesn't mean you have to make bad decisions. This is not your battle. I understand the girl wanting to see if she can find her mother, although…" and her voice lowers suddenly.

CHAPTER 3

Macia has heard enough. She stands up and quickly takes herself to the bathroom, eyes burning. So Gax's mother thinks it's going to be a wasted journey? Should she listen to them, trust their judgment? But what if her mother has been missing her all these years? It's worth it, just to see her mother's face one more time. But to go alone frightens her. Even with just Caecilia, it would be hard. She allows a little sob, knowing deep down that the only reason Caecilia is coming along is Gax. It's a good thing they're doing, taking the Message to Colchuyni as well as Downstream. Who knows, it might open the door to Colchuyni for more people from the Meeting House. It's not just about her and her mother; it's doing what the Mission School has been wanting to do for so long. She straightens her shoulders and walks back into the living room. And she's sure God will provide them with a place to stay.

Sonja and Greta aren't any happier, but more direct. "Why would you leave it all again? I thought people that desperate to get to Mataiox would be grateful and contribute to the society that gave them a second chance," Greta says, a frown cracking her makeup. "And how much do you know about the place you will be going? I have never heard of either of those places, but I know that going through a jungle takes preparation and isn't safe without a guide." She shudders, "Wanting to change people there as well? It's what those at Meeting Houses try to do. Change a culture and the way people live, rather than accept people the way they are."

Sonja adds, "And about finding your mother. What makes you think she will be happy to see you? She's started a new life, far away from people she knows. If she wanted to be part of your life, she would have come and found you, right?"

Macia shrugs, trying to keep her face pleasant, "It's not that easy," she answers Sonja, "To get back into Elabi would have been impossible, no matter how much she wanted to be back with her family. Finding her where she is might be the only way to be with her."

The night time brings doubts with it. Macia stares at the pale grey ceiling, and touches her sore thumb with her tongue. What if… She closes her eyes against the stinging, warm tears and tries to take her mind back to her beautiful pen and thick paper she used for her imaginary writing. "Dearest friend," she breathes, "what if my mother has forgotten about us? Moved on with her life? What if she is no longer alive? How will I find her?"

She turns over on her side, determined to imagine happy endings. Her mother smiling at her, embracing her, talking about the past years and how painful they have been, and Macia will be able to share the Message with her mother. Her mother will come with her and Macia can imagine one of the lovely white houses on the outskirts of Mataiox, her mother cooking in the bright coloured kitchen. Macia drifts off, happy dreams lifting her heart.

Friends at the Meeting House are kind, but sceptical. "It's understandable," Gax says as the three of them wander along the beach. "Last time I went to Elabi wasn't a huge success story, and this time it's even more unsure. Linu knew a little about Elabi, we had a key to the house and we had an outline of the city. This time, we know hardly anything, apart from the name of the village. We have nowhere to stay, which is something we need to pray about. The three of us going together has raised a few eyebrows as well, but the Mission School has accepted the situation."

Macia sighs. "And what about your mother and father?" she asks Gax.

"My parents find it hard, as we don't know what we will face. But the people at the Meeting House have agreed to pray for us every week, although not everyone is happy as people feel it could be dangerous. So the Mission School has been working on guidelines for us."

Gax looks away and Caecilia smiles at him, "I think we all struggle

CHAPTER 3

with the unknown and the questions," she says, not looking at Macia, "but a mother's love is special and as you said, it's another opportunity to share the Message with our people. Not many people in Elabi were interested," she touches Gax's arm lightly as he looks away, his face a little flushed, "but maybe it's meant to be, reaching Elabi from the old people down? Who knows how God will use us? There is the little mountain village as well. Nobody would have reached out to those people if it hadn't been for Macia…for us," she says, pulling the corners of her mouth up, standing tall.

Gax smiles back, and nods. Macia moves a little closer.

Gax is pleased that the preparation is proving him right in wanting to go Downstream. It won't be like his time in Elabi. For one, he won't be alone, and this time, they will be actively reaching out to people. God has given him a second chance at reaching the people of Elabi.

Chapter 4

Weeks merge into months. Caecilia ignores the feeling of fear that makes her hands shake and keeps her awake at night. "I want to go," she whispers to herself in the dark, "I want to be part of this. Macia will need me and so does Gax."

At least the trip shouldn't be dangerous. Not the first part anyway. "We'll be fine in Aniquist, obviously," Macia says over her shoulder, spreading something on her sandwich. "We should also be safe in Colchuyni, at least till we're getting better weather." That makes Caecilia feel better. "Look, you're just going along for the support and the adventure as well as sharing the Message," Macia says, taking a large bite, and waving her hand at the lunch staples. "There won't be any danger, until we start looking for the Downstream part."

Caecilia shrugs, "Of course I will come with you. It's not that I'm afraid of danger. It's the thought of what we might find that worries me. And the lack of solid plans." She flicks her hand at Macia, "I know we can't make those until we're there and we have got more information. I would love to know what housing arrangement we will find. What if we're in three different places around the village? But even if we have a place, what are we aiming for? Rescuing the elderly and rejected babies, setting up a secret colony, blowing up the boat, or what? I know the Mission School is working on guidelines, but they don't know what we will find either."

CHAPTER 4

Macia stops chewing. After a while, she swallows her food and says, "I'm sure God will show us the way forward." Caecilia nods, her eyes blank.

"Not long to go," Caecilia says, a few days later. She grins at Macia as the girl tries to shrug into her huge rucksack. "Do you think you'll be able to move through mud with that on your back?"

Macia pulls a face, "Hopefully the mud won't be too soft, I'll sink up to my knees within seconds otherwise." One more tug and the rucksack is in the correct place. She tightens the straps, rolling her shoulders to get comfortable. "It's the books," she grins.

"Yet you only have one, and I have more," Caecilia points out, "My maths book, books to help us whilst there and the copy of the Book."

"I hope I'll be able to get my rucksack on," Caecilia sighs. "These books are heavy and I'm not a pushup expert like you, so hopefully my shoulders will cope." With Macia's help, Caecilia manages to get into the arm straps. "It's not too bad once it's on," she says to her friend, "and I'm not planning on taking it off too often."

There is a knock on the door and Caecilia waddles as quickly as she can to answer it. Gax grins at her, his eyes taking in her struggles. "That looks heavy. Do you need me to take some of that for you?"

Before Caecilia has a chance to take Gax up on his offer, Macia's voice is rather sharp, "I'm sure we're fine, Gax, it looks heavier than it is." Caecilia gives a muffled cough to stop Gax from seeing the face she was about to pull. "We put them on to see how heavy it will be and to get used to it."

Caecilia bites her lip. Will she manage this great, heavy rucksack all across the mud path? What if she can't cope anymore after a few hours? "We really should have started working on it a few weeks ago," she groans as she shrugs her shoulders to get the straps off a rather tender spot. "The bags are fine, but will they still be fine by the time we get to Colchuyni?"

25

Macia frowns, "There's not much we can do about it now. And I have actually worked hard in the gym, focussing on my back and shoulders most days." Caecilia feels her face warming up, knowing Macia has hinted a few times that visiting the gym might be a good idea. "You'll be surprised how much you can do when you need to," Macia's voice is a little softer, "and then there's prayer. You know everyone back here will be praying for us." She smiles at Caecilia as if to make up for the barbed comments.

By the time Caecilia crawls into bed, her shoulders feel like they have had a bad quality massage. She gingerly touches the sore spot where the straps have hugged her for the last few hours and tears spring in her eyes. "Lord, I have no idea how I will cope. It's too much," she sobs quietly. She presses her lips together, grinds her teeth and tells herself, "You have no choice. You can't pull out now, you will have to simply see it through." Even lying down hurts and Caecilia squeezes her eyes shut.

At breakfast, Macia pushes a tube across the table. "Try this, just a few minutes before putting your rucksack back on," she says, her voice kind. "It might help a little. You'll manage, I'm sure, and we'll help you as much as we can." Caecilia nods and picks up the tube. Muscle cream. *An anaesthetic cream would have been better*, she grimaces but doesn't say out loud. Part of her rebels at Macia's patronising tone. She might not be as sporty, but that doesn't mean to say she's a weak lump!

Instead, she smiles at Macia, making her eyes as large and soft as she can, "Thank you, that's thoughtful. Hopefully, I won't need your help during the crossing, but I'll let you know if I need a piggyback." Both girls laugh and Caecilia makes sure Macia thinks the tears on her cheeks are from laughing too hard.

The day arrives that sees the trio get onto the early long-distance coach for the first leg of the journey. Caecilia smiles brightly at Gax's

CHAPTER 4

parents. "Thank you so much for everything," she gushes, and staggers onto the coach with her bag. She shivers. The early morning air is chilly and she's glad to find a place near the window. She smiles at Gax as he gets on the coach. To her disappointment, he takes the seat behind her, waving at his parents as he does so. Macia is the last one on, and after a moment's hesitation slides into the same row as Caecilia. Caecilia smiles at her, "Isn't it cold this time in the morning!"

After a full day on the coach, Aniquist is a whirl of colours, sounds and smells. Street vendors shouting at busy corners, their food sizzling and sputtering, and smoke makes the girls' eyes smart. "That smells good," Gax says with a large grin, "Maybe we should find our hotel, drop our stuff and find some food?"

"Maybe not from a street vendor," Macia cautions, "did you see that bit in one of the travel books? The last thing we need is food poisoning."

"I think I'm too hungry to worry about that," Gax laughs, "I'm sure if we bought something that looked very well cooked, we should be fine," he says. Caecilia shudders. Gax looks at the girls and gives a short laugh. "I suppose it's best to stay on the safe side," he gives in and both girls nod.

The hotel is basic but clean. The noise isn't muffled much by the windows and Macia says, "I can't decide between the overwhelming heat with the windows shut or the noise when the windows are open!" Caecilia agrees as she sorts out her bag. Streetlights flicker on and Macia sighs. "I suppose we better shut the window as this kind of place is bound to have mosquitoes."

Gax's knock sounds and the girls jump up to open the door for him. "There is a small restaurant downstairs, right next to the hotel. It saves us walking, as we're all exhausted."

They open the door to rain and quickly slip into the restaurant. Caecilia shivers, "It's a lot cooler straight away," she says.

The strips of barbecued beef with round potatoes and cornbread taste better than the girls expected. The beef is well-seasoned and Macia blinks back unexpected tears as the herbs remind her of Ignava. However difficult her stepmother was, her cooking was excellent.

"Those herbs are wonderful," Caecilia says, unaware of Macia's struggle. "I'm glad we didn't bring any with us."

In the morning, after a cornbread breakfast, the three set off through the city to find the office for the mud crossing. The route to the nearest office shows them some of the most beautiful doors they have seen.

"City of a thousand doors, it should be called," Caecilia sighs as they walk past another ornately carved door, set in red sandstone blocks.

Here and there women sit out of the rain, a blanket spread on the pavement, covered in woollen hats and scarves. The girls hesitate each time they pass one of the women.

"The scarves would probably come in handy," Macia says, "the evenings are cold, even now in the rainy season." Gax waits patiently for the girls but groans as the office appears to be closed. The door is simply locked, with no note explaining why and whether it's for a quick break, or for good.

Gax digs in his pocket, pulling out a list. "The next office isn't that far away," he says, hopefully.

"That's fine," Macia nods, "It's quite interesting, walking around Aniquist."

Caecilia looks away quickly, rubbing her face to hide her expression. Macia makes it sounds like she is some kind of anthropologist, studying the locals. "I'm glad we brought our waterproof along, as I'm not interested in testing the local rain," she grins at Macia who manages a chuckle. Gax laughs and smiles at Caecilia, making her rub her face again to hide the warmth.

The second office is open and manned. There is barely enough room for all three, but the girls squeeze in with Gax. He smiles at the man

CHAPTER 4

behind the counter, "Good morning," he says, trying to use the local dialect. Caecilia clenches her dress and looks at her mud-splattered shoes. *They're no longer white*, she thinks. "...the mud crossing," she hears Gax say, "and we would like to be on the next one."

The man doesn't say anything, just looks at the three young people standing in his tiny dark office, posters that must be at least ten years old clinging onto the walls. From the stack of paperwork on the desk to the dirty tiles underneath their feet, everything shows that his office has most likely been little used since the posters went up. Caecilia tries to pull a confident smile and Macia does the same, carefully inching away from the grubby wall. Gax stands a little taller until the man snorts. "Is one way only."

Chapter 5

Gax nods, "Yes, we realise we will have to stay in Colchuyni for the year before we return."

The man shakes his head, "No, ticket is one way only. You need new ticket, but in Colchuyni." He looks the girls up and down. "The walk is fast. No stopping and resting." Macia nods and Caecilia smiles, her heart beating fast.

The man grunts something and starts rummaging around, digging up a rather grubby paper. He writes Colchuyni at the top and glares at Gax. "Names. And date of birth." The paper is filled in, rubber stamped and the man taps on it as he hands it over to Gax. "They will leave in two weeks. Date is here. Shoes you need are there, time is there, guide not wait, so if you late, he will go. If you cannot do it, guide will walk on. Many people drown in last few years," he says with a sneer.

Caecilia shudders. Gax thanks the man and half pushes the girls out of the office. "I can't imagine any guide leaving people to drown," he hisses on the way out. "I think he was trying to scare us. All the same, maybe we should make an effort to get as fit as we can in the next two weeks."

Macia nods, looking pleased. "It won't take much extra training," she says, "although the higher altitude will take some getting used to."

They look at the mountains surrounding Aniquist, most of the

CHAPTER 5

summits shrouded in mist. "Even walking around Aniquist is harder than I expected, I'm constantly feeling out of breath," Macia continues, and she turns to Caecilia.

Caecilia raises her hands in protest. "Don't ask me, I'm out of breath when I walk to the shops in Mataiox, so no hope for me as your test subject, I'm afraid." The trio returns to the hotel, ready to make plans for the next two weeks.

Caecilia stares at the ceiling that evening. She feels exhausted, and her head throbs. She sighs and answers Macia's question, "Sorry, I have a headache, that's all. I didn't realise you were still awake." She can see Macia's shadowy form sit up.

"It might be because of the altitude," Macia says, "we'll have a quiet day tomorrow and just explore Aniquist. Maybe there is a library or something where there is more information about Colchuyni." She lies down again. "I hope you'll feel better tomorrow."

They wish each other good night and Caecilia closes her eyes. She misses her evening diary times but doesn't want to do it with Macia right next to her. She remembers what Macia said about her time in Elabi and writing the diary in her mind. Caecilia lets a deep breath out. "Lord, I'm so afraid… but it's more that I don't enjoy change. I don't want to be here, and I don't want to leave here for another new place. I want to be back in Mataiox, studying, going to the Meeting House…" She carefully wipes a tear away, making sure to even out the sobs.

"I'll be fine," Caecilia assures Gax two days before they are due to set off. "Although I might need a week to recover," she grins at him. He smiles at her, and she continues, "It reminds me of leaving Elabi and that's maybe one of the reasons I have found it hard to leave Mataiox."

"I'm glad you're both coming with me," he smiles, "as I can't imagine going to Colchuyni by myself. I know Nora from the Mission School was happy to come along, but it wouldn't have been the same. It's not about reaching Colchuyni and getting to know the people, it's about finding the link with Elabi. I'm excited," and he lowers his voice after a glance to see where Macia is, "I'm not sure we will find her mother, but I have been praying about it." He continues after a moment, "I hope Macia doesn't get disappointed. Hopefully, finding Downstream will be enough to make our trip worthwhile. I have been praying that we will meet the right people in Colchuyni to help us, especially with accommodation."

Caecilia nods, "Do you have any idea what to do once we find Downstream? If they know they're found out, won't they simply find another spot?"

"Maybe. We'll have to be careful and wise. I hope we'll find a way to help the people without alerting Elabi. I'm not sure there is much we can do. Many older people probably don't even want to be rescued," Gax says, "But they may want to hear from the Book and we should try what we can, especially for the babies." He sighs and smiles at Caecilia, the old Gax back for a moment.

Caecilia struggles to breathe, not because of the altitude this time. "I know you will do what you can," she says softly, "and I will help as much as possible. We prayed about this trip, and I know everything happens for a reason. Maybe someone in Colchuyni needs us, or maybe we need them. It will be an adventure if nothing else," she grins, suddenly feeling excited. "We'll learn a lot, not just about Downstream, but about ourselves and God as well. I'm starting to get excited," she admits, "maybe I needed longer to fully embrace the whole thing, but I can't wait to get there and to start our special year in Colchuyni. Will you tell people why we are in Colchuyni?"

Gax is quiet for a moment, then he says, "No, I don't think so." He stops and pulls a face. "Something in my heart tells me not to share the details. I don't think we should lie, of course, but we don't have to share all the details." He thinks for a moment, "Maybe we should use

CHAPTER 5

Macia's mum? We can say that we heard her mum had gone to this area, which is true, although we mean the back of Colchuyni rather than the village itself. That way, we don't have to lie and maybe they will be able to help us as well. There is a tiny chance her mum has gone to Colchuyni, who knows?"

At breakfast, Macia agrees that this is the best way forward. "We want the people to help us, and that sounds like a good way to garner support without troubles, in case they're not keen on people visiting the jungle." She waves her leaflet at them. "This leaflet says that the Colchuyni people avoid the jungle because of the insects and dangers. Surely some of them would go into the jungle? After all, there is food to be found and trees for wood, so why avoid it completely?"

"One more day," Macia says brightly, "and I want to buy one of those scarves and a large sunhat." Caecilia nods and says she saw a lovely woman selling near the hotel. "Yes, I was thinking of her too," Macia laughs, "I talked to her about the Book yesterday, but she wasn't interested. Hopefully buying from her will make her remember us, and she might remember the conversation as well."

The last day is a whirl of activity. They wash their clothes in the laundrette, buy their shawl and hats, repack their bags, and have a last special meal at the restaurant next door. "I will miss Aniquist," Macia says, leaning back in her chair. Caecilia begins to nod, then stops herself.

"I'm looking forward to living in a small village," she says, "especially after reading about farming. It can be calming, working outside, and seeing plants grow." Macia looks doubtful at that but Gax nods. "Maybe they do paddleboarding," Caecilia jokes with Macia who shudders.

"I don't think I want to ever stand up on a paddleboard again," she chuckles, "although fishing sounds like something we might have to do a lot, especially whilst waiting for the harvest."

The next morning, all three are up and ready before the sun is. The rain has stopped for now, but with the low-hanging clouds, it's impossible to tell if there will be more rain later. Before leaving the comfortable hotel, they pray. "...We need a place to stay, Lord, and we want to share the Book with the people..." They squeeze hands, looking at each other, eyes filled with tears as their adventure suddenly feels more real.

"It's so cold," Caecilia shivers as they step outside, tugging her coat tighter around her chest. "Hopefully, walking across the mud will warm us up." She shrugs her rucksack into a more comfortable position, tightens the straps a little and follows Macia through the town towards the water.

The streets are deserted, and by the time they reach the mud flat, Caecilia is warm enough as well as slightly out of breath.

"Can you see the guide?" Macia asks, not out of breath at all, Caecilia notices.

Gax looks up and down the deserted stretch of sand and points to a man with a large bag, not far from them. "That could be him, though it's not as if it's heaving with people," he says.

They walk over to the young man, who nods at them and holds out his hand for the ticket. He looks at the three, his face deadpan. Finally, he returns the ticket and says, "There are more people coming. My friend is coming. He brings more friends. We will walk fast, yes?" They nod and Caecilia wriggles her toes inside her shoes. Standing still on the cold beach has made her feet cold already.

Soon more people loom up out of the mist. One is another woman and she smiles at the girls. The guide grunts something, grabs his bags and sets off into the mist swirling over the water.

The woman walks close to the girls and says, "The mist goes. This time of day, it goes. And Riu is good. He knows the way very well." She nods a few times, then goes to walk in front of them. "Stay behind

CHAPTER 5

me, in my steps," she says with a kind smile. "Sometimes the path is narrow and hard to see. It gets cold when you are wet." The girls thank her, and Caecilia is glad with the pace set by Riu. It's not too fast, but they're walking at such a rate that they feel they're making good progress. Although it's hard to know as the mist hides their destination.

Gradually the mist thins out and a watery sun breaks through. Caecilia's white shoes are no longer white and Gax has one brown, muddy leg where he stepped in a puddle. Riu slows down for a moment and waves a hand towards a dark line emerging on the horizon. "Colchuyni," he says and carries on walking.

Caecilia gasps and groans which she turns into a cough. She smiles brightly at Macia and says, "Well, that won't be long then." Macia giggles and shakes her head. Caecilia sighs once they have walked for another hour. Wherever they look is mud. Mud and puddles, the odd little crab scurrying to a pool. Birds shriek at each other, protesting the invasion. By lunchtime, Caecilia's shoulders are on fire, but Riu doesn't slow down for lunch, simply pulls some food out of his bag. The others do the same and Caecilia struggles through some cornbread. She washes it down with water, her second bottle.

Just when Caecilia starts to worry about bathroom facilities on the endless mudflat, Riu stops near a large puddle. "First women," he says, gesturing for the men and the girls to turn their backs towards the puddle. He points at the woman who knows him and she turns towards the puddle. Caecilia cringes at the splattering noise, her face warming up. When the woman joins them again, Riu nods at Macia. Macia obediently goes towards the puddle, soon followed by Caecilia. She is relieved to have the opportunity but would have loved something more private. Once the men have all been as well, Riu grins and sets off again.

Macia smiles at Caecilia after an hour, the island clearer now.

"Nearly there," she says softly, her eyes looking concerned. Caecilia nods but doesn't look up. She knows if she looks at Macia, she won't be able to stop the tears. Everything aches and burns and even Macia seems to be a little out of breath. "We'll find somewhere to rest as soon as we can." Caecilia nods but with little hope in her eyes.

The ground starts to slope gently upwards, making the girls struggle for breath and Gax openly gasps and grunts. Riu grins at him. "On the way back, you will walk fast; you get used to it," he laughs. Gax pulls a face and laughs as well. The girls stay quiet, needing all their energy to breathe. Riu looks at them again and asks, "Do you have anywhere to live?"

Gax shakes his head and explains that they have come prepared to stay for the year as they're looking for Macia's mother. "We come from a larger city, so it would be nice to stay in a village and slow down for a year," he adds. "We will need to look for somewhere to stay."

Riu nods, "You will like Colchuyni and I hope the mother will be found," he hesitates but looks away after a few moments. When they reach the end of the mud he turns back to them. "My sister has a house. It is without people, as she married in Aniquist and stays there. She won't come until you are ready to go, so you can use her house." The three gasp and look at each other, and Riu shrugs, "She always asks me to have somebody stay in her house, use her field, but there are not many people in Colchuyni without a house. You can use it, but you must take care of it, it belongs to my sister."

Chapter 6

Riu motions for them to follow him. By the time they make it to the outskirts of the small village at the top of the hill, Caecilia can't feel her body anymore. There is a little breeze, smelling of cold rain and the green terraces on the hillside blur into a green mist as she staggers behind Macia and Gax. "The house is not very large," Riu says. "It's old but comfortable. There is wood left over for cooking and heating the house. Later this week I will show you where to find more wood and dung for your fire. Wood is hard to chop, but it smells nice," he flashes his teeth in a smile.

Macia grins back at him, trying not to wrinkle her nose at the idea of burning animal dung. One more turn on the path, and the little house looms up, the grey clouds so low, they're nearly resting on the black straw roof. The yellow stone house is built in an L-shape, the little windows shuttered. Macia's feet are on fire and one look at Caecilia makes her whisper, "Nearly there, just a few more steps. We'll get something to drink and eat, alright?" Caecilia manages to nod, swallowing back tears.

Riu pushes the door open. The blue paint is in desperate need of renewal, but Caecilia doesn't care. Riu waves his hand towards the terrace behind the house. "That is my sister's field. There will be space for you to grow most things. I will tell you soon where you will buy seeds, then you will be alright?" He looks rather doubtful as his eyes take in the girls, hardly able to stand up straight after the gruelling day.

Gax smiles, "Thank you, that would be helpful. I'm sure we'll manage, once we've had a rest. We're not used to so much walking," he apologises, his feet on fire and his left knee keeps giving way. He glances at the girls; neither seems to have noticed his struggles to stay upright.

Riu nods. "The work is hard, but it is still possible to plant and have a good harvest. There are people selling food in the village as well, only when it is very wet they will stay indoors. You go to the village in the dry times and you will find food." Riu walks around the small house, opening creaking shutters and pointing out the woodpile. "You will need more, especially for cooking and cold evenings," he grins and Gax nods, struggling to smile. He has spotted a couple of chairs inside and just wants to collapse on one of them.

Riu walks inside and the three follow him. He waves his hand around, "We look after this. We hoped my sister would come this year, but she has a man in Aniquist." He frowns but soon carries on, "So my family clean in here and sort everything for just in case she comes." The others nod sympathetically, wishing to try the soft-looking furnishings in one corner. There is no sofa, but a huge pile of bright-coloured cushions is piled up in one corner, and the idea of finally getting their rucksack off makes it hard to keep smiling at Riu.

He seems to feel it though, for grins and says, "I will let you rest. You go on up a few more steps and the village is there. There is a little store for special foods and drinks. Water here is good," and he gestures to a large pump set near the wall, next to a large fireplace. He walks to the pump and swings the large handle up and down. Water gushes out, and he grins. "It is cold and sweet," before gesturing at the fireplace. "Use the big pot for long cooking, like soup. There is an oven outside for bread and roasting."

CHAPTER 6

They nod and Caecilia pretends to look at the rough table, to wipe a few tears away. "Please, Lord, let him go, let us be fine for just tonight," she mutters quietly.

The prayer is answered instantly, for Riu spreads his arms out to encompass the house. "Please, have a healthy time here. I will come and show you where everything is and help you. You are new and I will show you our welcome for guests." He gives a low bow and then the wooden door squeaks shut behind him.

All three let go of their breath at the same time, making Gax and Macia laugh and Caecilia cry. "I'm sorry," she sobs as Macia hugs her and helps her undo her rucksack straps and slide the heavy burden onto the mud floor.

Macia hugs her again, "We made it. We're here, we're safe, we have a house and a field to grow food, and all our prayers for practical provisions have been answered." Caecilia nods and rubs her face. Gax groans as he lowers his rucksack and looks at the girls.

"All our worries about the house," Caecilia says, her voice wobbling, "all our prayers, and they've been answered in the most amazing way with this lovely house."

Macia says, "We have plenty of water and we have food in our large bags. I just want to drink lots of water, wash and sleep."

The others agree and Gax walks to the pump. He looks behind a bright curtain underneath a shelf and finds some stoneware cups. They look clean and he fills three of them with cold water. They sit at the table, looking at each other in the semi-darkness. "This water is good," Gax says, to break the silence. Macia nods; Caecilia simply stares into her mug.

They look around for beds. Behind several floor-to-ceiling bright red, yellow and orange patterned curtains Macia finds the bedrooms. Gax is given the tiny one containing just one bed. Macia and Caecilia claim the larger room. The beds are high and the small curtains underneath the lumpy mattresses show extra storage space. Macia nearly hits her head on the shelf above the bed as she climbs in. Caecilia is already asleep, she notices as she smothers her giggles. She lies down and the next thing she knows, the morning sun is shining on her face.

Macia sits up and smiles back at Caecilia who is sitting up on her bed. The girls shiver at the same time and laugh. "It's cold!" Caecilia exclaims and they get dressed quickly.

As they walk into the main room, Gax looks up. "I managed to get the fire going," he says in greeting. "I found a smaller kettle, so hopefully we can have a hot drink. I have teabags in my rucksack," he explains and tries to look humble as the girls express their joy. "We'll have a quiet day, I think," he groans as he stands up. "We'll have a look around the village and unpack. Anything else?"

Macia shakes her head. "I'm exhausted from yesterday and my feet are one large blister each. I'm not sure if I'll even fit in my shoes." She pulls a face at her feet and looks at Caecilia.

"Same here. It's not just my white trainers that are ruined," Caecilia laughs, "I would like to see the field though as we won't have long to plant. And I'd like Riu's advice on planting." Caecilia staggers over to her rucksack. "I'm sure I have the breakfast items in mine," she says, her stomach agreeing noisily.

A few minutes later, they are shovelling down cereal with powdered milk as if it's the best meal they've ever had. The tea is hot and sweet and they have a roof over their heads. A small fire has managed to take the chill from the room and Caecilia feels herself relaxing. "I have never been so tired in my life," she sighs, hugging the hot mug, "I thought I wouldn't make it. I prayed so much, I even prayed Riu out of the house as I couldn't stand up any longer." The others laugh.

Gax sips his tea. "Praise God for His mercies to us. I'm so thankful for the provision of this house. It's going to be an interesting year," he says, "and there is the task of finding our way down to the jungle

CHAPTER 6

area and through it." He pulls a face, "I'm running ahead of myself. I think I need to learn to live by the day, and not to worry about what tomorrow will bring, as it says in the Book."

The day is all they need. It stays mainly dry so they walk to the village together. They're pleasantly surprised when they walk into the shop. It's larger than expected, crammed with tins, bottles and packages from floor to ceiling. Some of the labels look older than the shop, and Caecilia peers at the numbers. She stands up, holding a tin with meat. "This is reasonable value," she says softly. Macia agrees and soon they have filled a basket with enough food for the rest of the week. "My feet are still on fire," Caecilia groans, "so it's good that we don't have to walk too much in the next few days."

Coming out of the shop, they make their way across the dirt road to a lookout point from where they can see the beach they came up yesterday. They stare down at the endless stretch of water, peering to try to see a dark line on the horizon that is Aniquist. The cloud cover makes it hard to tell. "It's strange seeing the water like that," Gax says, "it reminds me of when I was first in Elabi, feeling trapped, with no way out." He looks at the girls and quickly adds, "Not necessarily a bad thing. I propose that we study the Book every evening, or morning, whichever you prefer?" He can feel his face warming up as he looks away. They should have thought of that this morning at breakfast time. Not a good start, he berates himself.

Macia nods, "Maybe in the morning? I like to have the rest of the day to think about the words. We could maybe start when we get back?" Macia asks. "I must admit, the tiredness and the finality of it all is getting to me today. The shop is great and we have an amazing house as well as plenty of space to grow food. Everything has been provided for, but as you said, we're also trapped and I feel a little strange in this village."

Caecilia nods. "I noticed that the people are polite and pleasant, but not very talkative or outgoing. I tried to talk to several women and they smiled at me but didn't say anything. I'm glad we know Riu at least." Caecilia doesn't say anything about the dark corner in the shop. She wonders how she will explain what she saw to the other two. Caecilia continues, "Maybe I'm still tired and it's affecting me, or maybe the feeling we are so far away from everybody, but I feel… a little pushed down, if you know what I mean?"

Gax nods, "I had that when I first arrived in Elabi. I was excited, but there is a heaviness as well. Yes, let's get back to the house and look at the Book and pray together, that will lift us up." He turns away from the view with a slight shudder.

"I wonder if you can see the jungle from up here," Macia says. "It would be interesting to see, so we can picture things in our head."

"Some things are best not pictured for a while," Caecilia says and giggles at the dour voice that came out of her mouth. "You're right, it would be good to prepare our minds as well as our hearts, but not today."

They walk through the village and follow the winding path down to their little house. Wherever they look, there are terraces, green and covered in growing things. "Hopefully it's not too late in the season to plant our food," Gax says but Caecilia tells him they'll be fine. The clouds are lowering and by the time they reach the house, it's gloomy and damp, like a fine rain.

Gax shivers, "let's make some heat as well," he says but Macia nods at the small woodpile and he pulls a face. "It's not much fun wearing a coat all day," he grumbles, but after a cup of tea, which warms the house as well as their insides, Gax feels better. They put the shopping away and sit down with their Book.

Macia has a reusable paper and grins at Caecilia, "It's like being back in school."

Gax goes behind his curtain and reappears with a thin notebook. "I

CHAPTER 6

brought a few of these along," he says, laughing at the girls' reactions, "as I thought we'd need some more paper whilst here. There is paper in the shop as well, so we should be fine using this one for our time around the Book." He pushes the new notebook to Macia who glows and has the happiest grin when opening the thin black leather cover.

Half an hour later, all three lean back in their chair with a contented sigh, the first page of the notebook filled. The girls decide to make dinner together and Gax goes to check the gardening tools in the corner. "We will have to start preparing our field," he says over his shoulder whilst lifting a spade.

He looks up and grins as Riu knocks on the door and walks in.

Chapter 7

Riu smiles at them, "Hello again. I thought I better see you, maybe you have needs?" His eyes land on the Book and his smile is replaced by a wide-eyed look. Riu looks over his shoulder at the door, then touches the Book with his fingertips. "Is this your book?" he asks, "You bring it? Just one?"

He looks at them and as Gax nods he continues, "I am sorry. You will need to hide it, better destroy it." At the girls' gasps, he shrugs, "It is not allowed in the village. It will end our harvest and bring many diseases. Our elders say that. They always say that."

Macia and Caecilia look at each other, then at Gax. What will he say? Gax coughs, "We didn't know." He hesitates, as it wouldn't have made much difference if they had known. "We will be careful. What will happen if the elders find out?" He is curious but looking at Riu's face he wonders if that was a question best left alone.

Riu coughs as well, "I don't know for sure," he says slowly. "There was a girl. A long time ago. I think she brought it back. She came from visiting Aniquist for a season. She was taken towards the other side of the hill. The forbidden side. We never saw her again. I don't know," he adds quickly, seeing their faces. "Nobody goes that way, so nobody knows where she has gone."

"Why is nobody allowed that way? Is it a wilderness?"

Riu raises his shoulders till they nearly touch his earlobes. "I don't

CHAPTER 7

know. I have never been that way. The elders don't like people nosing. Anyone asking questions, or going up to village boundaries, they notice and can bring problems against you. I wanted to spend time with my sister in Aniquist, so I have kept in peace with them so my time away wouldn't be blocked."

Caecilia sighs. So much for the peaceful, idyllic village life. It sounds just like Elabi. "Will they watch us as we're new?" She wants to know where the dangers are.

Riu nods, "Yes, when you're out and being seen. They won't spy in a house or search your house, but if you have book out like that, they might see it. And you talk to others about the book or your God, there will be trouble for you. Although, as there are three, they might take you to the Khramuil."

The three look at each other, as it's clear from Riu's voice they should know what he is talking about. He grunts and says, "Khramuil is the holy house for this mountain, a special building. It is where the god of this mountain is made happy, he is served and his forgiveness is asked when we do wrong. Often, those who did wrong will be given to him." He opens his mouth as if to continue then stops and looks away.

Gax gasps, "You mean, the elders would give us to appease or please the god?" Riu licks his lips, looks at the door and nods. His face is no longer happy. "Does the god have a name?" Gax asks, wanting to know what they are dealing with. None of the travel books mentioned anything about religion.

Riu nods and lowers his voice, leaning towards them. "Wachshapah," he whispers, "but his name is sacred. Only our Head elder is allowed to say it. At other times, we refer to him as The Stream." Looking at their faces he explains, "He is like a dark river, bearing us all away, ready to roar and destroy or able to bring and sustain life."

Gax looks at the two girls. It seems like the stream has carried away their hopes, dreams and joy already.

Riu sighs and tries to smile. "I understand a little, having stayed in Aniquist. But this is my home, my people. I will not say anything, but I can't protect you when things go wrong and anger is started. This is not your God's mountain, so I don't know if he has power in another god's territory."

Riu stands up straighter, happy to change topics. He promises to help them with finding the right seeds. "It's not easy, the ground can be rocky, although I think your plot will be fine. My sister used it, so it's been growing before. You find the tools?" He spots the metal fork Gax discovered and grins. "Good, you need that to loosen the earth, dig in and remove the stones. It will make planting easier."

One troubling look at the Book later, Riu is gone, the door closed softly behind him. Gax and the girls look at each other. "I'm sorry," Gax starts, but Macia shakes her head.

"None of us knew, it didn't say in any of the books, did it?" She looks at Caecilia who shakes her head. Macia pulls a face and says, "Isn't there something in the Book about the floodwaters going over you and you won't drown, and staying unharmed in the fire?"

Caecilia sighs, "I don't want to even get wet, but I don't think that's an option, is it?"

Macia giggles and groans at the same time. "I have a feeling we're going to get wet enough. Will they expect us to go to that place, the Khra-something?"

"Khramuil," Gax says slowly and rubs the back of his neck. "I don't know. That could be difficult, as they might be suspicious or hostile if we are the only ones not going to ceremonies. We have to ask Riu what they think of people not following their god."

The girls look serious and Gax grins, "Well, I'm busy finding more implements for our garden plot, and we'd better hide the Book out of sight and the notebooks as well." He looks at the rather small windows. "Maybe we should close the shutters when we're looking at the Book."

CHAPTER 7

"That would look suspicious," Macia points out. "How will we stay hidden for a year? They will be watching us and we're sure to get found out. Maybe we should go into the wilderness earlier than we hoped."

Her voice trails off as she knows their time scheme is there for a reason. "We need to pray," she says after a quiet moment. Caecilia nods and the three of them hold hands as Gax prays. "Don't let the water frighten us," Macia adds when he finishes, "as we know what You promised in Your Book. Help us to be protected against the Stream." She gives Caecilia's freezing fingers a soft squeeze. Caecilia squeezes back and even manages a smile that nearly makes it around her face.

The girls hide the Book and notebooks and Gax collects all the tools he can find. The rain seems to have stopped so they go to the field behind the house. "It's a good size," Caecilia chatters, "so we should be able to do this. It'll be fun, won't it, to plant our own food. I wonder how long it will take in this climate. At least we won't have to worry about watering it if the rains come often."

Gax smiles at her, "I'm sure it will be good for us," he says and Macia hides her eye-rolling. She knows she is being unkind, but Gax's voice, sweet and slow, makes her cringe. "Anyway, should we simply start digging, do you think?"

They start in different corners and Macia is glad about the hard work. Soon her hands are hot and she keeps changing the grip on the small spade to stop blisters from forming on her hands. She can see Caecilia blowing on her hands. "My hands will be on fire in a minute," Macia groans and Caecilia giggles. "I could simply hold the kettle and boil water for tea." She bends down and makes a triumphant noise. "Look what I found!" She sniffs the herb to make sure, but she recognises the soft green leaves.

"Mint!" Caecilia's eyes look happy this time. Mint tea is one of her favourites and although Macia always has a heavy feeling deep inside when smelling the hot herby steam, thoughts of her stepmother Ignava accompanying the sweet aroma, she is pleased with the find. "That will save teabags as well," Caecilia says and looks closer to where Macia picked the leaves. "There is quite a lot here. Should we bring some inside, in a pot or something?"

Macia takes the leaves with her and looks around the small house, struggling to see in the late afternoon light. She finds a bowl in the end and takes it to their field. Together the girls dig out a clump of mint which is put on one of the windowsills. The fragrance soon fills the small house, especially once the kettle has boiled.

That night, Gax sits up slowly, straining his ears. He can hear something. Quietly he lowers himself again as he realises it's one of the girls crying. Probably Caecilia, he thinks, and he prays in the darkness, against the darkness. He mulls over what Riu said that afternoon. He misses a journal to write in, so he does what Macia told him before, writing in his head. "It came as a shock, although I should have been prepared for difficulties. I need to help the girls, do what I can to protect them." He stops there, "Even though I wouldn't know how to do that," he admits to himself after a while. His thoughts drift towards the sacred building, Khramuil, and he shivers.

The girls are quiet at breakfast, and Caecilia has dark shadows under her eyes. Gax groans as he rubs his hands gingerly. "My hands are too soft; by the end of the year, they'll look like farmer's hands. They'll never be the same again, and my mum will be horrified." Macia laughs and Caecilia smirks.

"I'm sure your mum will be glad you made an honest living," she teases and Gax laughs. "But I agree," she carries on, "I'm not sure how much digging I will be able to do today."

Macia nods then rummages around the sink area that seems to contain lots of useful things. She holds up some old cloths. "We could use those to wrap around our tools, as it will make it softer on our

CHAPTER 7

hands."

"Good idea, especially as I will need to chop more wood. I saw large logs near the woodpile. I might do that first whilst still able to hold a tool," Gax says. "Maybe we should look at the Book now, whilst the shutters are still closed. Nobody would think it strange at this time of day."

The Book open, notebooks still smelling new and crisp, the girls look at Gax. He takes a deep breath, forcing his eyes to stay away from the door, refusing to turn and look at a shutter creaking in the morning breeze. He is tempted to find some 'don't fear' passages, but yesterday they had agreed to work through a book in order. Slowly, Gax turns to the same portion they were looking at yesterday.

"Let us reason together, does that also include people like Riu?" Macia asks once they have read the first part of the chapter. "Surely what they do with that Khra building is wrong? Shouldn't we tell them and warn them?"

Caecilia fiddles with her notebook, "If they don't want to reason, there isn't much you can do," she says quietly. "Maybe like in Elabi, they will see the difference and maybe it will be enough? When they ask questions, that might be the time to reason."

Gax agrees. "I think Caecilia is right, there is a good chance they will recognise we are different."

"I wonder how long ago the girl was," Macia says, "as the elders might spot other believers a mile off if it was recent." Gax and Macia think it was a while ago, Caecilia isn't sure.

"Things like that stay in people's minds though. As Riu said, the fact that we're new means we'll be watched. Maybe we should instead focus on the next few lines, praying the promise and being willing and obedient, as God promises we'll eat the good of the land." She rubs her sore hands and laughs, "Being willing is maybe the easier part," she says quietly and shudders. "Being obedient seems to come at such a cost."

"I know," Macia agrees, then whispers, "What's the alternative? We left Elabi for the same reasons, didn't we? And it has been good; not easy, but good. This will be good too, but already it's not easy. We have to pray it will be good and that nothing will break that."

Chapter 8

Caecilia smiles, her face glowing with happiness. She rubs her cheeks as the smile is hurting her jaws. "At least this evening I can write something positive in my rubbing-out journal," she mutters to herself, then looks over her shoulder. She doesn't want the others to know how hard the last few days have been.

They have kept a very low profile, simply digging around their plot that seemed to grow each hour, chopping wood for the cold evenings and chatting about Mataiox in the evenings. Macia and Gax chatted, that is; Caecilia kept quiet.

Now, looking at their plot filled with seeds in neat rows, Caecilia feels herself relaxing, the knotted fear in the bottom of her stomach loosening a little. Riu grins at her. "You will have plenty of food," he says. Caecilia nods, keen to try out homegrown quinoa, a grain new to her, but popular in the village.

"Yes, thank you for all your advice," Caecilia answers, stealing a longing look to a far corner, her fingertips touching the smooth bag with seeds in her pocket. Riu had been so horrified when she had shown him the coriander seeds, she hadn't mentioned it again.

"I don't know why," she says over dinner. "I love coriander and it doesn't go too wild either, so I can't understand Riu's problem with it."

Gax wriggles his nose, "Maybe the Stream doesn't like it?" Both girls laugh, but he is serious all of a sudden. "I saw that mask you mentioned, Caecilia, the one in the corner of the shop." That stops the smile on Caecilia's face.

Both girls look at Gax with curiosity. "You know I went to the shop this afternoon, as Riu said we had space for one more row of potatoes. As I was waiting my turn, I wandered around a little. You were right," he nods at Caecilia, "that corner was smoky. Some kind of incense, making it hard to see. There was a horrendous mask hanging up, all black with green eyes like a twisted alien."

He tries to smile. "We can ask Riu when we see him again. Nobody else in the shop was going near that corner, so we won't look out of place if we stay away from it."

"We need to find out as much as possible," Caecilia says. "Should I plant the coriander seeds? There is something special about them, so we might have to hide them."

Macia looks at Gax, who shrugs. "I can't see how it can harm us," he says, "as long as you can't smell it in the house or on us." He thinks back to the shop. "There were plenty of herbs in the shop, so it's not something against herbs in general. Could we find a strong-smelling herb that would camouflage the coriander smell?"

Caecilia gets her herbs out and points at a packet. "Lemon balm," she says, "it smells quite strong and we could get more mint." She giggles, "The way we're drinking it, it's going to need more windowsills to keep us supplied!" Macia grins and raises her steaming mug with mint tea at the others.

Caecilia cries softly that night, trying to think of all the blessings, "Thank You for our garden, for Riu's help and for growing us as well." She digs around her mind, trying to remember why it had seemed such an important, urgent mission, a life and death matter. Death certainly seems a possibility. Even trying to remember the joy she felt in the garden doesn't help. All she can think of is the horrible mask she thought she spotted in the shop. Now Gax has confirmed it, and there is more, she could tell from his face, the way he looked away. The darkness seems to have spilt out of the shop to the whole village.

The morning brings more fine rain, but Macia and Caecilia venture out to get soil from their plot. They fill several dishes and pots that they have found, some chipped, discarded at the side of the house. "We'll keep the herb that shall not be named on the windowsill in our bedroom," Caecilia decides, making Macia laugh.

Apart from their study of the Book, double checking their plot, hoping to see the first leaves appearing, and tidying the little house, the days slip by one after another. Resurrection Days come and go, like an oasis. They all miss their Meeting House, the singing and the fellowship with others. They sing a few songs, quietly; hoping the rain rattling on their hut will keep nosy neighbours away and drown out any sounds.

Gax smiles, once the Book has been put away, and the shutters are open. The rain has stopped and the house smells of mint tea. "That was good," he sighs leaning back in his chair. "I wonder if Riu would be interested in joining one day. After all, he knew a little about the Book, and didn't seem too hostile."

Macia nods. "He said he wouldn't help us or stand up for us, but he wouldn't betray us. And he might know others that could be open to the message of the Book."

Caecilia can't help noticing how squeaky her voice is as she points out what Riu said. "He said our God wouldn't have power on this mountain, so I can't imagine him swapping sides. The more people involved, the more dangerous it is."

Gax smiles at her and in a soft, slow voice explains that it's important that people hear the message. "Sometimes it's worth taking risks. I'm not saying we knock on their doors or hang a sign up at the shop. I simply wondered if Riu would know someone who might be ready to hear the message. Sharing the message is one of the most important things to do," he adds, his face grave. "Maybe that is the reason Linu heard the noise, so we could take the message to this village."

When Riu appears one Resurrection Day, he looks pleased to see them. They go inside, and Riu sniffs. "You have a garden in here, too," he laughs. Caecilia shows him the tubs on the windowsills. Riu looks at the plants, rubs a bit of mint and tuts approvingly. "It helps with food. Food can taste the same all the time, especially near the end of the year. Just special potato." He gives an exaggerated shudder, making them groan in sympathy.

He looks around at the tubs, and waves at them. "I see no Eldergrass?" Caecilia looks at him and he nods at her. "The seeds you had the other day," he whispers, conspiratorial all of a sudden, "I said not to plant it. It is Eldergrass. Only the elders can grow it or touch it. I don't know how it got into the field." He slides his finger along the ceramic box.

"That one is mint and this here is basil. I have some chives, but these have been sheared as we used them last night," she laughs, making sure to look only at the few boxes near them. She can feel the coriander waving at her from behind their bedroom curtain. The tub is out of sight, in a corner of the windowsill with a picture frame in front of it, so it would be hard to spot. She doesn't want Riu to wander around the house on his way home though.

"Why is it called Eldergrass?" Gax asks, curious about the name.

Riu looks at him, "The elders use it for ceremonies. They…" He stops, uneasy to talk. "Anyway, why so much mint? You have a lot of mint."

Macia shows him her mug with a little tea left in it, the soft green leaves soggy and deformed. "It makes a lovely drink," she explains. "Simply put a few leaves in a mug, pour hot water on them and you have a drink." Riu accepts their offer of a mint tea, and soon they're

CHAPTER 8

seated around the table, steaming mugs warming cold fingers.

"Do you still have your book?" Riu asks and Gax nods. "Somewhere safe? Do you look at it?"

Gax nods again. "Every morning we look at the Book together," he smiles, "and every first day of the week we call Resurrection Day and we have a little meeting, like a ceremony. We dedicate that day to our God and praise Him and read the Book together."

"I saw those places in Aniquist," Riu says, "some of them were very big, with a lot of people going in. My sister sometimes goes to a small temple, although it has a special name. I didn't want to move The Stream. My parents have had many quiet years. I have had peace. My brother, on the other side of the village, he has a quiet life. I don't want the Stream to be moved, to leave its banks and find me and my people. I want the Stream as it is. The elders, they warn against putting obstacles in front of the Stream. I do not want that."

It stays quiet and Gax looks at the girls, wondering if he should invite Riu anyway. Before he can open his mouth, Riu says, "I know nothing about you having a book. I know nothing about special days and ceremonies on the first day. If they ask, I say no, they are just foreign with different habits and lives. That is all I will say to them."

Gax rubs the back of his neck. "Do you know anybody in the village that... who is like us? Different and maybe with a book?" Riu shakes his head and explains that after the last girl, nobody has mentioned the book or a different god.

"The harvests were very good, especially the summer after the girl went. So people listened to the Head elder when he explained."

As he is about to leave, he nods at the windowsill plants. "Eldergrass is used by the elders only. Khramuil is dark, they have masks, and some are new. They don't know. It is for safety, like a password or a badge. They hold a bunch of Eldergrass, so they know. Growing it is not possible. The Stream will devour you and everyone belonging to you if you grow it."

The door clicking shut reverberates in Caecilia's head all through a quiet dinner and even when she is in bed.

Chapter 9

Over breakfast, they discuss the Eldergrass. "I think we still need to grow it," Caecilia says. The others look at her in surprise. "I know," she shudders, "what Riu said made me feel ill, but I feel it is right to grow it. Maybe to show the Stream."

It goes quiet. "Do we believe the Stream exists?" asks Macia. She frowns a bit and says, "It's not real, surely, it's a false god they have made in this village."

Caecilia shrugs and says quietly, "Evil is real and the Evil one is real, so I think we need to be on guard," she stirs her mint tea, "but strong as well." She feels her face warm up. "I don't regret coming, but I don't think I knew what I was coming to either. But this morning, looking at those words in the Book, telling us for the Lord to be our fear and our dread, and He will be for a sanctuary. We don't know anything about Khramuil and what it is like. It is their holy place, but it can't be a sanctuary like God is. I felt that deep down." She tries to smile but her lips tremble too much. "I can't say I won't be afraid anymore, but it's no longer dark inside like it was before."

Gax nods, "Isaiah chapter eight is an inspiring chapter," he says, "and so true for where we are, where they look to the earth, but only find trouble and darkness, like it says at the very end of the chapter. I feel sad for the people here, having to live in such fear."

Days slip by and Caecilia feels each morning is not as light, not as warm as the previous one. "You wouldn't know," she teases Macia, "all that running around keeps you warm and you're studying too hard."

Macia laughs, and shrugs, "I don't want to fail when I get back. Running and keeping fit helps my mind as well. It clears my thoughts."

Caecilia looks serious then. "Soon it will be dark enough in the evening to go and see the other end of the village and find the way into the jungle. Or do you want to wait for daylight?"

"I'm not sure," Macia says slowly. "It will be easier to find out when it's light. We can see where we're going. On the other hand, in the dark, we will be left alone. I assume they will have a system in place to stop curious villagers from accidentally straying too close."

Caecilia looks around their plot, and says, "Where exactly is the jungle, do you think?"

Macia giggles," Not where you're looking, that's for sure. I would think it's past the shop, past the last few houses."

For the next few weeks, the three of them walk around most afternoons, even when it's wet. "We have to," Gax explains, "otherwise, if we want to go further, they will be surprised to see us and check up on us." Caecilia isn't keen on walking but has to admit the views are worth it and she feels good after they get back to the house.

"I wouldn't normally walk this much for fun," she laughs, "but coming home to a hot cup of mint tea and dry clothes has been lovely. Although I wasn't sure about that last path."

The path had been narrow, hidden almost, and Gax had hesitated to go in. "Are you sure it is a proper path?" Caecilia asked. In the end, they turned around after a few minutes. There was an odd quietness around them, the high grass felt like it was closing in on them, and all three had been relieved to get back onto the main path.

"Yes, that path felt menacing," Macia says, looking at Gax.

"I thought it was just too overgrown to be of help. It was a bit spooky though. Maybe we should take that path again sometime when it's better weather. It won't feel as dark and we're better prepared. Who knows where it leads to."

The girls nod, but not enthusiastically. "It does seem to go towards the jungle," Macia has to admit. "I wonder what kind of path it is. It seems too well-kept for an animal track." She sighs, "You're right, we must check it out. I can't say I'm looking forward to it. Maybe we should wait a while so as not to make the locals suspicious."

Gax brings it up one sunny afternoon. "Maybe today we should revisit that spooky path, and see where it goes to. It's quite warm, so most people will be resting and there is less chance of anyone seeing us disappear onto the track. We'll stay quiet, and simply pray." He laughs at their faces. "It was just a path. I don't think a path can be evil, that's left to people, I suppose, but we'll be careful and go slowly so we can keep our eyes and ears open."

The path is darker and more sinister than the previous time, Caecilia is sure. "I still don't think it's a good idea," she whispers but follows the other two anyway. The path goes on forever, rising and dipping with the landscape, twisting a little but steadily going towards the back of the mountain. The side where the jungle is supposed to be. After a while, they come to a small area like a lay-by. There is a fallen tree without its bark and Gax and Macia drop down onto the makeshift bench. Caecilia declines a seat. "I still don't like it here. And why is there a bench? This path must lead to something important." She swallows. "Do you think it goes to the special place?"

"The Khramuil?" Gax looks around the cut out area. "Maybe; it would be a bit small for the elders and villagers to all come this way though."

The path is long and Gax looks at the sky which seems darker already. "I'm not sure how much further we can go," he whispers, "it's getting late. This path could go on for hours."

Caecilia would love to turn around straight away, but having come so far… "Let's just walk for another ten minutes," she says, "and then we'll turn around. The mountain can't be that big, and surely this path has to lead somewhere."

Just ahead is another bend in the path and when they turn the corner, they stop. Caecilia claps her hand over her mouth to stop herself from making a noise, and Macia gasps and covers her face. In front of them is the most hideous building they have ever seen. It is built like a huge mask, a face contorted and angry, a tongue sticking out, made of snakes, twisted together to make a gangway into the gaping mouth, past razor-like teeth. The green eyes are evil, dripping with little green snakes and the ears are formed by writhing snakes as well.

The place is deadly quiet. No birds can be heard, and no scurrying other creatures. It is as if the jungle knows to stay away from this face. "The Khramuil, do you think?" Gax asks, and the girls nod, not taking their eyes off the building. In front of the face, they can see a wide path, like one of the main roads, leading straight to the horrible tongue and into the mouth. "That explains why the path was narrow and not much used. Do you think it's a secret way?" Gax looks back at the path and nudges the girls.

"We better go," he whispers, "it's getting darker by the minute. And it's a long way back. At least we should be able to walk faster, but we better stay quiet. We don't want to meet any elders." He tries to smile to lighten his words but the girls shiver and shake their heads.

It happens when they are nearly at the end of the path. The smell warns them almost before they can hear the footsteps. Gax spins around, his eyes wide with fear. Macia grabs Caecilia, and all three dash into the overgrowth at the side of the path and try to shrink into the background. Caecilia holds her chest, sure that her heartbeat can be heard. Macia clings onto her arm, and keeps her head down, not wanting her face to give her away with its paleness against the dark green shrubs. The dark figure slides past their hiding place, not

CHAPTER 9

making a sound, wearing a long robe and a hideous mask. The figure doesn't look to the left or the right but simply moves past them, a strong scent of coriander lingering along with the fear flooding them. They stay where they are for a while, shaken.

"That was close," Gax says, his voice a little higher than usual. "I'm glad we knew about the coriander," he adds, helping the girls to their feet. "It must have been one of the elders. I wonder if anyone knows who they are. We will need to be extra careful." He looks in the grass where they had hidden, but it's hard to see if they have left tell-tale signs.

Tumbling back onto the main path with relief, they almost bump into Riu. "Your god must have been looking after you just now," he whispers, looking over his shoulder, as well as theirs. "I saw the elder going in and then you come out. Only a little later. How did he not see you?"

Gax smiles and opens his mouth, then closes it again, his face red. "We realised someone was coming, so we hid," he says, trying to make it sound like a standard thing to do when out for a walk.

Riu shakes his head. "There are traps along the path, in the verges along the path. Snake traps, evil mouths, all kinds. You can't hide in the long grass as it will kill you."

The three look at each other and Caecilia can feel her hands starting to shake again. Gax looks dumbstruck and even Macia isn't sure what to say. "We asked our God to keep us safe," she manages in the end, "but we weren't expecting traps at the side of the path. We weren't sure who was coming down the path and we thought it better to stay out of sight."

Riu walks along with them, keeping a watchful eye out, and they realise he isn't keen to be seen with them. After what just happened, they can't blame him. "Did you get to the Khramuil?" he wants to know.

Macia nods, and with effort keeps back the words she was going to say. "It's an…unusual building," she says. "What is it made of?"

Riu looks at her in astonishment. "It isn't made," he says, "It has always been there. The Stream lives there, the Stream leaves the mouth and does what it will. We go in through the mouth to worship. We please the Stream. Then the Stream is pleased with us for more time. So we get better harvest. We have healthier children, better animals."

When they reach their house, Riu comes in for tea. He sniffs and Caecilia makes sure she rubs many of the leaves in the windowsill pots to spread their aroma. Riu turns his head round and wrinkles his nose like a rabbit, Macia steps in. "Do any of the other people go for walks? Just to enjoy the walk I mean?"

Riu is too polite not to look at her and answer her question. "No, but I saw it in Aniquist. People there walk. They walk in parks, and around the city. Always walking. Often with dogs."

By the time the mint tea arrives, the faint smell of coriander has gone and Riu has given up sniffing the air. The three look at each other over their steaming mugs. The coriander might be more tricky than they expected. Caecilia has dried some of it, but she is determined to have fresh coriander growing at all times. She isn't sure why, but seeing the elder this afternoon helps her to know that the three of them are not powerless or outdone by the people with the hideous masks.

Chapter 10

The three continue their routine of studying the Book, working in the garden and going for walks week by week, until at last it's harvest time. Caecilia smiles broadly, hauling in a sack of quinoa. "There is no chance of smelling the special herb," Macia agrees. "The whole house smells of quinoa. We will need the herbs to make it palatable though."

Gax hears her words as he staggers into the house with another bucket load of potatoes. "We will need to find a way to keep all this food fresh," he says, "and maybe grow more herbs?" The girls look around the living area and agree. Having to share the room with their entire harvest doesn't sound good.

Riu knocks and enters their house. "I see you have a good harvest," he says, smiling. "I show you the storage area," he says, and they follow him outside. At the side of the house is a very low lean-to, with a wooden lid, bent from the weather. The blue paint at the sides could do with another layer, but when Riu lifts the lid, they see sturdy steps leading down to a cellar.

The three go down and Caecilia exclaims at the space. "So much room for food," she sighs happily, "even shelves for jars. I saw the special canning jars in the shop."

Macia nods and points at the woven baskets around the room. "Perfect for potatoes and maybe quinoa in that one?" They all take some baskets up and shiver in the fresh rainfall when getting out of the cellar.

"Thank you," Gax says to a quiet Riu. "May we bring some of our harvest to you and your parents? For letting us use the house and the plot of land?"

Riu smiles, looking relieved. "That will be good," he says, "as long as you have enough. There are three of you." Gax waves off his words, pointing out that there is still more to harvest. He doesn't want to let Riu know that as food has been so cheap, they could afford to buy food as well.

Before leaving the house, Riu looks around one more time, then whispers, "Maybe your god has looked after you well," and slips out of the house, leaving the three to smile at each other.

There are no smiles when they arrive at Riu's parents' house that afternoon. They can hear the wailing before rounding the last bend leading to the bright-coloured cottage. Despite the heavy baskets, they run the last few steps, then stop in horror. Riu's mother is holding a little child, soaking wet. She cradles the child, weeping bitterly. The child is limp, and not responding. Macia sprints forward as she drops her basket, potatoes rolling against the red wall. She looks at Riu whilst kneeling next to his mother, her fingertips touching the child's cold face.

"The water. He was playing and then this. He was in, not long, but he is dead!" And Riu drops on the ground weeping, hissing at her through his hands, "Your god. I told you your book and your god would anger the Stream. Now water has taken my nephew."

Macia blushes, but takes hold of the toddler, looking Riu's mother straight in the face. "Let me. Let me help, please." The mother is too upset to fight Macia and she lays down the little boy, his round, sweet face still. Macia takes a deep breath and then closes her eyes for a few seconds, praying for strength, for courage and for the child to

CHAPTER 10

be revived. She covers the cold little lips and breathes, then pushing down firmly on the little chest, counts, pushes, breathes, pushes, in a determined cycle. All sounds fade into the background as she counts, "twenty-one, twenty-two..."

She feels it as she leans over the little face once more. Life. There is life! Quickly she rolls the chubby little body on its side and just in time too. A spasm brings up a load of water. Macia pats the tiny back, crying for joy, arranging the little boy to keep him on his side. She wipes his curly hair off his forehead and checks his breathing, his pulse, sobbing quietly with relief and gratitude. "Thank you, Lord Jesus, thank you," she whispers when leaning over the soft little face.

When she finally looks up, Riu's parents are staring at her, not sure what to think. There is joy at receiving their grandson back, but at what cost? Macia smiles at them. "It's a technique," she explains. "When someone drowns, there is a short time where you can often start their heart working again. If a person hasn't been in the water long, you can rescue them like that." She keeps smiling, hoping they will accept her explanation and not drag her off to the awful Khramuil to be dealt with for magic or whatever they believe she just did.

Riu is stunned as well. "You made him alive again," he says, his voice filled with awe. Or fear? Macia shakes her head and gives the same explanation, then adds that she has been studying the human body for her course and working with fitness requires her to know how to resuscitate a person. "But he was dead, we saw he was dead," Riu insists. He narrows his eyes at her, then looks at Gax and Caecilia. Caecilia is crying and smiling at the same time, Gax's grin looks like a permanent feature.

"Macia is right," Gax says quietly. "Yes, his heart will have stopped, but there is a small time window in which you can try to restart the heart, bringing oxygen into the body and sometimes people will then recover." He looks at the little boy and then at Riu, "Do you have a doctor here? For he could do with checking out, for there might be water left in his lungs. He can still get very ill."

Riu looks at his parents and his mother shakes her head violently, grabbing him by the arm. The three aren't sure what she says, as she speaks the local dialect faster than they are used to. Riu nods at his mother and looks at Gax. "No doctor. My mother says no doctor." He hesitates and says, "She doesn't think the doctor will like what you did. She is not sure she likes it. But Rociu is alive. She says it is all that matters. It will not matter to the doctor though. He might make trouble. They want Rociu, not the trouble."

Macia is relieved and seeing the little boy move a little, making a tiny whimpering sound, she scoops him up and lays him in Riu's mother's arms. "Here," she smiles, "keep him warm, and just hold him close." She touches the woman's arm. "It's not a trick or magic. I asked our God when I breathed into Rociu's lungs, yes, but it's also a normal technique doctors teach. Where we are from, many people can do the same thing." The woman nods and hugs little Rociu closer, kissing his little tanned face, and nuzzling his dark curly hair, still wet from the water. She walks into the house without looking back.

Caecilia helps Macia to pick up the spilled potatoes, and whispers, "Why did you mention God? Don't you think that was a dangerous thing to say? I saw Riu's father's face. What if he mentions it to anyone?"

Macia bites her lip. "I know. The words just came out. I had to give God the glory of what just happened. It felt like I was doing CPR forever and nothing was happening. I prayed and prayed, and I was just so thankful. I didn't want them to think it was just me, or just a technique. It was God, for drowning is awful and it could have been fatal. I don't know…" Her voice trails off but Caecilia hugs her.

"You are right," she whispers, "I shouldn't have given in to fear. Who knows how God will use this? Everything is for our good, right?" The

CHAPTER 10

girls smile at each other and hand the basket to Riu. "Here you go, some will be a bit bruised, I'm afraid," Caecilia says to him.

He nods, his face still filled with awe. He swallows, then whispers, "Thank you. I know what you did. It wasn't only technique. I heard you call on your God. He gave us Rociu back. The Stream has never given anything or anyone back. It simply devours, washes away." He turns round and together with his father carries the baskets into the house.

They return a few moments later and the father nods quietly and says a simple thank you. He goes back into the house. The four are left alone outside. Riu sighs. "I would like to invite you in, but I'm afraid to do so. My father... he isn't sure. I need to think as well. My nephew is here for the rest of the day but will be home tomorrow. He is often with us." He looks at the shallow pond near the house and shudders. "It was so quick," he adds.

After a few more moments with Riu, the three walk back to their little house. "Well," says Gax, kicking a small stone ahead, "who had expected that? I wonder if it will lead to anything?"

"The shop was busy this morning," Gax says as he comes into the house the next morning. "I'm not sure what people were buying, just more people around the shop than usual."

Just as he sits down to warm his hands, there is a knock and Riu peeks through the door opening. "Hello," he smiles, "I saw you coming back from the shop." He slips through the door after a glance over his shoulder. He sits down and accepts the hot mint tea. "I have come to tell you about the special time to go to the Khramuil," he says quietly, looking at the door again, making the girls feel nervous too.

"What will be expected of us?" Gax asks, as that is the most important thing right now.

Riu sighs softly. "I can't believe I say this. But your god is strong, stronger than what happened to Rociu. So here we are. In a few days, it is the special time. The time to visit Khramuil and pay the Stream. They will not count people. They think everyone will come so there is no need for counting. Everybody wears masks. Everybody brings something for sacrifice. So if you don't go, they won't know. But the elders will walk around the village. They bless all the houses. If there is light in your house or noise, they will know you are here. So I have a plan for you. You stay here, in the dark and totally quiet, away from windows. All the time. Till the morning. Sacrifices can last a long time. There is dancing and eating and it goes on until the sun wakes up. If they see you at home, they will know you were not at the Khramuil, as they would see you leave early. Stay in the dark until everybody is home at the middle of the day and it is safe to get up."

He breathes out and shivers, hugging the hot mug. What has he done? Will the Stream take him now, as he failed with Rociu? He looks at the three foreigners, and Gax nods.

"Thank you, Riu. This must have been hard," he says softly. Riu swallows, and Gax continues, "We will pray to our God to protect you and keep you safe. We will do what you suggested, and stay quiet." He pauses for a while as they all sip their hot drink, mulling over the dangerous days ahead. "How will we know it's the right day?" Gax asks and Riu explains that loud drums will be beaten all day. That evening, people will walk to the Khramuil down the main path, carrying their sacrifice and wearing dreadful masks.

"The masks have to be bad, to drive away bad luck, as the Stream doesn't believe in good. People do bad things, bad things happen in life, people die, animals eat each other. Anything pretending to be good, the Stream will devour. He wants real worship, so all masks are evil and people will make angry sounds and sing about bad things." He looks away. "You bring good, your god brings life to Rociu and you breathed into him," he says and looks at Macia. "I see the difference, but I live here. You are visiting, so maybe not going to Khramuil is

CHAPTER 10

better for you."

When Riu has left, Gax looks at the girls. "We better keep a low profile these days," he says quietly. "I could tell something was up in the shop, a sense of excitement."

Chapter 11

They set off for the shop early in the morning, hoping that it will be quieter. But it is busy already and Gax's heart sinks. He is worried someone will question them, but nobody seems to pay attention as Caecilia checks different herbs and Macia looks around for some smaller baskets. The shopkeeper grunts a welcome as he serves them and nods at a corner that holds masks and various tools. When Gax shakes his head the man shrugs but doesn't seem concerned.

When they get out of the shop, they realise that in the time they have been inside, a small market has been set up next to the shop. Judging by the noise, it is mainly livestock and Caecilia gasps at the bleating and squeaking. After hesitating for a few seconds, they decide to have a look. There seem to be mainly guinea pigs, goats and pigeons, but one man has a different kind of cage. When the girls look closer he grins at them, most of his teeth missing. He is chewing something which he spits out over his shoulder, then mumbles. The girls lean closer to the cage to see what kind of animals they are. "Ferrets!" Caecilia gasps. She has seen them when visiting a family from the Meeting House in Mataiox. "They're like the ones Cath has," she adds.

There are two ferrets in the cage, curled up in a corner where there is some dirty-looking straw. The man repeats the amount of money again and Gax offers a lower amount. It takes a while, but in the

CHAPTER 11

end, the price is acceptable. The girls lift the small cage and leave the market. They meet Riu on the way home, who stares. "We like ferrets," Macia says defensively.

Riu grins and says softly, "It's a good idea as well, as it makes it look as if you're getting ready." They stare at him and Riu waves a hand towards the shop. "They sell animals this week ready for people to buy as sacrifices. That way you don't have to give one of your animals or hunt for one." The girls stare at him, then at the two ferrets. "Those would have made a good sacrifice as they're hunter animals. Animals that are merely food are not so good. Animals that eat other animals are better-level sacrifice. You might get more protection or forgiveness."

The three are stunned and Macia holds the cage a little tighter. "Do you know what ferrets eat?"

Riu shrugs and scratches his head. "Probably meat as that's what they catch in the wild. Not sure what you will catch for them. Maybe buy some small animals at the market as well?"

The girls look at each other and Gax chuckles. "We'll have to learn to hunt, I suppose," he says, then adds, "Maybe we should use the traps we set for the rats and mice in the food cellar. We had two this morning, so we'll feed those to the ferrets next time." The girls shudder and Gax looks a little paler as well.

Riu laughs. "You could always release them, but maybe after the ceremony, otherwise you will have to buy them again," he says. "They will have been wild, so they can look after themselves. They might not like captivity anyway. Many animals do not like small spaces."

The ferrets turn out to be great fun. They are playful if not a little rough. Macia likes them a lot. Caecilia pulls a face. "It's their sharp teeth. They're too quick to use them," she says. "But they have such cute little faces and sweet round ears."

The ferrets come out when it's nearly time to go to sleep, making

Gax yawn. "I wished they loved the daytime," he groans, watching the two ferrets spin around, tumbling over each other in a whirl of paws and tails. "What are you going to call them?"

So far, the names have changed every day. Caecilia giggles as Macia says, "Tails and Paws. That's how they play, but their personalities are more like Tales and Pause, so it fits." Paws stops, and looks at her, his dark eyes shrewd, one little dark brown paw lifted in the air, paused. Tails jumps right over him, lighter fur streaked with blond, tail in the air. He turns around and standing proud, stares at Paws until Paws stops listening to the humans and sprints at Tails. Both girls shudder when it's feeding time. Gax dislikes it too, but it simply has to be done.

"The main thing is to stop them from hiding that last bit again like they did yesterday. That was revolting and if we hadn't realised it would have been more than revolting in a few days," he says with a shiver.

The following morning, after breakfast, the drums start up. A deep, pulsating noise that soon clambers right into their heads, making Caecilia want to hide under her blankets. The day has arrived. They look at each other, and Gax gets up. "What do you need from the food cellar today," he asks quietly although the door is still shut. Caecilia tells him, and Gax slips out of the house. He is back soon, shivering. "It's misty and cold," he says, rubbing his arms vigorously. "Staying under our blankets today won't be a punishment. I think it would be good to make it a special time to pray. We could pray for the village and our journey into the jungle."

As it darkens at the end of the day, they release the ferrets, whispering at them. The squeaking noises Paws and Tails make when getting their food cause Caecilia to hold her breath. "Do you think anyone can hear their noises?" She looks at the shuttered windows, expecting an evil mask to appear at any moment.

Macia doesn't think so. "The shutters are pretty good and although

CHAPTER 11

it sounds loud in here, they're only little voices. It's not like a dog barking." They're all relieved when Macia has coaxed them back into their cage though. The two furry bodies curl up together and they're soon sound asleep again. They whisper good night to each other and soon everything is quiet.

Caecilia is unable to sleep for a long time. She is sure that she can hear footsteps several times, once very close to the shuttered window of their room. She is glad that the window is shut as she suddenly remembers the coriander. Will they try the door and come in? Riu said they never do. "Houses are sacred. They will never come in a house. If they need you, they will wait outside your house." Caecilia had felt relieved, but what if they broke their own rule? Maybe this house wasn't seen as sacred as they didn't own it.

When she wakes up it is morning. She sits up and Macia smiles at her, placing a finger on her lips. Caecilia nods. "I think I can hear somebody," Macia breathes as she leans close to Caecilia. Caecilia's eyes widen and Macia shrugs, smiling again. Both girls stay as still as they can and Caecilia hears it at the same time as Macia: footsteps, just outside their window. The shutter rattles and Caecilia stares at Macia in a panic. Macia doesn't hesitate one moment. She slides out of bed, smooths her blanket down and lies on the freezing cold wooden floor. Caecilia does the same, shaking all over.

A small beam of faint morning light creeps across their beds, missing both girls by a fraction. The light stops moving and both girls hold their breath. They can hear a soft cough and Caecilia silently wipes away a tear, praying for whoever it is to go away. Another cough, and then, at last, the light beam shrinks again. They stay down as the shutters click shut again, the latch falling into place. The footsteps can be heard leaving their window. Macia releases a breath and Caecilia sobs quietly. She suddenly stops. "Would he have seen the coriander?" she asks in the quietest whisper, her hands framing her wet face.

Macia looks at the window and after a few moments shakes her head. "The wrong angle," she breathes, "he must have opened the shutter there," and she points, "so he couldn't have seen the coriander as it's there." She points at the dark, fragrant, fragile leaves.

Caecilia isn't sure. "He was there for a long time," she whispers. Nothing else happens and in the end, Caecilia agrees that he can't have seen the coriander.

"He would have come in, or knocked on the window," Macia says. Secretly, she isn't convinced. The elder wouldn't come in, because of the house being sacred, and they were supposed to be at the ceremony, so will there be a daytime visit soon? "I'm glad he's gone, as I was getting cold to my bones on that floor," she whispers, trying to chuckle. Caecilia nods and shivers as they get off the floor with some effort.

They stay under their blankets till lunchtime. Footsteps can be heard along the path in front of their house. It must be the families living further along the ridge, returning from the ceremony. Gax calls them softly an hour or so later. "I think it's safe to come out. We can have something to eat," he says as the girls emerge. "Maybe something cold, rather than make a fire." They eat silently, and the girls tell him about the elder opening the shutter and looking in.

"There is the Book and our notebooks," Caecilia suddenly says. They all look at the stack on the shelf.

Gax shakes his head. "It must have still been quite dark, so I doubt he could have seen what it says on the Book. Riu recognised it because he had been to Aniquist. I don't know how many others have been there. They might never have seen it or even heard of it. Anyway, I'm sure we are fine. He can't have seen anything, otherwise, they would have been back by now, lying in wait for us or something." When Gax sees Caecilia's face he bites his lip, catching the sigh before it escapes. "If you want, we can put the Book out of sight a bit more, and maybe put the coriander in a different corner?"

CHAPTER 11

Riu knocks early the next morning. He smiles at them. "I don't think you were missed," he says. "It was very busy. Many people were there. Only the Stream might know your sacrifice was missing. I don't know," he adds, and he shrugs. "Maybe your god makes the Stream not see. Then you will be fine. No elder put a note on your door either, so you are safe from what happens when they give you the note."

The girls tell him about the elder peeking in. "They are not normally to do that," Riu is shocked. "That is bad, as it can happen in the whole village. You cannot open a shutter to look in. That is not good." He thinks, a deep crease between his eyebrows. "But I don't know what you can do. You can't tell anyone. He can't tell anyone."

Riu explains that if a house has something suspicious or people go against the head elder, there will be a note attached to their door. "They hammer it on. The note will show what the problem is. You will then need to go to Khramuil to see the elders and explain. Maybe you step out of your hut and the elders will take you. That is only if it is very bad. Like a very bad thing you have done." He hesitates, then looks away. But the three know what he was going to say. *Like bringing a forbidden Book into the village.*

In the morning, soon after breakfast, Caecilia goes to check the door. The sun is starting to climb into view, making the cold less sharp. Caecilia looks at the view and she knows she will miss it. Even when they are back in Mataiox, she will miss this view and the clean mountain air. She will miss the smell of the wood fire and freshly turned soil. She won't miss the fear though. And the sooner they can get into the jungle, the better, as it also means that their time is coming to an end and before she knows it, they'll be back in Mataiox, spending time with friends at the Meeting House. She shivers in the cold air. So many hard steps to be taken first, it's weighing her down and she quickly wipes her eyes dry.

He stares at the fire, wondering what to do. They weren't at the ceremony, he is sure of that. But can he confront them? He has no proof. He rearranges his robe, and frowns. Why are they even here? They are different from the villagers, and they haven't blended in. That boy, Riu, is friendly with them, but that might be because the strangers are using his sister's house. He makes a deep, guttural growling noise. That is another young person that has left. He has to make sure nobody else from that family will go astray. There are rumours...rumours involving their grandchild. He slouches down. He will watch the strangers. And check on them, but after dark. Opening the shutter had been on the edge, and he can't take too many risks.

Chapter 12

Macia is sure last night saw the first frost. "We just need to wait a few more months, and then it'll be time to go. No need to pack yet," she grins as he can see Caecilia looking around the little house. "Although we might need to start thinking of what we'll take with us. Carrying our stuff here across the mud was hard work and this will be days and days of walking through the jungle."

Even Caecilia takes to walking in the next week. The small house is cold during the day when they leave the fire off, and the best thing to do around Colchuyni is walking. The scenery is breathtaking, the colours stunning even in the cold season. Caecilia's favourite spot allows her to look across the water where months ago they walked. It's a peaceful spot to pray as well. She has found a large, smooth stone in a cleft, where it feels relatively warm. "Lord, You know how much I want to be back home, and how scared I am. I still don't know why I am here apart from my fear of losing Gax. But I could easily be lost myself, killed in some remote village where nobody will ever find me."

They wake up with frost on the ground, making it hard for Gax to open the lid of the food cellar. "Maybe get tomorrow's portion out as well," Caecilia says.

After lunch, Gax sets off for the shop. "I might have a quick look around as well. There is a good view from the viewing plateau. I might spot the jungle."

"Make sure you're careful," Caecilia warns, "I'm sure we can enter the jungle just behind the Khramuil, as the place was so green and dense. That would mean the building is guarding the entrance, which makes sense. If they see you looking that way, someone might report you." She shudders. "I don't want a paper hammered onto our door," she says and pulls her mouth in a smile.

Macia isn't sure either. "Just be careful," she says. "We don't know if they are suspicious since the ceremony. The fact that the elder looked through the window, which Riu said wasn't acceptable, must be a sign they're not trusting us. If they see you staring in the wrong direction, they might take note."

Gax's cheeks warm up but he nods. "I will be careful. I often stand at the viewpoint, just looking around or rearranging my bags."

Macia pats his arm, "I know. It's just that the ceremony has made us a little wary. That's all. I think you're good at this kind of thing, like spotting the elder before he saw us on that path."

"That was a little too close for comfort," he says with a laugh, "so I won't be going on any quiet paths this afternoon, I can assure you!"

Macia waves one more time, then turns to Caecilia. "Shall we go for a walk as well?"

The girls set off, drinking in the views. They stay out longer than planned and it's only when Caecilia shivers in the cool air that they turn back. "That was beautiful, but it's getting colder in the afternoons," Caecilia says. "The sun goes down earlier, but the temperature drops before that. I'll start dinner soon, at least that will warm the house. The ferrets might need extra straw in their cage as well," she chatters as they walk back towards the house.

It's dark in the house and Macia lights the lamps whilst Caecilia starts the fire for dinner. Every little sound has her looking at the door and Macia bites her lip, frowning. "He'll be fine," she says in the

CHAPTER 12

end. "He might have bumped into Riu, who knows." Caecilia blushes but doesn't say anything. "Do you need more wood," Macia asks, her voice softer. Caecilia shakes her head and Macia rearranges some of their belongings that were left out. After a few more minutes, Macia looks out the window. "It's getting darker. Shall I close the shutters except for the one towards the road?" Her voice isn't as abrasive this time, more hesitant and Caecilia looks up from what she was doing.

"Do you think he's in trouble?" She stares at Macia who shakes her head, scowling.

"No, not at all. I think he has been delayed and I am annoyed because he knew we had been worried." She stomps outside and Caecilia flinches with each slamming shutter. "I'm tempted to shut the front ones as well," Macia mutters as she slams the door shut. "Serves him right if he struggles to find the house back." Caecilia laughs at that, although she isn't sure why.

Dinner is cooked. The girls look at each other, their eyes large in the flickering lights. "I think we ought to close the front shutter as well," Macia says quietly and slips out of the house to do so.

"We need to eat. Then think and plan as well as pray," Caecilia whispers, her eyes red. Macia nods and they sit at the table. The long walk has made them hungry but Caecilia is sure she'll be sick if she eats.

"We need the food," Macia says, her voice shaking, "for I have an awful feeling that we are in trouble. If they have taken Gax, they will come for us. We need to get him out as well as leave Colchuyni. We need all the strength we can get. Adrenaline alone isn't going to see us through. We simply have to eat, however horrible it... feels." Caecilia quietly swipes at tears.

Macia glances at the door. "We will need to leave the house, but when? Will they come this evening or will there be time?"

Caecilia sobs quietly then takes a deep breath. "I'm sorry," she says, "you're right. I presume they will nail the paper to the door first, so that might give us enough time to get away." She looks around the house. Biting her lip she says, "We better get the bags out and start planning. We won't need to take everything with us, but we must take food."

For the next half hour, they make stacks of the essentials. Caecilia says, "Maybe I should cook some food for on the way. It's not much point taking raw potato with us as it will be a while before we can make a fire and cook."

They open the door and peek out. It's quiet and the air is still. "Let's go together," breathes Macia and they slip out of the house. Macia lights the candle in the cellar and they collect what they will need. "We will have to carry it all, so we'll be limited," she warns Caecilia as she sees her filling several baskets. Seeing her friend's face she pats her arm. "We have to trust God to provide for us," she says. "There must be food in the jungle and we will be able to look for food once we're a long way away from Colchuyni."

Macia helps Caecilia to prepare food and distribute it over various containers. Just carrying the food by itself would be heavy. Add to that their clothes, sleeping bag, personal belongings… It's going to be a hard journey. Just when they have collected everything they can think of, there is a very soft rapping on the door. Both girls stand still, not daring to breathe. Is that the paper being nailed to the door?

The door opens, and Riu slips in, his face serious. "They have Gax," he whispers and sinks into the nearest chair, out of breath. The girls join him at the table. Riu looks at the chaos and back at the girls. "You already knew?" he asks.

"We guessed when Gax didn't return from the shop," Macia says.

Riu swallows. "He's in the special room in the Khramuil." He says, looks at the door then fishes a pencil and old paper from his pocket. "This is the main entrance to the Khramuil," he whispers and the girls

CHAPTER 12

lean closer, staring at the paper. "The main entrance is guarded and has many lights. This," and he draws a little blob on the paper, "this is a secret entrance, and from there, this long corridor takes you here. Now, this is what you will need to do. Not tonight. Tonight is fine. Not in the daylight. But when it is night again, this is where you will go..."

Chapter 13

Riu slips out of the house after promising to be back the following night. "I know I'm risking everything, but hopefully your god will protect me," he says, "even when you are gone. I will take you to the Khramuil, so I can carry Gax's bag. From there, you will have to go alone."

The girls sit in stunned silence after the door clicks shut. Macia leans over the map Riu has drawn. "We better study this and then burn it before we leave," she says and Caecilia agrees. "We need to pack soon," Macia continues, "as we don't want to move around too much tomorrow. The best thing is to stay out of sight."

It is nearly midnight by the time they have finished packing. Caecilia tries to lift her bag and bites her lip. "It's so heavy. How are we going to walk for hours and days with these?"

Macia looks at Caecilia and then averts her eyes. *I tried to tell you that for weeks, urging you to train*, she thinks. Instead, she says, "We'll get used to it. And once we're a bit further away from Colchuyni, we might be able to rest for a few days at a time." Caecilia is not looking convinced. "We have no other option," Macia says softly. "We have to take all this as we will need it for our trek to the other side of the jungle."

They wake up late, and breakfast is quiet. "We can eat the rest of the potatoes for lunch and have a quinoa salad," Caecilia says. "Should we

CHAPTER 13

store some for when we come back?"

"I don't know," Macia says slowly. "We might have to come back here to walk across the mud again. We also need to collect the rest of our belongings. But will we get captured if we return?"

They decide to ask Riu. "He might say the best thing to do is to sneak in under cover of darkness again, then hide near the mud walking point until it's time to cross. Either way, he will know."

"What about the ferrets?" Caecilia looks at the wooden cage. How is she going to carry that? "Maybe we should release them," she says, biting her lip. It would be sad to see the cute creatures go, but would it be cruel to carry them along?

"Maybe we should take them, and see how it goes. They might simply run away, in which case we have our answer."

Macia looks around the little house and points to a corner close to Gax's bed. "I'm quite sure they can't see into that corner," she says. "We could open the shutters, move the coriander and our bags and ferrets to that corner and we could sit down there. That way they can't see us but we can open the shutters and have daylight coming in."

Caecilia agrees and dashes to their sleeping corner to get the coriander. Macia rushes to open the shutters, worried she might be too late already. She hesitates at the door, turning the door handle slowly. Peeking through the crack, she can hear birds singing nearby. Does that mean there are no people to disturb the peace? She looks around and glances at Caecilia who stands in the middle of the room, pots with herbs in her arms, staring wide-eyed at Macia. "It looks ok," Macia hisses, then slips out of the door. She has never opened shutters that fast before.

When she gets back into the house, her hands are shaking and she sinks onto the edge of Gax's bed. "Horrible," she sighs and Caecilia shudders in sympathy. "I could do with some tea. Maybe we should quickly make some?"

Caecilia offers to make some, putting the kettle on to boil. She hides back in their little corner whilst waiting for the water to heat up. Hugging their steaming mugs, the girls lean back. The long wait has begun.

Just before lunchtime, they can hear mumbled voices. There is a knock on the door, and the girls huddle closer into their corner. More mumbling and then a hammering noise. Caecilia sucks in a breath. "The note," she whispers and Macia nods. "I wonder what it says," Caecilia says after a few moments. The hammering stops as if they heard her words.

The girls stay still, even when the voices have gone. "Should we have a look?" Macia asks.

Caecilia shakes her head, "They might have left someone to stand guard. They could grab us as soon as we open the door," she says, her hands shaking. She quietly leaves the corner to cook lunch, her eyes constantly swerving to the windows. Macia creeps out of the corner and whispers, "I'll keep an eye on the window, and will let you know if I can see something." Caecilia nods and glances at the door one more time. Lunch tastes like cooked straw but again, both girls force themselves to eat as much as possible.

They take a nap after lunch, knowing there won't be any sleep in the coming night. When they wake up, the light has nearly gone. "I better make dinner now," Caecilia whispers, "so we won't have to use too much light."

By the time dinner is ready, it's completely dark outside. "Do you think I should risk doing the shutters now? Riu will want to come soon, and it's easier if we can make a light in here," Macia asks, not in a rush to dash outside.

Caecilia swallows, then grabs Macia's hands, closes her eyes tight, and says, "Lord, we are scared. Everything is a mess and we want to

CHAPTER 13

get Gax free. We want to close the shutters and we are afraid we will be captured as well. Please help us, protect Riu especially. Overcome the Stream for him, Lord. Please give us courage." Macia smiles and pats Caecilia's hands once the girl stops speaking, and glides towards the door. She opens it, listens, and not hearing anything, slips out. Caecilia holds her breath as each shutter is closed with the softest of clicks. Moments after Macia joins her again, there is a barely audible knock and Riu slips into the house, just as Caecilia lights the first candle.

He grins at the girls, his face pale. "Are you ready?" He looks at the bags and takes Gax's bag with a soft grunt. "I hope your god is strong," he mutters. Macia shrugs into her bag and helps Caecilia with hers. Caecilia then lifts the cage with the ferrets and looks around the house one more time. Riu stares at the ferrets. "You take them to eat?" he asks and the girls glare at him.

"We hope they will hunt for us," Macia says. Riu shrugs and grins. Macia picks up the largest pot with coriander and Riu's face goes even paler.

"Eldergrass," he whispers. "I don't think it's on your note yet, but just for that, they would kill you. You better not get caught with that."

"We don't want to get caught at all, with or without Eldergrass," Caecilia says. Riu shakes his head and moves towards the door.

The night air is cold and Caecilia gasps. The ferrets make little squeaking noises, but not their usual happy ones. They follow Riu along the gravelly road, giving the shop a wide berth. Macia recognises the path that leads to the Khramuil. Just before stepping onto the path, Riu rummages in the bushes and produces three masks. The girls shudder as they see the ugly things but they put them on anyway. "You will need the grass now," he whispers.

Macia kneels, nearly losing her balance because of her heavy backpack. She breaks off as much coriander as she can and hands some to Caecilia. Riu shakes his head as she tries to hand him some. "My hands will give me away," he whispers, "as tomorrow and the day after, my hands will smell of Eldergrass."

The path seems even longer than the first time they went. There is no time to rest though. Just before they reach the Khramuil, Riu stops. "The Khramuil is just around the last bend," he whispers, "but there is a very narrow path that goes to the secret entrance. We will need to find it. Just don't leave the path, as there are traps in the undergrowth."

They inch along the path, staring in the dark at each bush and clump of grass. Caecilia finds it. "Look," she hisses, and points, then realising how dark it is, she says, "Look over there, between those trees." Riu peers into the darkness and grunts.

"You're right," he says, breathing out a very long breath. "Let's go." They follow him carefully as they shuffle along the narrow path. They're all panting and sweating by the time they come to the clearing. Riu leans back a little and they follow his lead. "I will leave Gax's bag here," he breathes, "and when you leave, he can pick it up from here. " He points and says, "Can you see my hand?" and when the girls make the right noises, he continues, "That is where the bad part starts, the forbidden part. Nobody ever goes there, only the Head Elder sometimes. It is bad, and…" he stops. There is no alternative and they all know it. Caecilia squeezes his shoulder and he sighs.

"I wish there were another way," he says softly, then slips the large rucksack off. He pushes it carefully underneath a bush and points out the bush to the girls. "Don't get confused in the dark," he says, "it's the bush here, by the large tree with no branches." The girls nod in the dark, and soon their rucksacks have joined Gax's. There is no point lugging heavy bags around the holy place. They straighten up, clutching the coriander a little tighter and Riu grunts. "That is better; I can smell the grass now." The ferrets make quiet noises, but the odd journey through the dark has them silenced.

CHAPTER 13

He touches their arms, breathes a "may your god keep you from being washed away," and he is gone, swallowed by the darkness. The girls touch hands, then set off, across the clearing, walking sedately like they have seen the elder do down the path, holding out the Eldergrass as a wand.

The small door into the Khramuil isn't locked. There are no guards and only one small, flickering candle set in a holder attached to the wall. The one nearer the door seems to have run out. "Should we take it," Caecilia whispers and Macia shakes her head.

"We don't want to be seen and it would be awful if we had to blow it out, the smell would give us away," she says.

They follow the corridor, trying to remember Riu's map. In the dark, in reality, it seems different from the pencilled drawing. They come to a fork. "Left, each time left except at the end," Macia murmurs, repeating Riu's accent. It makes Caecilia giggle, but the sound turns into a sob. They walk on, quietly, slowly, desperate to make a run for it, grab Gax and dash back out. Another left, more light. At the next left, darkness once more. Finally, the right-hand turn appears. They take a deep breath and shuffle into the dark corridor, feeling the ground slope downwards.

A cool breeze springs up, hardly noticeable, and by peering through the darkness, Macia spots an open door. "We're nearly there, this door looks like the one Riu described," she hisses. They walk on, even more slowly now as they don't want to miss the door. A noise. Was that a voice? They stop, head tilted, eyes staring into the dark. A voice, male. A cough followed by a groan. Gax.

"Here," Caecilia whispers and the door feels cold under their fingertips. The latch found, Macia pulls the door open and calls out softly, "Are you there, Gax?"

A gasp and a ghostly figure appears. "It's us," Caecilia giggles, aware suddenly of the ridiculous masks. "Come, we need to go."

Gax doesn't have to be asked twice, but he holds out his hands. "What about my ropes?" he whispers, "should we undo those first?"

Macia shakes her head and then breathes the word, no. "If we meet someone, we can pretend you're our prisoner, it's safer that way. We have the coriander. Come, quick." She can feel the muscles in her legs starting to shake. All along the corridor, she can sense slimy fingers grabbing at her clothes, entwining themselves around her legs. The darkness isn't from the lack of light only.

The three set off to the way out, Gax breathing heavily, Caecilia wording quiet prayers, Macia humming a song from the Meeting House over and over, barely audible, but somehow loud enough to dispel some of the darkness. Just as they are level with a turnoff, another masked figure looms up. Gax groans but Macia simply holds out the coriander bunch, giving it a little rub and a shake to waft the smell towards the other masked one. The masked one stops, steps towards them a little, and hesitates. Gax leans back a little, but Macia grabs his arm roughly, makes angry noises at him and drags him forward, away from the figure. Caecilia does the same, tears silently rolling down behind her mask.

It works. The figure doesn't stop them. They walk on, calmly, and authoritatively. Only at the next bend does Macia dare to glance back. The masked one is still there, staring after them. Knowing they're nearly at the exit she hisses, "Quick now, in case he raises the alarm. He was still staring at us and clearly didn't trust us. Let's hurry."

They run as fast as they can without making a noise, Gax gasping for breath and limping a little. "I'm ok," he snorts, "just hurt my foot, that's all." Struggling for breath after those words, he stays quiet, until they reach the little door.

Chapter 14

Voices. They can hear mumbled voices behind them, not far from where they just were. Macia dashes back to the one candle and blows it out, plunging them into darkness. She stumbles back, and hisses, "Open the door, but not too wide." Caecilia pushes the little door but it won't budge. Panicked, she pushes harder, a sob escaping. Macia reaches her. "Here, let me," she whispers, tugging at the door, twisting the doorknob, pushing... Suddenly the door flings open and they tumble out, shutting the door behind them.

"Stay close to the building," Macia says, her words barely audible. She shivers, not just from the cold night air. This reminds her too much of another escape. They stand still in a dark spot and Macia digs out a knife from her pocket and starts cutting at the ropes around Gax's wrists. It takes longer than she hoped and she is desperate to have a look around, to get going, but doesn't dare to take her eyes off Gax's wrists.

Now and then, Gax gives a muffled cough. "They made me breathe in something. It sent me almost to sleep. I know I said a prayer whilst being nearly out. That stopped the smoke," he says and coughs. His eyes look huge in the faint moonlight and he sniffs.

"There, done," Macia says, relief nearly making her drop the knife. She stuffs the ropes in her pocket and looks around into the darkness. "There, look, the tree without branches. Our bags are there."

"Bags?" Gax manages to squeak out.

"Yes," Caecilia says, her voice calm despite the tremor in it, "we had to leave the house. We packed our bags, Riu carried yours. We'll manage," she says, smiling and swallowing a sob at the same time.

Gax is stunned. They expect him to walk into the jungle tonight with his lungs on fire, his foot…who knows how bad his foot is? "We might have to hide for the night and maybe a few days," he says, but Macia shakes her head.

"Look," she breathes, "we need to get going. It won't be long before a whole bunch of elders will come out of this door. With our heavy bags, we won't stand a chance."

She sets off for the tree and the other two follow, Gax has his hands balled in fists, limping and fighting tears. Should he tell them how much he has been hurt? Will it change anything? The girls seem very determined to get out. "Lord," he breathes, "I suffered for Your Name and the girls are just thinking of getting out, away from trouble, running into the jungle." His face is wet by the time they find their rucksacks.

Thankfully, the ferrets make the little whiny noise they make when they think food is coming their way or rather, should be coming their way. Macia chuckles. "Good helpers," she croons over their cage, whilst struggling into her bag. She helps Gax and Caecilia and whispers to the latter, "I'll go in front, shall I? You go to the back. I think Gax is upset about leaving and he is limping as well." She can vaguely make out Caecilia nodding, so she turns towards the path and follows it slowly, not wanting to miss the turn.

It is Gax who finds it, accidentally. He coughs and coughs, struggling to catch his breath, at the same time trying to muffle the sound as much as possible. The girls have to wait, and it is then that Macia spots the small gap between trees, an old gate blocking their way.

Caecilia, looking behind her, gasps. "Quick, I can see lights. They'll

CHAPTER 14

be here in a minute for they must guess this is one of the ways we could go," she hisses, nearly pushing Gax down the track.

Gax doesn't seem to be in a hurry. "They'll easily overtake us," he whispers, "there isn't much point in running anywhere."

Macia looks at Caecilia and can see the girl's eyes widen in the faint light. She grabs Gax's arm, "Let's go," she says, "keep praying and keep moving. We will do this," and she pushes the gate open. They follow the narrow track and within a few minutes, reach a steep staircase. The steps are slippery in the cold air, and they have to be careful not to lose their footing.

Caecilia was relieved to see steps going down, but after a few minutes, she realises that going down steps is nearly as difficult as going up. The constant strain on her legs, coupled with the heavy rucksack, makes her feel exhausted before long. There is no sign of anybody following them, but they go as fast as they can.

Just when Macia thinks she can't possibly take another step, there is a little resting place, similar to the one along the path from the village. She hesitates. Should they waste precious time or would it pay off in the long run? She decides they will need to rest if they want to be able to continue. The three sink on the log. Gax groans and coughs and sits hunched up like an old man. Caecilia dries her face, her legs shaking from the strain.

After a few minutes, she drags herself to her feet. "We will need to keep going," she says softly. Macia nods and gets up. "This path can't be much further, for why would anyone want to go this way, then have to go all the way back?" Gax says nothing, but once the girls have helped him up, he follows Macia down more steps.

Soon the steps stop and they're on a narrow path. Macia releases a long breath. Until she sees the junction just ahead. Which way should they go? Peering down one branch of the path, she sees nothing but shrubs. The other path seems to lead to a small building. "That

Head Elder's place, the one Riu mentioned," she whispers and Caecilia agrees. "The jungle must be the other path, at least I think so."

Gax grunts. "Maybe we should hide in the hut? They won't expect us to go there."

Macia shakes her head. "It has to be the right path. If we stay in the Head elder's hut, we are still in danger. I don't think they will follow us into the jungle."

Gax suddenly lowers himself onto the muddy path. "Well, I can't walk any more," he says, "I am in too much pain to stand here and think about it. Why don't you go and check the start of the path? But I can't go there tonight. I have had nothing to eat for ages, you don't know what they did to me. Everything hurts and I did say I wasn't able to travel right now. I have tried my best, but I can't move any further." And he sobs, his head on his arms.

The girls look at each other, stunned. What are they going to do? Caecilia says softly, "I think he's had it, he sounds exhausted. His limp has been getting worse, so I believe him. Should we briefly check the path, then try the hut? Gax will need food and rest, we can't leave him behind."

Macia sighs. For a moment she wonders if it's worth asking Gax to catch up with them once he has recovered, but she realises it's not going to happen. They will have to spend time in the Head elder's hut. Caecilia leaves the ferrets with Gax and the girls go to the start of the overgrown track. They peer into the darkness, trying to see as much as possible. "This must be it," Macia says, "it looks awful but there is no other path that I can see."

Gax looks up as they come back. "It is definitely the path," Macia says, "but we'll go and see the hut. Hopefully, we can stay there." Gax nods and tries to get up. Both girls have to help him and tears are streaming down his face again by the time he's standing. He limps behind Macia towards the hut.

CHAPTER 14

When they reach the clearing, they stop and stare at the hut. The outside is decorated very much like the Khramuil, with evil-looking snakes covering the low hut. The red snakes contrast with other evil faces, painted black with golden tongues sticking out. There is no door, just a doorway and there are no windows that they can see. "We will be trapped in there," Macia whispers. "If anyone comes, we won't be able to get away. Maybe we should sleep near the hut, rather than inside."

They stand there, hesitating, till Macia says, "I will have a look inside. There might be a door at the back so we can get out unseen." She gets to the door opening and stops. Will the place be covered with traps? She looks all over the door frame, trying to find out where danger could come from.

In the end, she decides to shuffle inside carefully. She pulls her torch out of her pocket, relieved to have some light. Once she is in, she can see two windows as well as walls and doors into other rooms. Maybe staying here would be an option after all, as long as they can ignore the grotesque statues all over the hut. As she turns to leave, a life sized figure by the door makes her jump. Still shaking, she reaches the others.

"There are a few rooms inside and windows," she says softly. "We might be safe enough, although there are some horrendous pictures and figures inside. A huge one, next to the entrance."

Caecilia giggles then looks serious again. "Do you think the statues are safe? Those snakes look so evil, but do you think it is safe for us to be inside such an evil place?"

Macia bites her lip. Part of her says no, but they're just made of wood, so why would it matter? It's merely unpleasant, surely? "I don't know," she says slowly, "I'm sure God can protect us but I think we need to pray, for the place does feel dark and horrible."

They enter the hut cautiously and choose the room to the left as it's larger and has a window that can open. "Maybe we should open the window," Caecilia says, "as we might have to make a run for it. Should we put our rucksacks outside, just in case?"

Macia nods slowly. "I think we should. If we have to leave, it's most likely going to be in a rush." They take a few necessities from the bags, then the girls take the rucksacks outside to hide them. "This tree would be good," Macia says, "we can put everything on those branches. They might not be spotted as easily either." To get the bags up sounds a lot easier than it is in reality, but groaning and sweating, the girls manage to get all three bags up.

"Do you want food now," Caecilia asks as they're together inside. "Gax must be starving, but maybe we should eat as well."

Gax has to force himself to eat slowly. "I'm glad you brought food," he says, trying to smile, but his face won't move. "I am so exhausted, but how will we know someone is coming?" The girls agree to take turns watching. Macia will go first, then wake Caecilia after a while. "I can take the third watch," Gax says, "for by then, I will have had a good rest. I'm not sure we'll be able to outrun any pursuers though," he says quietly, not looking at the girls.

"We have to pray and trust God to help us and protect us," Macia says and gets up quickly. She decides to sit near the door opening, so she can see out, without being seen. She frowns, thinking of Gax. Maybe they should have gone as soon as they realised he'd been captured. They could have come back to the house, grabbed their stuff and hidden in the village somewhere for a while.

"It's quite light," Macia whispers once Caecilia is awake. They're standing in the entrance room, Caecilia doing her best not to see the large statue. "I haven't heard or seen anything, so hopefully they have given up. They might be waiting for daylight, so do keep a good eye out," she pleads. Caecilia nods and shivers. How awful to get overrun!

Macia can't keep her eyes open, but she listens for noises. Birds,

CHAPTER 14

grunting noises, the ferrets rummaging now and then, Gax snoring. No footsteps or shouts, nothing to say they've been discovered. She knows she has to trust Caecilia and get some sleep, but what if...

Caecilia hesitates. Should she wake Gax? He looks shattered, even when asleep. She creeps away again, not wanting to leave the doorway too long, in case they will come. A few times she is sure she can hear something, but nothing definite.

Gax wakes up, stiff and sore and looks around the room. Staring at him is a thin, contorted face, its golden tongue mocking him. He shudders. What a place to sleep. He does feel better and looking at Macia, he realises Caecilia must still be on lookout duty. Quietly, he creeps from the room, making sure Caecilia can hear him once he opens their door. He doesn't want to startle her.

Caecilia smiles at him and Gax smiles back. He lowers himself to the floor next to her. "Just like old times," he croaks and she giggles. "No wolf this time, just some weird...person," he says and they stare out at the greenery around them for a while. Just when Caecilia looks as if she's going to say something, they both hear it.

It's not a loud noise, but people are coming down the path. "They're still on the stairs," Caecilia whispers. She gets up. "I'll wake Macia. We might be safest in here, but I'm not sure."

Gax stares at the trees, no elders in sight yet. Will they capture them? Will he be back in their clutches again? Or will they simply push them down the jungle path, to be dealt with like that girl before them? Riu had said they would most likely sacrifice them as there were three of them. His breathing is fast. There is no way he can fall into their hands a second time. Will he be able to walk fast enough and far enough to outrun them?

He slips back into their room the moment he sees the first figure shimmering between the trees.

Chapter 15

"What should we do?" Caecilia whispers, glancing at the window behind her. "Should we run and hide, or are we actually safer here?"

Gax isn't sure. Nothing seems certain anymore. Their plan had been so good, he knew it had been God sending them to Colchuyni. Now? He has no idea. Why would God arrange for them to travel through the jungle in the wet season? Why not wait a few more weeks?

Macia clears her throat. "Maybe you both stand close to the window, ready to get out. I will peek through our door, and at the first sign of trouble, we'll slip out. There is only a problem if they split up and surround the hut." She tiptoes toward the door and pushes it slightly ajar, making sure to stay away from the crack.

Caecilia and Gax grab their belongings and the ferrets. Caecilia looks through the window and gestures to Gax. "I will hide the ferrets underneath the hut," she whispers. She climbs through the window and then reaches for the cage. The cage fits underneath the hut as the ground slopes away. Caecilia manages to get back in but freezes as she can't do so without making a noise.

They hear no alarm raised, and soon breathe a little easier. But they can hear the voices coming closer. Macia hardly dares to blink, afraid she will miss the critical moment. The masked figure appearing in the main doorway takes her by surprise and she clamps her hands over

CHAPTER 15

her mouth to stifle the gasp, her eyes fixed on the short, stocky figure. He waves a lantern around and chuckles. She isn't sure what he says, but as soon as the words leave his mouth, he turns around and leaves. Macia breathes a sigh of relief until the next masked character enters the hut.

The man opens the door to the other, smaller room, and responds over his shoulder to the stocky one outside. The door clicks shut, and he turns around slowly, waving the lantern to shine in each corner. Macia is tempted to shut their door but decides against it. Hopefully, he won't notice it's ajar. "Yes," he growls to the man outside, "yes, I come. I look first." He starts towards their door and Macia moves back slowly, still keeping her eyes on him. Gax and Caecilia have slipped out of the window but are looking at her.

She is about to signal to them to make a dash for it when the stocky man calls out again and the man close to the door stops. He reaches for the door handle, and Macia scoots, just as she hears his answer. "Fine. Is fine. You say to him then." The door is pulled shut and heavy footsteps walk away from the door. Macia sinks to the ground, shaking. The rooms are now the safest places in the wide area.

All day they stay huddled under the window, quiet and dozing off but never sleeping. They eat the cold potatoes with some vegetables, not yet hungry enough to turn it into a tasty meal. "That is all the food from my bag gone," Caecilia says, her voice shaking a little. It had seemed such a lot and after one day on the run, her food has gone. That leaves Macia and Gax's meals. Another two days before they have no more food. In a dangerous jungle.

Just before it gets dark, they can hear the men returning from wherever they went to search for them. Their voices are harsh, and they walk a lot slower than they did this morning. Macia keeps an eye out and although one man looks through the door opening, the stocky man grunts something and they walk past the hut without stopping.

Macia wipes her damp hands dry and smiles at the others, giving them the thumbs-up sign. She walks over to where they're sitting down and says, "As soon as they're gone, I'm going to have a quick look in the other room."

"I think it's pretty safe to wait here till morning. They might come back to search again and they might search the jungle path this time, so it's a risk we need to be prepared for, but they have quite a long way to go to get down here, so if we leave at first light, we should be able to stay away from them."

She decides to explore the other side room. There is a table just above the ground and some cushions. A tall cupboard stands in the corner and Macia can see tins and jars like they sell at the shop. She hesitates, then remembering Caecilia's face when she shared that her food had all gone, she takes several tins and returns to the others. "There are lots of tins," she says, "I think we'll call it payment for our hasty retreat and Gax's ordeal." The others laugh, relief all over Caecilia's face. "I have money in my pocket, so I will pay for the food, leaving some money on the table. Anyway, we can use the cushions to sleep on, as it will be more comfortable."

Caecilia smiles at Gax. "As it's quiet, maybe we should look at your foot?"

Gax swallows, and nods. "My left foot feels not too bad, but the right one hurts." He takes his shoe and sock of. The foot is red, and seems a little swollen.

Macia returns to the side room where she has seen some cloth. She hands the cloth to Caecilia who wraps Gax's foot in the cloth. "It should feel better in a few days, although the walking won't help." She smiles at him and he smiles back, his lips no longer trembling.

They take turns standing watch, just in case other elders will come to search at night. Gax smiles a little as he plays with the ferrets. They let them go hunting to find food, but just as he settles down to keep

CHAPTER 15

watch, they return, making soft squeaking noises. They play near him, nudging him with their noses, their dark, shrewd eyes looking up at him as if wondering what he is doing on this strange journey. "I don't know either," he whispers at them, "not any more, that is. Maybe I will know again in a few days. Or weeks."

In the morning, they open some of the tins with a jar of fruit for a delicious breakfast. Macia puts the money on the low table and Caecilia returns the cushions. They grab their belongings and leave the dark, sinister hut, glad to get away from the red wooden snakes and black gargoyle-like faces. They repack things as quickly as possible, and then they're off, into the jungle. The path is damp and spongy, and leaves brush their faces as they go, making the ferrets protest.

"Shush, I'm not doing it on purpose," chides Macia as they whine at her for another shower in their cage. "Be grateful you have fur to keep you warm." Caecilia chuckles but Gax says nothing, he merely frowns when looking at the path ahead of them.

He is walking in front, as his foot is still bothering him. The bandage helps a little, but it still hurts. Caecilia has found him a large, sturdy branch to use as a walking stick. "If you walk in front, you can set the speed," Caecilia suggested, so here he is, limping in front of the two girls, feeling their looks digging into his back. Is there pity in their eyes? Or do they think he's weak and a moaner for making such a fuss?

The path slopes down a little but not enough to make it uncomfortable. If he wasn't in so much pain and aware of the long, dangerous journey ahead, he would have enjoyed the path. "Watch out for those branches," he says over his shoulder, ducking and glancing behind them at the same time. He doesn't feel safe, for if the elders follow them down this path, they have no way to outrun them. It would all be a waste of time and effort.

Just ahead, Gax can see a fallen log. "Maybe we should have a quick break," he says, and the girls agree. The log is damp but it's better than sitting on the grass.

"I think we made a good start," Macia says, smiling. "We have been walking for some time and not heard anything or anyone, and it's getting muddier. That must be a good sign." Caecilia nods, not too keen on the muddier bit.

A few times they have to step across little streams running across their path. Soon, the path is nothing more than an animal track. Through the trees they can see a dark glistening stream, hardly moving, simply staring at them. Floating branches resemble the snakes and Caecilia shudders and looks away. She spots a few yellow flowers, dangling down from a climber plant hugging the trees. Their beauty is in stark contrast to the dark, glowering stream.

The day drags on, their shoulders on fire with rucksacks that seem to double in weight each passing hour. The path has improved, making walking less arduous. The dark woods make the day seem even shorter, and they will need to find shelter soon. Macia points out a small grove of trees on higher ground.

"I'll go and explore it," she calls to the others.

The thick circle of trees are woven with climbers and Macia can see it won't take much work to clear the undergrowth in the centre, making it into a natural den. "Maybe we should turn that into a hut for the night," she says, "as we won't have to build anything. It looks like a place made for us."

They stop to look closer at the den. The shelter is hard to get into, and they use their rucksacks to block up other openings. Inside the hut, the ground is covered in moss. Rather damp, but soft. "Should we look for something to eat? There might be fish in the stream." Gax doesn't sound too keen and neither are the girls.

"The first day is always hard," Macia sounds as if running away from masked elders by hiking through dark jungles is a regular activity.

CHAPTER 15

"We can eat some of our food tonight and tomorrow morning. During the day, we will be able to look out for things to eat." She rubs her sore shoulders and stretches, contorting herself to straighten out unhappy muscles.

Caecilia says, "I brought that tree guide. It seems to include jungles of this type, so it might tell us what we can eat." She slumps down on the dark green moss, checking it for moving creatures. "I'm not looking at it tonight though, my eyes have gone to sleep already." Macia laughs and after a quick, cold meal, they unroll their sleeping bags and make themselves comfortable.

"Should we keep watch?" Caecilia asks, not too keen on staying awake any longer, listening to the quiet noises of the jungle.

"I think we should be alright," Macia says slowly. "There are wild animals, I suppose, but this den should protect us enough, I think." Gax simply snores, and the girls giggle softly before joining him, whilst the ferrets set off for their evening meal. The girls have left the cage door open, so they can come back if and when they want.

The masked figures look at each other, studying the money on the low table, seeing the empty spaces where jars and tins used to be. They have seen the signs of people going down the jungle path but didn't risk following. They will ask the Head elder, but it seems that the three foreigners have decided to die voluntarily. The stocky one makes a cutting sign along his throat, and the other man agrees. A pity he didn't look in the other room yesterday. It will be hard to explain that to the Head elder. He looks at the door, but the stocky one shakes his head. No, they couldn't have known. Anyway, it's too late now. They take the money for the Head elder and slowly start the never-ending ascent up the staircase, hoping the Head elder agrees with their judgment that the three young people will never be seen alive again.

Chapter 16

Gax is the first to wake up. He sits up and stretches, feeling a little better. His body still hurts, but some of the dark clouds seem to have lifted a little. He looks at the still-sleeping girls and decides to turn over a while longer. He is fast asleep again by the time the girls wake up.

They eat some of the prepared food, as it won't stay fresh much longer, and then sit down in their little den. "What should we do?" Macia looks at the other two, wondering what their plan is. "This den is nice, it's comfortable," she explains. "Maybe we should stay here for a few days? I can't imagine the elders following us this far in. Why would they?"

Caecilia looks around the green den. "It's comfy here and I slept well. My shoulders hurt from my bag, so it would be lovely to have some time to relax and wait for the right season to be a little closer. We could maybe fish and collect some food as well. It will give me time to look at my food book," she laughs.

They agree to stay a few days. This will allow Gax's foot to heal, for them to collect food and to be better prepared to face the real jungle. "We might need to keep an eye out for the elders," Macia says, "just in case they are determined to get us, although I can't believe they would come this far."

They spend the entire day making the den more comfortable and

CHAPTER 16

hiding all traces from the outside. Caecilia reads the book and with Macia, starts looking around to see if they can find the various trees and bushes mentioned. They find one bush with edible berries, and even though there are just a few berries ripe, they treat it like a victory. They feel a little better equipped to face the journey, however long that might turn out to be.

By the time they sit down for their evening meal, as the shadows in the woods are turning too long for comfort, there has been no sign of the elders. The girls found some herbs that the book told them would protect them against mosquitoes. Their den was wonderful and they had slept well, but they all have several mosquito bites. "Tonight, we'll be better prepared," Caecilia says, and she hands out some of the leaves. "The book says dried mint can be used, but I wanted to keep those for tea. Dried lemongrass is different though, so even if we can't find any more, further on the journey, we have some dried leaves we can use."

She uses some of the climbers to hang the leftover leaves for drying, spreading them out around the den. Gax wrinkles his nose, "Just the smell should be enough to kill any mosquitoes entering the den," he laughs. "It's not a bad smell, but pretty strong in here. Let's hope it helps, for some of last night's bites have been itching the entire day."

They sleep well, feeling safe and excitement is starting to creep in. "Our last potatoes and just in time as well," Caecilia says, sniffing the cooked potatoes. "I opened a tin of meat to go with it. Once the tin is empty, we can put other food in it, or use it to cook our next meal."

Gax smiles, "You're good at this camping thing," he says and Caecilia blushes. Macia looks away. She was the one that got them this far and it's a lot more than a 'camping thing' as far as she is concerned.

"Let's read the Book," she suggests, knowing they have to work together and they're one in Jesus. This trek is not going to work if they are petty, so she smiles at Caecilia and thanks her for the food.

Gax opens the Book, "It feels like we were thrown into something we were not prepared for. I do feel better now we have had a rest, we found some plants we can eat, and generally have more time to think and get our minds in the right place. Maybe I should have trusted God more, though," he admits, speaking slowly. "I don't know… maybe I wanted it to be our decision when to go into the jungle. Maybe I needed this rush and the time with the elders." He swallows a few times before his voice is steady enough to continue.

"Nothing made sense for a while. My throat still hurts," he pulls a face as the girls nod. His coughing has been nearly constant that morning, "It was smoke the elders waved in my face that started this cough. When I lie down it's not too bad," he says, "but it made me feel very faint and unaware of what I was saying exactly. I know I shouted some kind of garbled prayer, and they stopped the smoke immediately. Maybe it was some kind of truth serum idea," he says, rolling his eyes.

Reading the Book together feels like a calm in their worries. After they put the Book away, they decide to collect more food. "I think we ought to carry on tomorrow," Gax says. "We don't want to stay here too long. I know we can find food, but we don't want to stretch our time in the jungle too much. It's better to get to whatever we will find Downstream."

The girls set off with some small baskets to find some nuts and roots. Gax has managed to rig out a fishing rod and will try to catch some fish. "We might have to cook that as it won't stay fresh long enough," he warns. "Hopefully, it will be safe enough to do so when it's nearly dark."

"Mmm, some wild kind of potato and fresh fish for dinner," Macia chuckles, "we'll sleep well after that."

They set off, agreeing to simply eat some lunch when they can. "I don't know how quickly the fish will bite," Gax explains, "and it would be good to catch enough for this evening and tomorrow, so we can walk most of the day without having to find more food."

CHAPTER 16

Macia and Caecilia decide to stay together. "It feels a large wood," Caecilia says, looking around with wide eyes. "I can see myself getting lost in here."

"Maybe we should have used something as a marker," Macia says when they stand up from digging up some more roots. "The clump of trees is still visible, but I'm scared we might turn a corner and lose sight of it."

Caecilia bites her lips. "Maybe we should veer a little more towards the den in that case," she says. "We could search that area over there, so we cover a square, rather than get deeper and deeper into the woods."

Macia bends over a bush to find a few more berries when she is sure she hears a noise. "Did you hear that?" She looks at Caecilia, who is standing up as well, a few berries rolling out of her hand. Both girls stand still, ears tuned to catch the sound again. "There!" Macia says and Caecilia nods. There was definitely a noise, wild, like breaking branches. "Let's get back to the den," Macia whispers and Caecilia nods again, not moving.

"Again!" Caecilia suddenly manages to walk. Swiftly, they move towards the den, not daring to run as the noise would give them away. Macia looks at their baskets. They have done well.

"We should have enough for tomorrow and even the day after," Caecilia agrees when Macia mentions it. They reach the den, which looks so peaceful. Once they're in, Macia grabs a large fern branch they kept in the den on purpose and sweeps the ground outside the den. She isn't sure, but isn't that supposed to wipe out footprints?

"I hope Gax will be here soon," Caecilia says softly. "He must have heard the noise as well but maybe he is investigating, rather than hiding." Macia pulls a face. The last time Gax went to explore, it ended with him in captivity. Hopefully, Gax will have learned hiding makes a better choice some days.

Footsteps can be heard and heavy breathing. The girls look at each other, Caecilia in shock, Macia finding herself thinking, What now? Gax slips into the tent, tears streaming down his face, clutching their largest tin filled with fish, blood everywhere, dripping on his shoe. The girls gasp and jump up to help him, but when they open their mouths to ask all the questions, he stops them, sobbing.

"The elders," he whispers, struggling to catch enough breath to speak, "they're nearly here." The girls stare at him, and then Macia looks at his leg again. "A crocodile," he sobs, "I was just getting some fish sorted. It appeared out of nowhere. I ran, and it clipped me. I nearly fell but managed to dash between some trees and it returned to the stream. I'm not sure how bad my leg is." That explains the noises they heard.

Macia nods then dashes back to the entrance with the trusty fern to wipe the entrance smooth again. Good thing too, as there are wet, red spots where Gax's leg has dribbled. As she pulls the fern in, she can hear voices. The elders are coming. Will the den be safe? It's a rather obvious shelter, she suddenly realises, and they're bound to investigate it.

She looks at the other two; Gax is being helped by Caecilia who is tying strips of his old shirt around his leg. "Hopefully, the blood will have cleaned it enough," she whispers, then notices Macia. Her eyes widen and she turns pale. Even Gax stops crying. Macia looks around the den and decides there is nothing they can do. Their stuff is rather spread out, their sleeping bags rolled up neatly, baskets with food in the middle of the den. And there is no other way out.

"We'll have to just pray they won't check this place," she breathes to the others, who nod. They hold hands, although Macia can't close her eyes. She can feel Gax's hands shaking wildly.

The men are not coming in secret and they don't seem to be expecting the young people. "Surely they'll have died by now," one grumbly voice sounds. Macia rolls her eyes. The stocky one, who didn't want to check the hut too closely. He's clearly not keen to make

CHAPTER 16

much effort for a few stray youngsters.

Another voice answers; a harsh deep voice. "We need to find them, dead or alive, although dead is so much better." Macia starts and Caecilia squeezes her hand, as the voice continues. "We have made a promise to shelter the sanctuary and these foreigners must not disturb its peace." The voice makes it clear that's all there is to it.

"I agree they must be dead by now." A female voice joins in. "Why can't we simply leave them to the Stream to deal with? The Stream can be trusted, surely, to protect his domain. Aren't we at risk, entering into this place, intruding?"

To their horror, the group seems to have stopped just beyond the den. If any of them look around, they might realise what a wonderful hiding place the den makes. "Just trust me," the harsh voice answers, "I communicate with the Stream, Wachshapah, regularly, here, in his domain." There is a small gasp from the group and Gax shudders. Caecilia looks like she is going to be sick any moment.

"Something is going on in his lower sanctuary, somewhere where even I would never enter. It's part of his dominion. It's hidden from me exactly what, but when commanded, I agreed. I promised to do my best to shelter that part of the sanctuary. That was many harvests ago, years have come and gone and I have kept my promise. That is why Wachshapah has blessed us so abundantly. He has been worshipped and sacrificed down in the lower regions as well as in our village. If these young people reach the lower area, who knows how Wachshapah will punish us? He can destroy all we hold dear, just for the sake of a few foreign young people. Everything is at stake here and they must be stopped."

Wide-eyed, the three stare at each other and Gax manages a watery grin. The man must be speaking about the Downstream area.

"It is getting late," the harsh voice sounds again, "we will return." The three stay as still as possible, not even breathing. When the voices move away, Macia creeps silently to the entrance and tries to peer out. Just then, one of the masked figures turns back, looking directly at the den. Macia freezes, narrowing her eyes, hoping the gleam of her eyes will be hidden. The masked figure hesitates, looking over his shoulder, and then back at the den. After another quick glance, the figure throws something in the long grass and raises a hand to his hips as a kind of wave towards the den.

Macia looks at the other. "What do you make of that?" She asks and they look again at the object she has retrieved once the group was far gone, probably back at the Head elder's hut by then. It is a glass bottle with cooking oil. "Why would he do that? He must have known we were there, but why didn't he say anything? How did he know, and who was he?" No matter how many questions they ask each other, the answer never arrives.

"We just have to say, The Lord has provided," Gax says and he smiles, his eyes bright for the first time since his rescue. "Maybe we will know one day, maybe not. I suppose it doesn't matter, but we should pray for the person who is helping and protecting us."

That night, Caecilia dreams of the Head elder and his awful voice, the stream turning into a mighty flood filled with crocodiles. Just as she is about to scream in terror, the flood is swallowed up by a small glass bottle with gold-coloured oil. She laughs herself awake.

Chapter 17

"We'll have to leave first thing tomorrow morning," Gax says, trying to raise his leg, his face pale. "It sounds like they will be back. We can't risk it, for that Head elder sounded determined to get us."

The girls nod, and Caecilia sighs. "It's such a lovely den," she says, touching the nearest tree for a moment. "At least we have some food to take with us. Do you think it's safe enough to make a fire to cook the fish?"

Gax hesitates then shrugs. "They won't be back tonight, I would think, and they will see the remains tomorrow, but hopefully we'll be a long way away by then."

Dinner is delicious. After so many cold meals, eating fresh, hot fish with some cooked roots is great. Macia chuckles. "If anyone in Elabi could see us now, they wouldn't believe their eyes." They certainly look a state, especially Gax. He licks his fingers and grins back at Macia, then looks away. His leg hurts and he has a splitting headache. Will he be able to walk fast enough in the morning to stay ahead of the elders?

Macia touches the old strips of shirt they have boiled in the water and says, "They're cooled down and so has the fresh water." They didn't want to use the sterilisation tablets, as there might be times when they won't be able to boil the water. Caecilia and Macia work on the dirty strips, trying to get them off Gax's leg. Gax whimpers and tears roll down his face as the soaked-through bandages come off inch by inch. Macia can feel her stomach do funny flips as she looks at his mauled leg, but Caecilia is busy cleaning off the blood, pouring clean water down his leg. Once it's clean, she pours some of the oil on the leg.

"This oil is such a special gift," Caecilia says, but once the leg is bandaged again she adds, "It's hard to tell how your leg is." She starts to reach out to him but pulls her hand back as she sees Macia looking away. "I will keep my book handy, as we might see different things on the way tomorrow."

Macia nods. "Good idea. We'll keep this basket handy as well, so we can fill it with goodies. We might not have much time to look for things, as we need to stay ahead of the elders. I wonder how long they'll try to find us?"

None of them knows the answer. "The Head elder sounded determined to get us, so they might follow us for several days," Caecilia says, her face pale. "I don't like the idea of having to rush for days and days, simply to stay ahead of those elders." Gax closes his eyes, the idea of having to rush making him feel ill. "Anyway, Caecilia continues, "we'll have one more night in our den, and hopefully, the rest will do us all good."

In the morning, Gax is sweating and shaking. Macia looks at him, her eyes dark. "I'll be fine," he tries to smile, his eyes red-rimmed. "I'll take some of my tablets and after breakfast, I'll feel better." Caecilia makes breakfast, and then with Macia, she cleans up the fire remains and packs the sleeping bags. Macia's eyes keep going towards Gax, who does seem a little better. They set off when the sun is barely up and although they're not rushing, they do try to set a good pace. Caecilia finds herself glancing over her shoulder, then at Gax right in front of her, limping badly, his shoulders slumped, his hand gripping

CHAPTER 17

the walking stick tight, knuckles white.

How long they need to walk each day is hard to tell. Macia spots a fallen tree up ahead, just off the path, closer to the stream. She looks over her shoulder and seeing Gax, she knows they will need to rest. "Let's have a break," she says and smiles. "We can sit down here for a bit, and have some of those berries maybe?"

Gax slumps on the tree and isn't interested in berries, turning his face away. "I don't feel like food just now," he says, his voice small. Caecilia hesitates. He does look ill.

"I think you should try in a minute," she says softly, "for without food, it'll get worse. These berries are good for you as well." They all drink some water and Macia takes the basket as she has spotted a bush like the one they found yesterday. There are plenty of berries as they're closer to the stream and especially higher up the bush, there are large, juicy ones. Gax is persuaded to have a few and soon, they're back on the gently downward-sloping track.

By lunchtime, Gax is shaking again. He forces himself to eat some lunch and takes another tablet. Macia closes her eyes, to force herself to rest, rather than fidget. She knows Gax will need longer, for the tablet to kick in and to catch his breath, but valuable daylight hours are slipping away.

Macia looks down the path, frowning. "I just feel like the elders are closing in on us," she says. "Maybe we should sit down and pray. I just feel…slow and heavy." The others agree and they sit down together, Gax peeking through his lashes every time he hears a noise from the direction of the stream. The idea of having to walk all afternoon makes him sweat even more.

"…Gax especially, as he is in so much pain, and we pray for special help for him." Gax bites his lips. He doesn't want special help; he wants to be better, to be out of this jungle, to be safe at home. But he says amen anyway.

He looks around the den, lowering his head towards the ground. It is clear the young strangers stayed here. He growls softly, knowing he will need to write. Let him know strangers are traversing the jungle. Will they go far? Are they aiming for...for the other side of the jungle? He frowns. They must be found. He has to stop them, at all costs. And soon. He smirks at the dark, rust coloured splodges around the hut. One of them must be injured. Maybe the Stream will kill them before he has to. It will also slow them down. Between Wachshapah and his elders, they should be able to catch up and deal with the strangers. Before they reach the territory of the Elutera... He shudders. He has to be fast. He bites his lip, staring ahead. Yes, they will return swiftly to the village, retrieve what they need, then make all speed down the path, before it is too late. He will send a messenger down tomorrow if necessary.

The afternoon seems never-ending. They have several short breaks and by the time they find a place for the night, Caecilia and Gax are close to tears. "This is probably the best we'll get," Macia says, pointing at a large tree with a thick bush around it. "We can use those large branches to make some shelter." She starts dragging branches towards the bush. Caecilia helps; Gax simply sinks onto the forest floor, too tired to care where they'll sleep and how many elders will find them.

Once the hut is done, Macia says, "That looks pretty inviting. I'm exhausted." Caecilia nods, simply lying on the soft forest floor, staring up into the treetops. Macia gets up again. "I am going to find some firewood so that when it's getting dark and we know the elders won't be anywhere nearby, we can have a fire, boil more water, and cook some food."

Caecilia sits up. "I will get some water," she says, almost sounding like it's a question. She retrieves the large water bottle they have been using and walks towards the stream. She's in two minds between stomping and making a lot of noise, or quietly creeping up to the river,

CHAPTER 17

getting water and dashing back. She ends up doing neither. Keeping a sharp lookout, she fills the water bottle and carries it back. Standing near the den, she bites her lips. Having fried fish was wonderful and it's still light. Not for much longer, but it might not take very long to catch some fish.

Gax is looking at her and she smiles at him. "What are you thinking about?" he asks, smiling back. When she tells him, he loses his smile. "Are you sure?" He hesitates, licks his lips, and struggles onto his feet. "I will come with you. Two will be safer than one, and that way, it will be easier to keep an eye out." Caecilia is relieved and the two of them set off for the stream with fishing gear. They can see Macia through the trees and they wave at her and point at the river. She waves back, and soon the dark, slow-moving water is close. Gax takes a deep breath and starts putting the fishing rod together.

Between them, they manage to catch enough fish for two days but when the darkness starts to edge in, they spot a ripple in the stream. "A crocodile," Caecilia says and she backs away. Gax nods but forces himself to stay, to grab the tin with fish, and their rod. The crocodile is quite some distance away and doesn't seem interested in them at all. Gax takes the fish behind the den to clean them. Caecilia and Macia get the fire going, and Macia shows some of the roots she found.

They boil extra water and repeat the bandaging job. Caecilia bites her lip. The edges of the wound do look red, but that can be simply trauma and not necessarily infection. What if the wound gets worse? They use oil again, and she says, "I wonder if there is anything in the book about leaves for wounds and infections," trying to sound as if she's simply being curious.

They sit around the dying fire as long as they dare, quietly, thinking their own thoughts, and Gax reads a little from the Book and they thank God for another day. A day closer to their goal and a day further away from Colchuyni and the elders. A day without accidents but still an exhausting day. Once they're in the small den, they look at each other in the darkness. "Should we have a guard, now that we know the elders are looking for us?"

Gax groans but says, "I think you're right, for we don't know if they're only travelling in the day. They might follow us in the night as well." The girls feel their spirits droop. Dinner was lovely, the den is cosy, they have water to drink, no accidents today and Gax seems a little better. But there are enemies out there, ready to grab them and kill them.

Macia says, "I'll take the first watch, then I'll wake Caecilia, you can come after that and I'll take the last watch." She looks around their space and says, "I'm going to sit in the door opening that we made. That way we can see out and hear what is going on, without being seen." She gasps as one of the ferrets chooses that moment to come back in, climbing over Macia. "That gave me a fright," she giggles, and sliding into her sleeping bag, she settles in the door opening. The other two lie down, and Caecilia is asleep before she's horizontal. Gax takes a little longer, listening to the night noises, the soft noises the content ferrets make and Caecilia's breathing.

Macia rubs her eyes, having been woken by Gax. It feels a little silly, sitting out here in a sleeping bag, watching the jungle do its early morning thing. Maybe she should go back to sleep, they have at least an hour before they need to get up. Just as she starts to scoot further back into the den, she can hear something. It's not a loud noise, and for a moment she thinks she has imagined it. Then the noise comes again, followed by what sounds like a voice. A quiet one, but a voice for sure. Macia freezes. What should she do? In the end, she crawls back into the den. Gax sits up and she quickly moves to his side. "People coming," she breathes.

Gax struggles out of his sleeping bag, pulling faces as his leg hurts. He looks out of the den, listening carefully. He can hear the voices

CHAPTER 17

and soft footsteps. No light shines and he moves back into the den. "No light. I don't think they will be able to spot our den. We covered the fire."

Macia nods. They should be safe, as long as Caecilia doesn't make a sudden noise. They might be suspicious as it looks like a good den. It is a little similar to where they stayed before. Have they discovered that one? They might be on the lookout for something similar.

The footsteps sound nearer, the low voices clearer. "They can't have gone far," and Macia recognises the Head elder. "They will need to find shelter and food, so we must be well past them. We will get shelter just before daybreak. We can rest till noon, then carry on, unless they pass us in that time. That will save some trouble." They can't hear what the other elder replies, as they have gone past the den. Gax and Macia sit still but they watch the men walk past them. Just before daybreak isn't very long from now. That means that they will pass them soon after they start walking.

Macia crawls back into the den. "What should we do?" she speaks very quietly, and Gax shrugs. "If we stick to our plan, we'll walk past their den within a short time. We might see them and avoid them, but we might not find out until it's too late." She can feel tears burning.

Gax yawns and gives a soft groan. "We better wake Caecilia. We will need to start walking soon."

They keep breakfast a quiet meal, eating leftover fish with some of the cooked roots, washed down with water. Gax tells Caecilia about the nighttime walkers. "What should we do?" she asks and Macia shrugs.

Gax leans closer. "They feel safe enough and they want to catch us as we walk past. That means they will need to be somewhere close to the path. They might not even hide as they hope we won't expect them. Once we see them, we can make a detour, like going closer to the stream. I know," he continues quickly, seeing the girls' faces. "But it will be just for a short time, so it should be safe enough. Once we're past them, we can follow the path again. The men will sleep till noon, so that should give us some time to get ahead."

The girls aren't happy, but cannot think of an alternative. "There are likely to be other elders behind us," Macia says, her shoulders slumped. "The Head elder only had one other person with him. I think they split up. They probably aimed to get us in between, so we must get ahead of the Head elder. Let's go and see if we can get the plan to work."

They pack up their camp, trying to destroy all traces of their stay, then quietly follow the path. Macia spots the figures first. Just as Gax suspected, they are simply rolled in a blanket at the side of the trail. They turn towards the stream, grateful for the undergrowth. Until they have to walk through it, close to the water's edge. Macia hesitates. The plants are hard to deal with, and some of the branches are sharp. Gax taps her on the shoulder, holding out a thick stick. "Use this," he says and smiles. Macia grabs the stick and uses it to push branches aside, leaning on the stick when the ground is rocky or uneven. Gax keeps a close eye out for crocodiles. The last thing they want to do now is have to run for it. On and on they struggle, sweating, the sun shining directly above them.

Chapter 18

They walk until lunchtime, when they sink on some soft, but damp moss. Caecilia hands out the food and they chew in silence. Gax shivers now and then, struggling to swallow his food. "Will we be able to stay ahead of them?" Caecilia asks, looking over her shoulder. The noises are constant, and in her head, she can almost hear the quiet footsteps of the pursuing elders.

"We can't leave the path," Macia says, and Caecilia swallows as that's exactly what she was going to suggest. "We'd be lost within five minutes," Macia continues. "We need to keep moving as much as we can and pray the elders will stay behind. I don't think they'll be able to keep pursuing us much longer, as they have lives to live. Surely, if they're gone for weeks, people will start looking for them, and that's the last thing they want."

"I hope you're right," Caecilia says, then smiles a little, "it does look as if the stream is wider and shallower here, so maybe that's a sign we're getting near the end?" She looks at the stream and pushes the thought of getting back to Colchuyni away. The elders will need to walk back, but so do they, eventually.

"There must be a different way home," she whispers, her voice no longer supporting her thoughts that have gone back along the path anyway.

"I wouldn't be surprised," Gax says, then adds more quietly, "the idea of going all this way back doesn't sound too appealing. I never thought it would be this far! But maybe we should trust God with the outcomes again, and simply live each day, without worrying about the next day?" Caecilia nods but looks away. She remembers the worries about getting a house, and feels her face warming up at the memory.

All three have to suppress a sigh when the food is eaten and there is no reason to stretch their lunch break any longer than necessary. Gax gives a little sob as he stands up, but tries to smile as the girls look at him with concern. "It'll be fine, once I have a good night's sleep," he says, and the girls pretend they don't hear the wobble in his voice. "At least walking on the path makes it easier," Gax says, and Macia nods, and chews the corner of her nail.

Caecilia stands outside their latest shelter, looking around, not knowing where to start looking. Dry wood? There isn't anything dry around them, not even the air is dry. Gax grunts and shrugs. "We will see what we can find," he says to Caecilia. "Let's have a look over there, as there are a few trees close together. There might be some dry leaves or smaller sticks." Caecilia bites her lip as she spots Gax wiping his eyes now and then, his shoulders hunched and shaking. There is nothing she can say or do to help him, and she allows herself a few quiet tears as well.

By the time Macia returns with the water and some berries, there is enough firewood for a small fire. "We'll have to be careful how we cook everything," she bosses, "for that's not a large stack of wood." As there is still a little daylight left, she hunts for more wood without much success. "Maybe we should carry some with us, as soon as we find some," she suggests and glares at Caecilia as she protests about the weight. "We need wood. We need it for so many different things and this is taking ages to sort out. That makes everything harder, so carrying just some wood for a while is easier than this mad rush of trying to get enough for a meal and clean water."

CHAPTER 18

They finalise their camp for the night and once it's dark, they sit and listen. "I don't think they're nearby," Macia whispers in the end. "Let's make the fire, but be careful." The fire soon burns, and Macia keeps a sharp lookout, to make sure no fuel is wasted, and Caecilia listens for the Elders whilst keeping an eye on the roots being cooked.

Macia sits in the doorway, wrapped up in her sleeping bag. Not because she is cold, but to keep mosquitoes away. The leaves help, but not enough. Caecilia is right into her sleeping bag. "Lord," she sobs quietly, "I can't do this. Gax is... I know he's struggling, but he is so different. Macia is her old self again and I just want a hot bath, clean clothes and normal food. I want people, I want to read Your Book openly and just for all this to go away." She makes sure the others can't hear her. Gax spends every free moment lying down, complaining about his leg, the mosquitoes, and how sore everything is. Tonight, it was too dark to read the Book, the elders too close. Caecilia sniffs softly, but soon sleep overcomes her.

Gax wakes Caecilia near the morning and they sit together for a moment, sure the Head elder will come past soon. "I'm surprised they haven't passed already," Caecilia whispers, "as we didn't go very fast and we had to make that detour along the stream to avoid them." Just then, they can hear noises. "Here they are now." She withdraws into the shelter a little, covering her face and hands to stop them from showing in the dark. Gax does the same.

"They're earlier than yesterday," he breathes, "which might be a good thing. It means they might get further away from us, and eventually, they'll be far away enough, that we won't have to worry anymore."

The two men pass their shelter. The Head elder stops just beyond the spot where they can be seen. "...smoke..." is all they can hear as they're too far away. They keep their eyes on the little lights the two men carry. After a while, the lights move along the path. Both lights, Caecilia notices and she releases the breath she'd been holding, chuckling as she can hear Gax do the same.

"They'll be careful, so we need to be careful as well," he says softly, as he wriggles further into the shelter, ready to go to sleep now he knows where the two men have got to.

Caecilia rolls her eyes, then settles down to keep an eye out for the other two or the possibility of the Head elder returning to check out the smoky smell. There is no breeze, so she isn't surprised the smell of smoke lingers in the air. It's a good thing they're further away from the path, she thinks.

"We might have to camp close to the stream tonight," Macia says over breakfast, as soon as she hears what happened in the early morning. "We can alternate where we stay the night, so it's less predictable and they won't look for us in the same spot." Gax glances at his leg and she looks away. "Clearly, we'd find a crocodile-free spot or one higher up maybe. There might be a way to make a shelter in a tree. We just can't be predictable, that's all I'm saying." She knows her voice is sharp, but why hasn't Gax thought of the same thing? He must have forgotten how badly they treated him. "The thing is," she tries to make her voice as slow as possible, "if they catch us now, they'll most likely simply kill us. They're not going to take us back to the Khramuil, are they? So they'll simply feed us to the crocodiles, and say the Stream has sorted us out."

They set off, after dealing with Gax's leg. Caecilia tries to catch Macia's eye as she cleans the leg with some precious water and newly washed bandages, but Macia looks away. The smell makes her feel ill. Caecilia avoids looking at the quietly sobbing Gax, who is clutching his upper leg and rocking himself. "I'm sorry," she whispers, but he shakes his head and Caecilia washes the dirty bandages in the used water, so they can be boiled later. If they can build a fire, that is. Caecilia looks back at their shelter a few times, wishing they could have stayed a little longer. She mentions it. "Maybe we should find a

CHAPTER 18

good shelter and stay a few days. Stock up on food, rest a bit and let the elders all be in front of us."

Macia rolls her eyes. "Who knows how long the walk will be," she says, "and we have to get back in time for the mud crossing unless you want to hide for another year in Colchuyni." She takes a deep breath, feeling her cheeks heat up. "I'm sorry," she says, "I would like to rest as well. It's just that we have no idea how much further it is and what we'll find when we get there. The best thing is to keep moving for now, and maybe rest once we know where we're at?"

More trouble starts soon after lunch. Gax is the first to hastily excuse himself and dash behind a bush. He re-emerges, looking pale, his face wet. "Sorry," he says, "I just needed to go."

The girls find themselves making quick getaways soon after. Half an hour later, they decide it's time to find shelter. With lots of private spaces. "I will get some water," Gax says, before doubling over, holding his stomach. A few moments later, he is off to the river to fetch water, his leg dragging more than ever. The girls are grateful for the firewood they all collected during the day. The extra weight had been hard, but now they're relieved they won't need to look for any.

They store the wood inside their shelter, to keep it relatively dry and just relax in their sleeping bags, with quick dashes outside. As soon as the sun has gone down, they start the fire, boil water and have a small meal. None of them is hungry, but they will need to drink. Once the water has boiled and divided between the water bottles, they turn in, the clean drying bandages a reminder they need to get help soon.

The night is long and sleep is broken. No elders can be heard although Gax saw dark figures pass quietly along the path, going downstream.

"There are clearly more elders, they must have caught up with each other," Macia moans in the morning. She is tired and her stomach still hurts. Gax grunts that they didn't look like elders. Out of all three, he has been the worst affected. "It must have been the water," he says, "it had the little bubbles all over, so I took it off the fire."

Macia stares at the ceiling which is made of huge branches held together with creepers, their flowers smelling sweet. She bites her lips. They'd been so careful purifying the water and one careless moment made them all ill and set them back. There is no way they can travel today and maybe tomorrow is in jeopardy as well. All those days are wasted because the water hadn't been hot enough. She can feel her eyes burning with tears but she mutters to herself, "It's all in God's Hand, nothing you can do about it." Midmorning, she gets up. "I will get some more water," she says, "and some firewood as well."

Caecilia looks at her with a pale face and nods. "I will help you in a bit," she whispers, and Macia smiles at her. Poor Caecilia has a hard time as well, but soon after Macia returns from the river, she gets up and helps her look for firewood and food. They keep a good lookout for the elders. After lunch, they can hear voices. Another two elders pass by, without looking in their direction. They're chatting, seemingly happy to simply walk through the jungle. Macia is relieved. At least now they're behind these elders as well.

Gax is very sick for the rest of the day, but Macia feels better already. Her legs are a little shaky and food has to be handled carefully, but that's all. They have plenty of clean water, as Macia has gone again after boiling the first lot. Now the elders are ahead of them, they feel safe enough to make a fire in the daytime as well as when darkness comes. Macia is glad when Caecilia helps her to get more firewood. She wonders if she should go fishing, but the idea makes her stomach protest. There is a little food left over.

That night, the girls take turns watching. "I will help," Gax says, his legs shaking and struggling to carry him. "I feel better now I've been to the toilet again, so I could watch. I feel punished for taking it off

CHAPTER 18

the boil too quickly and I'm sorry you're dragged into it with me."

Macia pats his arm. "It can't be helped. I'm feeling a lot better and we'll have another rest day tomorrow. It might mean that we've lost the elders for a while, which is great news. Go and sleep, we'll keep an eye out, in case they come back this way."

She looks at him, taking in his tanned face, his profile manly against the evening light, the breeze from the bay ruffling his hair. She rests her head against the wooden lounger, taking a sip from her cold drink. One more night, then she'll need to return. She sighs and he looks up from the letter. "I'm sorry, my love," he says, and taps the letter. "It's from the mountain village. He says there are strangers walking across the jungle. They might be looking to settle, join the Elutera or even be on there way here." He frowns and she shudders.

"The Elutera don't need trouble added to them," she says. "Why would they be coming this way? Strangers?"

He shrugs, and tries to smile. "He doesn't say much in his letters, as you know. He says he will deal with them. Let's hope he does. Anyway, my love, we haven't much time before you need to return. Let's not waste it on strangers in the jungle this evening," and he takes her hand, waving at the man near the door to refill their glasses.

She's not so easily distracted. The Elutera are unpredictable, but useful for difficulties like this. Maybe she should leave them a message, stir them into action. She can't have strangers upsetting her life. They must be stopped and she doesn't think she trusts the mountain elder to do the job properly. It won't be the first time he failed.

When she mentions it, he shrugs. "Maybe he could be taught a lesson as well. The arrangement is clear. And three people went into the jungle, unhindered? Something needs to be said about that," he agrees, stroking her arm, showing his white teeth in a smile only for her.

Chapter 19

Caecilia stares out into the dark jungle which is noisy. Noisier than she expected. Everything is different from what she expected. Gax was ill all day, preventing them from travelling again. Macia had shrugged it off, but Caecilia knows how much Macia wants to travel. She's surprised Macia hasn't set off alone yet. She sighs and thinks of Riu's words. Maybe he was correct. Maybe this is the Stream's territory and they are powerless against disasters happening. Otherwise, why would Gax be so ill? And injured by the crocodile. Hurt by the elders.

Caecilia sighs again. Maybe the Stream is more powerful than they had banked on. She tries to look up, but the branches are too interwoven, blocking out the sky. She swats at a few mosquitoes and wipes tears away at the same time. Macia's voice makes her jump. "Let me take over. Gax seems to be sleeping better, so hopefully, we'll be able to travel soon. We will need to as well; it's getting harder to find food and firewood."

Caecilia nods, too tired to be chatty like Macia. "We could travel just a short way, maybe after lunch. That way, we would be able to find food and new firewood," Macia carries on. "We will still move forward, but it will be easier.".

In the morning, Gax feels well enough to read from the Book, even though the girls have to strain to hear his voice. Caecilia can feel her

CHAPTER 19

face warming up. "Fear not," he reads, "for I will pour water upon him that is thirsty." She pulls a face. Gax looks up and smiles at the girls. "This is just what we needed to hear," he says, "we need this water and at least it's always pure."

Macia smiles, "It's hard not to fear when everything goes wrong, which is why I missed the Book so much when I was by myself in Elabi." Caecilia looks away. Gax brought God to Elabi, but couldn't stay. Macia had God in Elabi, but couldn't stay. Now they brought God to Colchuyni and they'll be lucky if they make it out of the jungle alive. Never mind their mission to find out about Downstream and possibly put a stop to whatever bad is happening there. Evil is dealing with them; how could they ever expect to fight evil here, on its own territory?

Gax nods that he's well enough to carry on walking. It will be several hours till it's too dark to travel. Macia and Caecilia look for firewood and food, and Gax concentrates on staying upright and moving forward, one footstep at a time. "I can see a shelter, on the other side of the path," Macia says quietly, and points. There is a large tree with bushes around it. Caecilia shudders as she can imagine the stream close by. Will they be in more danger there, as they're closer to the water? Or will the Stream not dirty its own patch?

They decide to go a little further, walking cautiously. Macia is quiet and looking sombre, chewing her lip, Gax is struggling, sweating and shivering, Caecilia is silently wondering about the Stream's power. She shivers. "We'll have to find shelter soon. We haven't got much food so we will need to get some fish," she says, hoping Gax will manage to help out this time. Caecilia doesn't like fishing. Macia is good at it but she needs Macia's energy to find more firewood and to collect water and maybe more berries.

"I should go," Gax says, sounding as if they probably won't expect him to do so.

"Good idea," Macia says. "At least it will give you a chance to rest, and Caecilia and I will do the water and more firewood." Gax's shoulders slump a little more and Caecilia frowns as he stumbles a little. Doesn't he realise they get tired too?

She sighs, "We'll help you if you want," she says, "and Macia is right, we do need more food. We don't want to get too weak as it will make everything harder."

"I know that," Gax says shortly, "I don't think I could get much weaker as it is, and I will need protein to build up some strength. Maybe we should take another whole day out tomorrow and stack up on food and firewood as well as some needed rest for all of us."

Caecilia frowns. What does she say to that? They don't need rest, they need the jungle to end, to reach their destination and they need more food. "We'll get food cooked as early as we can," she promises, "so you can have a longer night." That's as far as she will go. She isn't in the same rush as Macia, but she wants to get away from the Stream sooner rather than later.

Macia keeps looking around, not taking part in the conversation anymore. Gax sniffs now and then, swiping at his eyes. Caecilia looks away, irritation making her walk faster, so she has to keep slowing down to avoid bumping into Gax. She notices Macia looking around and soon, Caecilia feels uneasy as well. Most likely because of Macia, she tells herself, but no, something has changed.

"I don't know what it is," she starts, but Macia flaps her hand at Caecilia to make her stay quiet. At a rather sharp bend in the path, Macia dashes behind a few trees, beckoning the others to hurry as well.

"There is something," she breathes, as they stand close together. "I don't know what it is, but it's making me feel itchy." Caecilia nods and opens her mouth to agree, but Macia carries on. "I don't think it's the elders, but it could be. I just feel watched, if that makes sense. It

CHAPTER 19

doesn't feel like an evil watching, just being stared at."

Gax tries to grin, but Caecilia shakes her head at him. "I agree," she says quietly, "I felt it the last bit. It wasn't there earlier, but after we stopped for a quick break, it started. I thought it was because Macia kept looking around, but it wasn't just that. I couldn't see anybody, or hear anything. Do you think it came from the stream area?" She looks at Macia who hesitates.

"It felt like that," she says slowly, "but at other times, it was more in the woods itself, as if it had moved." Caecilia doesn't want to say anything, but surely there could be another stream further on in the jungle? As they're further into the jungle, maybe the Stream becomes more powerful. The water itself is certainly wider than it was when they first set out along the path. She glances around as Macia is talking, still uneasy. "Maybe we will hide for a moment," Macia whispers, "see if you can notice anything."

The three stand hidden by the large tree, its long leaves dropping the odd waterdrop on them, making Caecilia shiver. Nothing moves, and although birds and other creatures are scuttling along branches, nothing is menacing. Gax sighs and in the end, they give up. "Let's carry on, but keep our eyes open," Macia suggests. Gax hasn't said anything all this time but hasn't moaned either. Caecilia is glad, for she knows they felt something.

They walk on slowly and Caecilia's hands are shaking by the time they stop to seek shelter. "I kept thinking I heard something, it was making me so jumpy," she whispers to Macia, "and every time it was just a bird or some other animal. Once I heard a crocodile slide back in the water, I'm sure, that's how much I was listening out!"

Macia giggles but looks around. "I know," she says, her smile slipping. "I don't think it's the elders as they make more noise, but what it is, I don't know. Maybe we're simply tired and need a good rest, a hot bath, clean clothes and a large meal," she says, tugging the corners of her mouth upwards, but Caecilia can see her swallowing.

"We'll have to break into whatever building there is Downstream," she whispers to Caecilia that night as Gax is keeping the first watch. "I need a bath, so we will have to use their bathrooms when they're asleep." Caecilia giggles and Macia continues, "as well as find clean clothes and new shoes and a whole lot of other things." She suddenly sighs, "Do you think we're nearly there? I have lost count of how long we've been walking through this awful jungle."

Caecilia sighs as well, her voice shaking as she says, "I have no idea. It's the idea of having to walk back to Colchuyni that makes my stomach go funny. My shoes won't hold out much longer."

Caecilia suddenly thinks of the water they are heading towards. "Gax knows how to build a coracle," she whispers, and Gax turns his head around as he hears his name. He scoots a little further into the shelter to hear what's going on. "You could build a coracle and we could help," Caecilia says, her voice higher than usual. "We could row or sail all around till we got back to Colchuyni. That must be easier than traipsing through the jungle for another few weeks on rotten shoes, eating half a root and a few herbs each day."

Gax opens his mouth to say it's not that easy to build a little boat, but he stops himself. How easy has it been to walk through the jungle? He's sure he's got a temperature and his leg hurts worse every day. So does the foot that was damaged by the elders. He is constantly thirsty but doesn't dare ask for more water as it was his fault that the water wasn't cleaned properly, making them all ill. He wants to get back home, and soon. If they all built a boat together, that might be sooner than hoped for. So he grins instead, "We'll see what we can do," he whispers. "Maybe we'll build a coracle with a sail this time."

He looks out of the shelter, as he is sure he heard a noise. Not a loud noise, a stealthy one. He doesn't move but signals the girl to be quiet. There, the noise returns. Gax peers through the darkness,

CHAPTER 19

trying to spot a moving shape. Nothing can be seen, and he leans forward a little to have a better field of vision. Is that a moving shape? A bird flies up, the branch swaying wildly and he rolls his eyes. Maybe he imagined the noise. Until he hears it again. It's something large, moving slowly around, not that far from their shelter.

Macia slips out of her sleeping bag, unable to stay still any longer. She nudges Gax as they both see it. Dark shapes, walking slowly along the path. The darkness hides how many shapes there are, but Macia is sure there are more than four.

There is a low whistling noise, like a flute and the figures stop moving. Gax swallows. "Our fire," he breathes and Macia shivers. The fire has long been covered, but as always, the smoke seems to linger in the damp air, clinging to dripping branches. Soon, the flute sounds again, longer this time, and the figures set off once more towards Colchuyni. Macia realises her teeth are chattering and she is shaking all over. To see those figures glide by in the dark is frightening. She glances over her shoulder but Caecilia is hidden in her sleeping bag. "Nine," Gax whispers, as a ray of moonlight manages to filter through, outlining the various moving heads. Gax counts and nods, he is sure of his number. "No elders," he says, making sure to leave the last sound off as much as possible."

If not the elders, then who are these people? The flute sounds again, low and sad. Gax and Macia stare at the figures who suddenly disappear, swallowed up by the jungle. Simultaneously, they swing their heads back downstream. Noise again. Louder this time. Voices, one deep and sounding unhappy, easily recognised. The Head elder.

Chapter 20

Caecilia sits up as well, and the three listen, holding their breath. They can't tell what the Head elder is saying. Only his voice is clear. The elders aren't going fast, and seem to take a lot more care in looking around.

They pass their shelter, and although one of the elders hesitates, looking towards the clump of bushes around the tree, none of them stop. Soon, the voices fade, and the jungle is back to its normal nocturnal sounds.

Macia says, "They're gone now. Do you think the elders will carry on like that all the way to the village? That would be good. Hopefully, this means they have given up. I don't know who the others were."

Gax says, "They might have been the Head elder's friends, the ones he talked about. He said he'd promised to keep their secret. So maybe he has warned them and they're looking for us as well." Caecilia bites her lip. That is just what they need. Not just elders, but another group hunting them.

"I'll keep watch," Macia says, "you better get some sleep, for we ought to make good time tomorrow. That way, we'll stay away from the elders and hopefully the others as well. We don't know where their base is, so they might be coming back this way. I will let you know if I hear them again."

Caecilia struggles to sleep. She is exhausted. She is sure that she can

CHAPTER 20

hear the stream in the background. Can it read her thoughts, like their God? She can feel her face heating up inside the sleeping bag. The others would be horrified if they knew her thoughts. It is only because of the accidents and the trouble they have had, she defends herself. And Riu had said that their God might not be able to do anything in this area. Why does that make her feel like her soul is drowning?

They start early. Caecilia keeps looking over her shoulder, Gax is wiping at his eyes and even Macia is breathing hard. "We just need to push through," she pants, "the elders could return and so could the others. I keep looking for a well-hidden spot where we can rest for a moment. I don't think we can simply flop down near the path. Not today."

Gax sniffs. "My leg hurts. I know it always hurts after the bandage has been changed, but it's hurting a lot today. I'm not sure how well I can do this afternoon, without setting us back again. I'm sorry to be such a burden," he adds, his voice shaking.

Caecilia pats his arm, not looking at Macia. "We know you're doing your best," she says softly, "we'll try to get as far as possible, and maybe we could have the fire a little away from our shelter?"

She looks at Macia who nods, her cheeks red. "We have to get further," she says to Gax, "we'll stop as soon as we find a safe shelter for the night." She helps Gax in his rucksack then sets off again. She glares at the path ahead. Every day in this jungle she has been walking in front, leading them all. The other two have moaned every day about how tired, how hot, how hungry they are. She hasn't said anything; what could she say? She has tried to sympathise, but really? Walking carefully, checking both sides of the jungle, she gets out some lovely paper in her head and a green pen.

"Hello dearest," she starts, the title always able to make her smile, "I know I have been quiet, so I hope you don't mind me talking to you now. Life is rather hard. I feel so bitter. With everything and everyone, really. It started in Colchuyni, maybe even the first day." She thinks back to that first day, and Riu's reaction to the Book. "Yes, as soon as I realised that we would have to live hidden all that time, my heart sank. It was the best thing about Mataiox, the freedom we had to share about the Book, to speak to others…"

She can hear Gax stumble behind her, and she looks around, grabbing his arm to stop him from falling flat on his face. His walking stick has snapped in half. "My leg," he moans, tears pooling in his eyes. Macia sighs quietly, but he must have heard it. "I'm so sorry," he says, his face warm. "I feel so weak and useless and guilty. If only I had prepared better and taken more notice of what we were told."

Macia tries to smile. She gets it. She had simply thought of their goal, not facing up to the steps in between. "We've all made mistakes on this trip," she says, "I still think we're nearly there, for the jungle feels different."

Gax nods, looking less pitiful. "Maybe we should pray together," he says, suddenly, reaching out his hands. "We haven't done that. I know, we pray when we look at the Book, but we haven't really properly prayed, I feel." The girls take his hands, although Caecilia hesitates.

"Should we move away from the stream a little before we pray," she whispers. The others stare at her.

"Why would we do that?" Macia says, then clamps her lips together and takes a deep breath, making Caecilia blush. "It's water, maybe not very clean, but that's all it is. The Stream that the villagers worship isn't this water. This water hasn't got ears, so we should be safe to pray." Caecilia nods, her face red, eyes lowered. Her hands are cold and shaking. Both Gax and Macia give them a reassuring squeeze.

Gax stares at his toes, his shoes beyond hope and looking as if they won't take him much further. He has let the girls down, that is clear. Even Caecilia is starting to believe in the Stream, not wanting a river to hear them pray. He is the one who has followed God the longest,

CHAPTER 20

has been to the Mission School, and this is already his second mission. So how could he have let the girls go so far out of touch with God? His face glows as he remembered how he'd allow them to interpret Hezekiah's fifteen-year promise to their situation.

He takes a deep breath, squeezing his eyes shut, "Lord God," he starts but Macia gasps and shakes them both, her eyes wild.

"They're coming, quick, oh no, they must have seen us!" They run towards the river as it's closest to them, helping Gax as much as they can. Macia calls, "There is a little path here." They follow the path around a bend, and the stream suddenly narrows, with debris blocking the water. Macia spins around, and points. "Look, that tree, it has made a bridge across the stream. Should we risk it?"

Gax glances over his shoulder, expecting the elders to come crashing through the bushes any moment. He nods, and points. "That side looks denser, we might be able to hide. As long as we make it across before they spot us."

Macia takes a deep breath and steps on the tree. It's slippery and she hesitates, but realising there are no other options, she keeps shuffling sideways across the tree trunk, onto dry ground. Caecilia is right behind her and they hug briefly as they're safe. Gax is nearly across the branch collection when Macia spots movement in the stream. Crocodiles. She opens her mouth to warn Gax, then changes her mind.

Caecilia's eyes widen as she spots the movement too. "Gax," she hisses," then stops as Macia touches her arm.

"He's going as fast as he safely can," Macia says quietly, "if we make him panic, he might lose his balance." Caecilia nods and shivers, staring at the small eyes, just above the surface, gliding towards the makeshift bridge. "Quick, Gax, quick," and she grabs his arm as he wobbles off the end of the bridge, and the three dash into the undergrowth, looking for a path to follow.

They're hidden from the elders. Will they realise they crossed the stream? "I don't think they'll follow us," Macia says, with a giggle. They all look back. The two crocodiles have made themselves comfortable on top of the branches, their dark bodies barely visible against the dead wood.

Gax is pale. "I am glad I didn't see them when crossing," he says, shivering. "I would have lost my head, and probably my balance at the same time." They look up as they can hear a noise. The elders. Their masks are clearly visible against the green backdrop. Caecilia makes as if to move, but Gax stops her. "Don't move now, they'll see the movement. I don't think they'll be able to spot us.

They sigh with relief as the elders turn away. "We will follow the stream, but we can't at the moment, not with the elders looking for us. And once it gets dusk, it'll be too risky because of the crocodiles," Macia says. She points ahead. "This is kind of a track. As long as we keep the stream in sight, we will be alright. If we lose sight of the stream, we'd get lost within minutes."

They all find a stick to keep branches out of their faces and set off along the narrow track. Calling it a track is an exaggeration, but there does seem to be a way to get through the greenery all around. Macia keeps a sharp lookout and points to a clump of dark undergrowth. "Look, that could make a good shelter and it's a bit hidden. We should be able to make a fire just there," and she points again, "as it can't be seen across the stream and it's not right next to our shelter."

Caecilia points out they're the other side of the stream. "We don't know if they'll follow us across," she says, "They might wait till the crocodiles have gone, then come across the same way we did."

In the end, they simply use one of the purifying tablets, eat some cold leftovers and slide into their sleeping bags, too exhausted and frightened to build a fire. "The smoke hangs in the air," Gax says, "and it's a risk as the light can be seen a long way off. We don't know where

CHAPTER 20

they are and there are the other people as well. We need sleep more than anything," he decides.

When Macia takes over from Gax again, it's been a standard jungle night. "One of the ferrets hasn't returned yet," Gax says, looking worried. "They usually come back together or at least soon after each other." Just then, the little ferret's face appears, squeaking and nudging Gax. He grins. "I'm glad you're back," he whispers, "I don't think they enjoyed the journey today. The running wasn't their thing, they were shaking and looked unhappy when we were about to cross the bridge," he tickles the nearest one and yawns.

Caecilia has buried herself in her sleeping bag. Having done her watch stint, she struggles to get back to sleep. They were about to pray to God and instead, they ended up fleeing across the stream. Was that a warning? A punishment? A tiny whisper suggests it might be God showing His power over the Stream even before they asked Him. It doesn't feel like that, though and she struggles to keep her sobs quiet.

He looks at the message. People in the jungle? He sneers. They know that already, they don't need that woman telling them. The picture with masks is clear enough, and he shows it to his right hand lad, who chuckles. "We will teach them alright. They deserve some teaching," the boy laughs. He shudders. Maybe the boy is getting too hard-hearted. Maybe he will leave him behind this night.

He looks around their hiding place, counting in his head. They won't all need to come. He will allow the dark boy to come along. He did well yesterday, tracking. He deserves a reward. He looks at the message one more time, then pushes it into the small fire, picking up the stick with the cooked bird pieces. Yes, they will take back their jungle. Not because of the woman. But because nobody causes the Elutera unrest.

Chapter 21

Macia wakes the others at first light. "We should start soon," she says, "I don't feel safe here, it's too close to the crossing." They don't dare to make a fire. There is a bush with edible berries nearby so they help themselves to those.

It is the hardest jungle day. The track is overgrown, and they all end up scratched, despite their sticks. The ground is more uneven and Caecilia sprains an ankle. "Let's have a short rest," Macia decides as she sees the tears on Caecilia's cheeks. "We started early and it's been quiet all morning, so the elders might have given up." She doesn't believe it but would love for it to be true.

Caecilia takes a deep breath and smiles. "I'm alright," she says, "it's not too bad, it only hurt for a few moments." They stop for lunch, but soon they're on their way. "I'm sure that noise was a crocodile," Caecilia says softly, trying to see past the bushes hiding the stream from view.

When they can't walk any further, the girls help Gax to set up an extra long stick, as he doesn't want to be visible on the other side of the stream. He keeps a sharp lookout for crocodiles as well. Gax glances over his shoulder, not wanting the girls to see him struggle. He looks up the stream, but the bridge they used to cross the stream is no longer in sight. The jungle is quiet, as far as human sounds go. Once it's nearly dark, they light a fire, cook the fish and boil the water.

CHAPTER 21

Their shelter is hardly visible from where they're sitting and Caecilia keeps glancing at it, worried to lose it in the darkness.

They cover the fire, and Gax is determined to take first watch. "I'm fine, as I rested whilst fishing," he says, "you two get some sleep. I feel warm and full for a change," he grins, rubbing his stomach.

Caecilia is about to drift off to sleep when she hears the noise. She opens her eyes, wondering if it's simply an animal, but seeing Macia get up, she follows. "What is it?" she whispers.

"No idea," Macia whispers back, "I'll have a look. Probably elders, as they're making a lot of noise." It's true, and Caecilia can hear their voices. "They're coming this way," Macia says after a while. Caecilia shudders and closes her eyes, knowing it's not going to stop the men. Closer and closer. "They must be hacking a path," Macia says quietly, "hopefully they'll carry on for a long time, it will make tomorrow easier." She goes quiet as the men are coming closer.

Gax can hear them near their fire. It has been covered up, but he hears the Head elder shout, "It's still warm!" They have found the fire, however well they covered it up. They had scattered the ash, so how could they find the warm spot?

He slides back into their shelter and moves their belongings closer as well. In the dark, he can hear Macia put a few items in her rucksack. "Good idea," he breathes and gets his bag ready as well. He hesitates over the sleeping bag. Should he put that away, ready to make a run for it? But the elders will easily outrun them.

The men are close. Too close. The three huddle as far away from the entrance as possible as if that will make a difference. Caecilia sobs, her head buried in her sleeping bag. Macia squeezes her eyes shut, allowing the tears to trickle out, praying silently for protection, for safety, for rescue. Gax is numb. "It's all my fault. I should never have joined this mission," he forms the words with his mouth, "Lord, please forgive me for thinking we could do this, that I could do this. We should have taken more students from the Mission School."

The steps stop. "...nearby," the Head elder says, his voice suddenly lowered. Gax tries to look at the girls. Should they defend themselves? They have their walking sticks and the men might not be able to get to them easily, as the opening is narrow and low. Silently, he reaches out and grabs his stick. Macia's eyes widen as she sees what he does. She hesitates, glances at Caecilia's form huddled in the sleeping bag and grabs her walking stick, putting Caecilia's near the girl.

They can hear stealthy footsteps around the path, closer...closer. Gax grips the walking stick in both hands and moves closer to the entrance, his hands shaking. Suddenly, the jungle is filled with noise. Horns are blown, a clash of wood on wood, and shrieks louder and more terrifying than a human could possibly make fill the night air, making the ferrets flee for their lives. Gax drops his stick and the three clutch at each other, Caecilia's crying and whimpering drowned out until she hides into Macia's shoulder, dimming the sounds.

Running, crashing, shouting. The noise seems endless, but it's moving further into the jungle. Macia jumps up and grabs the others, shaking them. "Quick, run. They will know where this shelter is but we can go back a little. There was a hiding place not far from the fire. I didn't want to use it as it was too close to the fire, but now we can. They found the fire and they think they found us. They'll be back." She helps Gax and Caecilia and, wrapping their sleeping bags around their necks, they hobble through the dark jungle. "Stay on the path," Macia says. Soon, they reach the fireplace. She hesitates, peering into the darkness. "There," she hisses, pointing at a dark shape. "Quick."

They stumble through rough undergrowth, Caecilia gasping at the scratches and stumbling over the uneven ground, Gax whimpering softly every time his leg touches a branch. They get to the new hideout and Gax has to admit that it's a safe-looking place. "Let's move as far back as possible," he whispers. "They might start looking again, but

CHAPTER 21

they might not come this way, not expecting us to go back."

They try to listen to the noises, but it's unclear what is happening. Caecilia can hear the odd shriek or shout, but she blocks her ears. She is shaking all over, her ankle burning and her head throbbing. Are the elders teaming up with the others or are they fighting each other? She gets her sleeping bag out and hides inside. It's warm and dark, the material soft and comforting. She doesn't want to be here, she wants somewhere safe and comfortable, not smelling of mud and smoke, desperately needing a wash.

Gax peers into the darkness. He glances over his shoulder at Macia who is sitting close behind. "What do you think?" he asks her and she shrugs.

"I have no idea," she whispers, "it sounds like they are fighting each other. I thought they were the Head elder's friends. Maybe they are angry that he didn't catch us or keep us out of the jungle?" Gax nods. That makes sense.

"Do you think they'll come back looking for us tonight? They might have given up, and wait till daylight," he says, suddenly exhausted.

"I'm not sure," Macia says slowly, "I could keep watch if you want and wake you if something happens."

Gax nods, his shoulders sagging with relief, "Sure, thanks," he says, "as long as you're alright with that?" he adds quickly, not wanting Macia to think he isn't capable of standing watch. Macia grins and makes herself comfortable near the entrance of their new shelter, the forest quiet once more.

She can hear the soft breathing, Caecilia's occasional whimper in her sleep and Gax snoring softly. Just as she turns back to the entrance, she can hear someone coming. Someone running. Her eyes strain through the darkness, with only a little moon light. She is sure she can see a moving figure, staggering along the path. He is near their fireplace. The person doesn't slow down or even look around. She hesitates. Should she wake the others? In the end, she decides to leave them to sleep. The person doesn't seem interested in them or anything else for that matter.

Just then, the figure moves through a clearing and moonlight falls on his face. Macia clasps her hand over her mouth to stifle the gasp that slipped out. It is the Head elder but without his mask. She recognises his dress and figure. He is leaning on a large stick, limping and moaning. A few times she can see him stumble but quickly get up again. He glances over his shoulder, and Macia can see the terror on his face as he looks around wildly, checking for danger. Macia stares at his disappearing shape, sure that what she saw on him, covering him, was blood. He must have been beaten up. Pretty badly, too. She looks at Gax and Caecilia, but leaves them to sleep.

Over breakfast, held inside the shelter, Macia explains. "It was the Head elder, I'm sure of that. He didn't have his mask on, and he seemed hurt. He was limping, falling down a few times, but was rushing as fast as possible back towards the bridge. It was dark, but the moon shines through that patch over there," and she points towards the path. "I could see him for a moment in the light, and I am quite sure he was covered in blood."

Gax frowns, "Why would he be alone and hurt? Are you sure?" He stops as he sees Macia's face. "I'm not saying I don't believe you," he protests, "I'm more thinking out loud, I suppose. The Head elder, hurt and running away upstream towards Colchuyni. He will have to cross the stream again as well."

Macia nods. "We heard the screaming and shouting. Who knows what happened?"

Caecilia looks towards where they are supposed to be going today. "Should we go anywhere today?" She bites her lip. "Maybe we should have a rest day and wait till they have all moved on?"

It does sound tempting, but Macia sighs in the end, "I think we ought

CHAPTER 21

to carry on. This shelter isn't too good and yesterday, the men got too close for my liking. I want to get this trek over."

After breakfast, they set off, slowly, down the path. "At least the path is more visible, unlike yesterday," Gax grunts and Macia gives a nervous giggle. They stop every few minutes to listen and look around.

"I feel watched again," Caecilia whispers as they stop, and Macia nods. They try to stick to some kind of cover, and Macia keeps looking around. Caecilia feels her eyes burning, she simply wants it to be over. In a way, coming face-to-face with whoever is watching them almost seems better than this.

Just before a bend in the path, Macia stops. She sniffs the air and looks at the others. Gax nods once, "There is a funny smell," he says and they all stand there, sniffing the air. Gax goes pale as he whispers, "It smells like my leg did after the crocodile snapped at me." He starts to reach out to Caecilia who has given a small gasp but he lets his hand drop, feeling awkward all of a sudden, and he glances over his shoulder. Maybe the girls are right. Maybe they are being watched. The place feels heavy in the jungle heat, with things buzzing around all the time and birds fluttering. At the moment, it feels very still. Everything feels wrong. He glances around, looking for the perfect shelter spot. "Do you think we should seek shelter for the night and hide for now?"

Macia shakes her head and even Caecilia looks doubtful. "I don't like the idea of finding somewhere to spend the night when it feels like we're being watched," she breathes. "Let's just carry on, but be careful." They grip their sticks a bit tighter and slowly move around the bend.

Caecilia gasps and moans out loud and Macia covers her mouth. Gax stares, unable to move. Bodies and blood are everywhere, the ground churned up and branches spread across the path. Nearby is a shattered mask, another one clutched by a smaller body. Critters scamper as they appear, making Caecilia whimper and she leans over the bushes near the path to throw up. The sound makes Gax's stomach flip and he takes a deep breath, regretting it instantly. His stomach heaves and although he tries to stand tall, soon he doubles over and wastes his precious breakfast as well. Standing up straight, he looks at the horrendous scene again, blinks a few times, and realises there aren't as many bodies as he first thought. He looks at Caecilia who is shaking violently, her face grey. He touches her arm and she glances at him without responding.

He looks at Macia who turns back to him, her eyes wide, face white. "I can see some of the elders, look," she points carefully, "he still has his mask half on. But there are others as well."

Gax looks at the still forms and says, "Maybe the attackers were killed by the elders? The Head elder must have escaped, presumably by fighting his way out." Macia nods and points with her chin towards a discarded mask.

"There is his mask. It's more elaborate than the others," she says and takes a careful breath. "What should we do? We can't bury them, we have no tools and the attackers might still be around."

Gax shudders. "We can't leave them like this either," he sighs, "although I have no idea what to do."

Caecilia whispers, "Maybe drag them into that bush, the one that looks like a shelter? I know it makes no difference, but this is too awful." They can hear the tears in her voice and Macia nods.

Carefully, they move closer and Caecilia throws up in the bushes again. Macia turns to Gax, "Maybe you should look after our rucksacks and keep an eye out," she whispers and Gax almost manages a smile as he looks at Macia, his face warm and not just with the fever. Caecilia and Macia work together, both shaking with the horror of it all, not looking at the injuries or faces, trying to not be there in their

CHAPTER 21

minds. Until they come to one of the elders, slightly to the side, half hidden by some grass. They grab him and straighten up at the same time, staring wide-eyed at each other.

"He's still warm," Macia gasps.

Chapter 22

Caecilia and Macia stare at each other for a moment. Macia tugs at one arm, trying to use the man's knee to turn him over so they can see. "Riu's dad," Macia gasps, as the battered face becomes visible. "Oh no, how bad is it, do you think?"

Caecilia kneels next to the unconscious man and shrugs, looking at Macia. "I have no idea. He's breathing, but that's all I know. He must have been unconscious for a long time, so I'd imagine he's badly hurt." She simply stares at the man and then points at the broken mask nearby. "He is the one that threw the oil to us," she says, "look, that must be his mask." They stare at each other again. So many questions, but it doesn't look as if they will have any answers soon.

Macia reaches over and rips part of the man's shirt, making Caecilia sit back. "I need some cloth," she says and uses it to wipe his face and clean off some of the crusted mud around his nose and mouth. There is no response; Riu's dad isn't showing any signs of life, apart from his shallow breathing.

Gax appears, breathing hard, looking pale, making Caecilia jump. "Sorry," he whispers, "I had to come and see. Is he alright?" When he leans over Caecilia's shoulder to have a look, he gasps. "Riu's father! What was he doing in the jungle?" Macia points at his mask and Gax stares at Caecilia. "You mean he was…is…one of the elders? Does Riu know? What will he say when his dad comes back to the village?"

CHAPTER 22

Gax looks at Macia and Macia says softly, "I don't think he'll be back in the village any time soon, if ever. He looks badly injured." Caecilia's eyes fill with tears and she looks at Gax again.

"You're right," Gax says after a moment, "maybe we should use some of our water? His mouth looks so dry."

Macia nods and pulls her bottle out. She pours a tiny amount on a clean corner of the cloth and tries to moisten the dad's mouth. Twice, three times she manages to wet his tongue and he swallows, a sign of life. Riu's dad groans and they all sit back, elated. Macia cleans his face a bit more with the cloth, smiling in anticipation. He opens his eyes, unfocused, and sees them. His face twists in pain and he mutters, "...sorry...tell Riu...evil..." His eyes change, even the colour of his face seems to change and Caecilia grasps Gax, who holds on to both her hands, eyes wide. Macia's hand with the cloth drops to the ground as she stares at the face that is now still and blank, empty.

"No," she whispers, "no, no, please don't go," and she grabs the hand, then lets it slip through her fingers. Riu's dad has gone, and no begging or asking will make him return to them. Macia's shoulders slump. How will they tell Riu what happened to his father and where his father is?

"What should we do?" she asks after a moment. "We can't leave him here, at the mercy of wild animals as well as those people." She glances at the shelter where they have carried the other bodies, but she can't bring herself to add Riu's father to that place of horror.

They glance around, and Gax points at a shallow ditch. "We could place him in there and push the rest of the soil on top of him," he explains, "then add some large branches to stop animals," he trails off as he sees Caecilia go pale. Macia nods, as it's the best option. Together they carry Riu's father to the ditch, and Caecilia drapes the dirty cloth over his face, sobbing.

Using large branches, they scrape the soil over the body, and Caecilia keeps an eye out as she collects more sturdy branches to spread over the top once they have covered the man. They work quickly, worried about staying in one place too long.

Caecilia gives a loud, desperate gasp and Macia and Gax look up. Caecilia is facing a young lad, who is glaring at her. "Don't you dare," Caecilia shrieks, waving a twisted branch at him, and she growls at him like a mother tiger defending her cubs.

The young lad takes a small step closer, and pointing with his chin says, "What are you doing?"

Macia stands, rooted, the large branch in her hand. She rubs her eyes, her breath coming in quick, shallow gasps. Can it be? But how? Her eyes take in every detail of the young, strong face. She swallows and whispers, "Halit?"

The young man's head comes up with a shock and he stares at her, wide-eyed. "Who are you?" He takes in the picture, Macia's matted hair, dirty, stained clothes, and face streaked with mud and blood. "How do you know me?" He glares, "Who told you?"

Macia drops the branch, and with a small sob, steps towards the angry lad. "Halit? I'm Macia. I'm your sister Macia. Where is Mother? You lived? Did she live? They let you both live?"

Halit stares at her. "My sister? From Elabi?" he says in the end and Macia nods, fighting against tears. Her little brother, her sweet darling little brother, standing in front of her, a young man, tall and handsome, looking strong. "You are from Elabi?" He looks over his shoulder as if expecting an entryway from Elabi.

"I left Elabi," Macia says, gesturing towards Gax and Caecilia," "We left Elabi. We came to look for you and Mother. I wanted to know what happened to you, to her. Did they let you go, or is Downstream simply this, living here?"

Halit curls his lips back, "No. No, it isn't. They didn't let us live, they didn't let us go. Mother went, she escaped as soon as we arrived

CHAPTER 22

and never looked back. That is what she says."

Macia stares. "You escaped? So where do you live and what happens to people from Elabi?" She looks around, the jungle green and dense as ever. "Where do you live?" she repeats.

Halit hesitates. "Why are you burying the man?" He asks, raising his chin at Riu's father.

"He was the father of a good friend," Macia says. "He helped us, and I don't know what happened, but he died. We want to bury him, because of his son." Her voice shakes a little, as she is well aware that Halit was likely part of the group responsible for the deaths. She doesn't want to anger him or scare him into attacking them, but she doesn't want to lie to her little brother either.

"They came on this side of the stream. With their masks," he says, as if that explains everything, and justifies the deaths. Seeing their faces, he says, "They are not allowed on this side of the stream. We don't allow anybody on this side. The other side," he waves towards the stream, "the other side has a good path to Felix, who is in charge of the Requipacem facilities." Macia shudders at the dreaded word. She knew that is what Downstream was for. Why had she thought they would let people live?

"We saw you. Then the masked ones followed. They crossed the stream. I don't know why they wanted you?" he asks and Macia sighs.

"We escaped their village. We came to their village because we wanted to find you and Mother. They captured Gax," and she raises her chin at Gax, "and so we rescued him and ran straight into the jungle. They were determined to capture us. We overheard the Head elder, he's the one with the large mask, that he had agreed with someone that nobody would come that way."

"That must be Felix," Halit agrees. "Felix would not like to have his work interrupted," he sneers. "No wonder they were so desperate to stop you." He looks pleased, but Macia looks sad.

"Your friend's father," he says, remembering what she had said and he does his best to look less pleased. "I don't know what happened." He frowns, "Not sure what to do next," he says, "for you should not be here. But you have come to see us," he says, and his face brightens. "That should be fine then. I will take you to Mother. She might not be there," he warns, as he takes a step back, "for the boat is due to arrive and they try to rescue who they can. Sometimes it's nobody and sometimes it is many people. Then we're all busy."

Gax looks back at Riu's father. The work is nearly done, and he hesitates. Macia sees it. "We need to finish this, but we're nearly done. Just wait a few minutes," she says and picks up the large branch again. Caecilia helps, not having said a word. They heap up the soil as much as possible, then cover the body with branches. They step back and again, Macia feels sadness. She can imagine Riu's face when they tell him. Or will the Head elder tell the family? Nobody is to know who the elders are, so can he tell their families now the other elders are all dead?

They shoulder their rucksacks and follow Halit. He uses a stick to make a path, walking through the jungle. Ahead, the jungle seems less dense, and Caecilia brightens up. Are they at the end of the jungle? Halit turns round, and says, "The stream goes wider and other streams join. We need to go that way," and he points deeper into the jungle.

They leave the water behind. Caecilia is relieved, glad to leave its menacing presence behind. Although the Stream seemed to have attacked its servants, rather than them. Maybe God was stronger after all? The trees all look the same, the vegetation is thicker than ever, the ground is uneven and the humid air drains their energy. "We will need to rest and have lunch," Macia says as she looks at Gax and Caecilia.

Halit frowns. "Can't you wait? We haven't walked very far."

Gax opens his mouth, but Macia beats him to it. "No," she says, "we can't wait. We only had a very small breakfast and we have heavy bags

CHAPTER 22

to carry. I don't know how much further we have to go?" Halit looks away, and Macia swallows. Why won't he tell them? Is he taking them to safety or can she not trust her little brother? She peeks at him as they're eating.

Lunch doesn't take long, simply because they haven't much to eat. Halit looks at them, rolling his eyes. He opens a pouch he has dangling off his belt and hands out food. A kind of bread, some baked flat cakes and some kind of grain rolled inside leaves. They eat as quickly as they can without completely abandoning manners. Macia swallows twice, nearly choking on her mouthful. "Thank you," she says, "we just had roots we found and fish. We couldn't fish yesterday because of the elders looking for us." She doesn't want her little brother to think they are incapable of looking after themselves. Truth be told, Halit's gift was very welcome.

They set off again, and Caecilia smiles at Macia. The girls get Gax to walk directly behind Halit and Caecilia whispers, "He's still got that dimple in his cheek, the one your father used to frown about, remember?"

Macia remembers and she grins. "He does look like father a little, but I love the dimple. It looks sweet on a tall lad," she giggles.

"Walking is so much easier with food inside you," Caecilia sighs after a while. "I do hope we're nearly there. It's been uphill for ages, and my shoulders are aching."

Macia nods. She is exhausted as well. Not just the walking, but the emotional drain from their gruesome find this morning, having to handle those men... her stomach twists and a little bit of bile rises in her throat.

Halit shakes his head as Macia points out plants. "There is plenty of food in the camp," he says. "We have people who collect food every day."

Macia nods, glad about the extra information. They live in a camp.

Life is organised. There is food. "On the other hand, a little help would always be welcome, right?" She smiles at her little brother, who stares at her.

"Why would we collect food when we're not part of the collection team?" He frowns, "Why would you confuse everybody?"

He carries on walking, and Macia can feel her face warming up. She stands a little taller. Caecilia touches her arm. "They're from Elabi," she whispers. "They're all from Elabi. They didn't leave because of the Book. They left to escape death. They will know nothing of what we know, and they will not understand kindness and helping each other. Maybe they do a little, because of their circumstances. But they don't have the Book."

Chapter 23

Noises can be heard up ahead, voices and the soft hubbub created when people are together. They have reached the camp. Halit glances over his shoulder and seems to slow down a little. They follow him through a gateway set in a wooden palisade around huts. Huts of different sizes. People can be seen, mostly elderly and a few children.

Looking at the number of people she can see, Caecilia decides they're quiet. "They don't seem to make much noise for the number of people here," she hisses at Macia, who nods to show she heard. "Those children," Caecilia continues, "they must be the ones sent on the boat with defects." Caecilia looks around. She doesn't think her mother ever sent a child Downstream, not during the time Macia's mother has been gone. She can think of several classmates whose parents sent more than one baby away on the boat.

Gax glances over his shoulder at the girls and opens his mouth to ask something, but Halit stops and looks at them. "This is our hut," he says, pointing at a large hut. "Mother and I share it and sometimes we have an extra baby to look after as well. At the moment we are by ourselves. We have a separate room, where the baby normally stays. You girls can have that room and you," he looks at Gax, "can stay with me. The rooms aren't large, but it's better than where you have been staying." He pulls a face as he looks at the state they're in.

Macia can feel her face warm up. Before she can put her little brother straight, Caecilia ask, "Is there somewhere where we can get clean? We have been travelling for days and days, and although we managed to wash our clothes, we didn't dare go into the stream because of the crocodiles."

Halit gasps and opens his mouth, then shrugs, "There is a washhouse. Let me get some soap and cloths and I'll take you there." He hesitates, "Do you want to go in first, so you can leave your bags here?"

They look at each other and Macia giggles. "Maybe it's best to go and get clean first, rather than walk around the house like this." Halit rolls his eyes but disappears into the large hut. The wooden door, unlocked, clicks shut. He reappears, carrying a basket.

"This is the soap and cloths," he says and walks away. They follow him to a large round hut, "It isn't hard to work, just look," he says and they crowd around. "The water comes from here, there will be plenty in the tank, but not enough to stand there and just let it run," he warns. He points at the tank on a higher platform next to the hut. "The water is in there. We can fill it up once you are done." The tank looks huge and Macia can imagine the work it takes to refill the barrel. He holds out the basket to Macia and turns round, leaving them standing in the middle of the village.

Macia lowers her rucksack and grins. "I can't believe we're about to get clean," she says and opens her bag to find some relatively clean clothes. The others do the same. "Do you want to go first?" she looks at Caecilia and smiles. "We can wait out here, as it's cooler in the shade." The village feels hot compared to the jungle. It's still humid but the sun is burning down as well, making it harder to breathe. Caecilia smiles and grabbing her things, heads inside the hut. Soon, they can hear water splattering and Macia feels better and cleaner, just from hearing the shower!

Gax sits in the shade, slumped against the wooden wall. He tries to

CHAPTER 23

smile as Macia says, "I can't believe we are here. If only my mother was here as well. At least she'll see us cleaner than we were." Macia looks at Gax and frowns a little. "You look very pale," she says softly, the joy slipping from her face. "Is it the last bit of walking we did, as it was quite fast?"

Gax shakes his head, and opens his mouth to explain, but decides the effort is too much right now. He shrugs and tries to smile again, but instead, his eyes fill with tears, and he slides down a little further.

Macia looks around and is relieved when Caecilia appears from the bathroom hut, glowing. Caecilia gasps as she sees Gax slumped against the wall and kneels with Macia. "He needs help," Macia says and Caecilia nods, swallowing hard. Macia glances at the bathroom, the chance to feel better so close, but it will have to wait.

Halit is walking towards them, frowning. "Gax is unwell," Macia says, waving her hands towards a softly moaning Gax. "Is there a medical room or someone who can help?"

Halit looks at Gax and shrugs. "They might help, or they might take him to the stream," he says ignoring Caecilia's shocked gasp. "Why haven't you had a shower yet?" he continues, glaring at Macia, who explains that Gax suddenly became unwell. Halit rolls his eyes and hesitates. "I will go and ask the people in the medical hut. They might be too busy, or they might see him. You go and clean up, and I will get someone."

Macia nods and after a last look at Gax, she briefly touches Caecilia's arm and grabs her clothes and the soap. The water feels amazing, but all she can think about is Gax's grey, sweaty face. She can hear voices just as she is getting dressed. Tugging at the damp clothes, she rushes to get ready, ending up almost as hot and sweaty as before the cool shower.

When she gets out, Caecilia smiles at her, her face wet with tears. "They will take Gax, but they aren't very hopeful," she whispers as

Macia stands next to her. Two older men and an old woman stand around Gax, their faces long and their voices quiet.

The woman straightens up and looks at Macia. "We will take him. This girl says he was bitten by a crocodile. Normally, when someone is bitten by one of those, we send them to the stream straight away, as we can't waste time and resources on something like that." She glares at Macia's shocked face. "A crocodile bite leads to trouble. Too much trouble and our resources are scarce and precious. Anyway, Halit says you are his sister, and as you have taken so much trouble to get here, we will make an exception. But he will need to recover well, as there is no second chance."

The two older men haven't said anything, but as the woman finishes, they bend down and drag Gax onto a kind of stretcher, made out of wooden beams with cloth holding them together. Halit and the woman help as well, but the woman shakes her head angrily as Macia and Caecilia step forward to help. Halit pulls a face and says, "Go back to the hut, I will come as soon as I can. It is better for you not to see and help." He points with his chin in the direction of the hut and then Caecilia and Macia are standing alone, in the middle of the village, the quiet noises of village life humming around them.

Caecilia bites her lips and Macia touches her arm again. "Let's get to the hut and drop our things. We can have a quick rest, for the water will need to be topped up, and I'm exhausted. There is nothing we can do for Gax." She swallows, as she was going to add 'but pray', but they have both been praying and saying it out loud sounds strange. So the girls turn towards the large hut. Macia hesitates as they get to the door. "This is the right one, I hope," she says, trying to smile. Caecilia nods but doesn't smile back.

Inside, the windows do let some light in, but it's still hard to see properly. Macia sees a dining table, a sideboard and a few doors. The first door they enter has a bucket with a structure built over it, and a

CHAPTER 23

jug and bowl to wash your hands. "At least there is an indoor toilet," she says. The second door reveals the guest room, at least she assumes it's the guest room. Not wanting to get it wrong and upset Halit, they leave their bags in the main room, and perch on the edges of the dining chairs.

Halit returns and scowls at them. "Your friend will need more help, but there is nothing for me to do there." He scrunches up his face, and adds, "Others will help. We need to refill the water and make your beds. The grass we use for the mattresses can be collected just outside the camp." The girls nod and follow Halit out of the hut. Walking to and from the village well with large buckets makes them as sweaty and sticky as they were before their shower.

They wash their hands with the last load and Macia quickly splatters some water on her face as well. She is still not sure what to think of Halit, and she peeks at him through wet fingers. He is looking away, arms crossed, chewing something. He reminds her of some young people in Mataiox, hanging around on street corners, not knowing what to do with themselves. Back at the hut, they grab large bags, and Halit takes them out of the village. "This is the grass we need," he says and waves his arm towards thin, stringy-looking grass. The girls are relieved to see lots of it. The grass is soft and breaks easily, and soon they are collecting large handfuls, stuffing the bags with the aromatic herbs.

"It smells nice," whispers Caecilia. She has no idea why she is whispering, but Halit's face seems to have a frown as the default position. Macia nods, and Caecilia continues, "It reminds me of the fields near the lighthouse," and her eyes fill with tears. Macia points out some of the berries but Caecilia shakes her head, suddenly grinning, swiping at her eyes. "No more berries," she says, "I will never look at berries the same way ever again."

Halit comes closer and hears the last words. He snorts, "I still don't know why you travelled so far to find us," he says, "or why you left Elabi in the first place. Where did you go?"

They tell him a little about Mataiox but Halit looks confused. "So many people? Not just one city? It sounds all too big and with so many people, there must be a lot of problems."

"True, but also a lot of people to help those with problems," Macia smiles, but her brother doesn't smile back. She stops the sigh from escaping, remembering the awkward days in Elabi after she started reading the Book. She will need to find that same patience and love all over again, it seems. She grabs more grass, stuffing her bag faster than ever.

At last, the mattresses are filled enough, and Halit shows them how to close the buttons on the end of the bag to keep the grass in. They return to the village, where it is quieter than before, with people staring at the girls and looking away as soon as the girls look back at them. Macia feels uneasy. The atmosphere in the village has changed whilst they were collecting grass, it seems. She waits till they're back in the hut, putting the mattresses on the bed frames. "People in the village suddenly changed, at least that's what it feels like," she says to Halit.

He nods briefly. "Some will not agree with treating your friend," he says. "Everyone is involved in collecting what we need and to have a guest come and use up time and resources on the level he will need, well, people will resent it. They'll soon forget though, as long as he doesn't… I mean, as long as he stays alive." He lights a small light in the main room and turns to the girls.

"We collect our food from the kitchen," Halit says, "but it's maybe best if you don't both come along. Macia can come, as I can say she's my sister. I will explain about you," he continues, looking at Caecilia, "but people don't need to know the full story. If they hear you were on this side of the stream, they might insist you're dealt with. After all you have been through, that would be a shame." Macia blushes at his tone. Her brother scoffed at emotions, but hatred, or even despising someone to such an extent that you're rude all the time, that's an emotion as well, she thinks.

"Later, when Mother is back, we can see what needs to be done, as well as about your other friend, if he is still here. I still don't know what you were hoping to achieve," Halit says, as he walks out of the door, Macia having to follow him.

She glances back at Caecilia and pulls a face. Caecilia rolls her eyes and grins making Macia stand taller as she gives Caecilia a tiny wave. She walks fast to catch up with her brother, bursting with all the questions she can think of. She decides to start with the easier ones. "How many people live in the camp?"

Halit shrugs. "It varies. Lots of the older people who are rescued die, so we have a burial team. Some people are very ill, and although we look after some of them in the clinic, they might still die. The children usually stay, but some of the teens go and join the Scitabi, the other camp."

His voice sounds harsh as he mentions 'the other camp' and Macia frowns. "There are two camps in the jungle? Do they go and rescue as well?" Halit nods and explains that the Scitabi are very active.

"They used to rescue whoever they could get out and attacked the boat. This has led to armed guards being sent along with the boats. It's made Mother's job harder. We don't want anyone to come into the jungle, but the Scitabi are harsher."

They arrive at the kitchen, a large, open hut, where the villagers queue to get their food. They wait their turn, and Halit explains who Macia is, why she is here and that Caecilia and Gax have come along as well, adding that Gax won't need any food for a while, if ever. The woman behind the large cauldron sniffs. Macia can see her left arm isn't working well. "You're lucky we have extra in that case," she says.

"We made the same amount, but your mother isn't here and neither are some of the others in the pickup detail. You can have their rations. In the morning, I will add your friends and relations to the list," she adds, not looking too happy about the change.

The three eat in silence, although Halit glances up a few times as there seems to be more noise outside than usual, but the girls are too exhausted to hear or care. They help to clear up but are relieved when it's late enough to go to bed. Halit grunts something as they wish him goodnight.

Macia stares at the ceiling, missing the evening reading from the Book, wondering how Gax is, and if they will tell them how he is, or whether he will simply disappear. No, she has to trust God to keep Gax alive and to look after him. She sighs, "Dearest friend…" then trails off, as she doesn't know what to say, or where to start.

Chapter 24

Macia opens her eyes to the darkness of early morning. At first, she can only think how comfortable the bed is, but then the memories of the last few days crash into her consciousness. What have they done to Gax? She recalls her brother's stony expression and feels her chest clench as she wonders if she will see her mother today.

Caecilia stirs across the room. "Oh," Caecilia yawns, "so nice to sleep through the night with no guard duty." Then, in the dim light, she catches Macia's pensive look. "Oh Macia, I can see it's sad to be back to Elabi thinking. We lived it for so long and now it sounds strange. There is no mercy, no kindness. I wonder how they will feel about the Book?"

Macia sighs. "And yet they are open with negative emotions. Halit is an emotional young man. The way he reacts to everything, and the woman in the kitchen openly rolled her eyes and complained."

The girls laugh at the memory. Then Macia continues, "They have allowed emotions, but still say they don't want emotions. So yes, maybe it will be the same for the Book. They might not like the idea, but tolerate us reading it."

Caecilia agrees. "I wonder what the Scitabi is like. They must have been the ones killing the elders."

"It sounds like they simply do whatever they'd like to do," Macia replies, sitting up in bed and stretching her arms. "I don't even know if Halit described them properly. They were loud and violent, but they never came near us, did they? There is something strange going on," she says, then giggles. "That sounds like one of those books Gax's mother likes to read," she says, sadness suddenly stinging her eyes. "I have no idea what I thought Halit would be like," she whispers, her voice shaking. "He isn't at all like I thought he would be. He was so sweet and smiley as a little one."

Caecilia reaches over and squeezes Macia's fingers. "He has been through a lot and living in a camp in the jungle for most of your life can't be easy. I wonder what his job in camp is?"

Macia knows. "He works around the village, tidying, finding food, cleaning, and all the odd jobs. He says he likes it as it's important for everyone's wellbeing; at least that's what he said."

"It doesn't sound like he enjoys his job. Maybe that is why he's angry a lot," Caecilia suggests and Macia agrees. Caecilia continues. "He's also pretty stuck unless he wants to go to the Scitabi. There is no way back to Elabi and no way out the other side of the jungle. He has nowhere to go and no future. Although they all work and live together, it doesn't feel like one large happy family. We might have to pray for a way to help."

Macia nods in the dark, pressing her lips together. "You can only help people who want to be helped." Her rude little brother doesn't seem to feature high on that list. "Maybe my mother will be more open," she says, "after all she has been through, she must see how broken the whole Elabi system is. She goes to rescue people, surely that means she can see a better way?"

Breakfast is awkward. Halit doesn't say much, other than his job needs him today. "We thought we would check on Gax today," Caecilia starts.

"No, they will tell you when he is ready," Halit says between

CHAPTER 24

mouthfuls, "Try not to mix too much with the others. They might not like the idea you were found in our side of the jungle. And most of them don't like the Scitabi. They won't like the stories of the attack and the fact they didn't attack you."

Macia wonders about the Scitabi. "Would they go across the stream?" She looks at Halit, who frowns. "It's just that we saw them before, so many of them. We thought they were looking for us, although they most likely were looking for the elders."

Halit's face turns a darker red and he looks away. "No idea," he says, and gets up, telling the girls over his shoulder, "The bowls need to be washed. Next to the kitchen is a washing up area. Take the cloth there," and he points. "The rest will be available when you get there."

They stare at each other as the door slams shut after the young man. Macia stirs her breakfast and swallows. Before she can apologise, Caecilia touches her arm. "I know he's your brother, but none of this reflects on you. He might change once he's got used to us." Macia smiles at her friend, and sighs.

After they finish their breakfast, Macia says, "Let's read the Book, find our notebooks and use this time before we're stopped from reading altogether again."

Just as they lean back, the Book still open on the table, Halit returns. He stares at the open book and notebooks with pencils and frowns. "What is that?" He points with his chin at the Book.

Macia clamps her fingers together underneath the table, but answers, "It's a book."

Halit frowns. "A book. What does it do?"

It goes quiet. The girls don't want to look at each other, but is Halit serious? "A book is a collection of words, of writing," Macia says, slowly, not wanting to be patronising, but wondering where the conversation is heading. "You can have books with stories or books with instructions."

Halit sinks on a chair, looking at the Book, then their notebooks. "And those," he waves his hand at the pencils and notebooks.

"They're notebooks. They're empty books and you write in them with a pen or a pencil," Macia says, and she shows Halit the page she was writing on. "I can write down what we were talking about and what I was thinking, so I can look at it again at a later time," she explains.

Halit leans over the pages of the Book and sits back abruptly. "They're little…figures," he says, "how do you know what they mean?"

Macia explains that you learn to read. "That way, you can read words, put them together into sentences and form stories. You can write messages, you can label things and you can read or write for pleasure," she says, smiling softly as she thinks of the diary she wrote in her head when beyond the hills. "You could draw a picture and write something underneath it. That way you could learn new things. There are books about plants," she points at the book Caecilia is holding up. "That is how we knew what we could eat and what to look for."

Halit's eyes are huge as he looks through the book with pictures of life-like trees and bushes. He turns each page carefully. "This is amazing," he says in the end, looking at them. "What does it say," and he points to a tree and its description. Macia reads it out to him. Halit stares at the page. "So much information, in such a small space," he says softly.

Caecilia says, "Some books have important information. It helps you to know about life and the world around you."

Halit shrugs. "I like the book with trees," he says, "but we already know what we can eat. It doesn't matter if we don't know the name. We know enough. And life? Life in this camp tends to be short, and we don't want to think about that." He stops, brows furrowed. "The older people that come, they can read. I have heard them talk about it. I just didn't know what they meant. They never bring anything with

CHAPTER 24

them, as they have escaped the boat in a hurry."

Macia bites her lip; should they say anything? "This book is very special to us," she starts, "as it tells us why we are alive." Halit stares at her, and she swallows. "Reading this book and following its teaching is what caused us to leave Elabi. Rather, we had to leave Elabi."

Halit's eyes open wide. "You mean, you can't stay in Elabi if you read certain books?"

Macia nods, "That's right. There are a few books you can read, but there are many books that are banned. This Book is one of the banned books, so I was taken beyond the hills but I managed to escape and join Gax, our friend, and Caecilia in Mataiox."

Halit rolls his eyes. "Sounds too complicated for me," he says. "First, you tell me about books, then there are banned books and you end up escaping. From where? What hills?" He stops her before she can explain. "I need to get back to work. I will come for you when it's lunchtime." At the door, he turns around. "Maybe don't say anything about your book to anyone just yet, especially the old people. They might still think of books as forbidden. I'm sure Mother will care less about books."

When Halit is gone, the two look at each other. "Should we try and teach the younger people to read and write, using the Book?" Caecilia asks. "Should they even learn to read, I mean, it's not as if it benefits them in the village, is it?"

Macia frowns, "It must be good for everyone to be able to read," she says. "They might not need it right now, but what if they travel to Colchuyni or even out into the world? We might be able to sail around the headland to get home, and some of the other young people might want to do the same thing. They must have leisure time as well; it would be good if they could read."

Macia stares at her fingers and adds, "Surely we ought to tell them about God and they should be able to read the Book? It's important, isn't it? It's about their souls."

They're both quiet. "Yes," Caecilia says in the end, "yes, it is important, you are right. It's dangerous as well, and we don't know what will happen. The older people will know it's forbidden teaching, but they might not care anymore by the time they're here. I suppose it depends on what your mother says."

Halit doesn't mention the book for the rest of the day. When Macia tries to bring the subject up over dinner, he shakes his head. "I'm not that interested in your letter thing. Book," he says. "Life here is simple. We rescue people, we fix the sick ones, and the babies we bring up. Whoever stops living is dealt with. We like our life that way. People who want more join the Scitabi." He glares at the wall, "They take more chances, get themselves in a lot of trouble and often bring problems on the whole of the jungle. We won't stop them, and we can't stop them, but we don't need change. We have a smooth life, and that's how we like it."

"But then you die," Caecilia says softly, "and what happens then?"

"Then you get dealt with by the camp," Halit shrugs.

"But what happens to you?" Caecilia says, "To the person you are inside, your soul?"

Halit frowns at her. "How does that help you? That's just emotions wanting more and longer and better lives. It doesn't do anything for a person." He stands up, "Anyway, I am getting some sleep for tomorrow or the day after, Mother should be back. With new people. It will be all hands on deck, as they're usually in a state. Not just the boat journey, but also escaping and getting to the camp. Some of them die on the way, so we will need to go back along the route to deal with them."

Macia touches her cutlery and looks at Halit. "You said this morning not to go to the medical room, but how is our friend? Won't Gax worry if we're not there?"

CHAPTER 24

Halit looks away. "I don't think your friend is worrying at the moment," he says, pulling his lip in a sneer, then he adds, "They're using strong herbs to keep him asleep. They did...they had an operation on him yesterday; he'll be glad to be asleep. That was the noise yesterday evening." As he sees the girls' faces he shrugs, "I'm surprised you didn't hear it. I thought he would be gone this morning, but he's still alive. The people working in the clinic aren't too happy, as they'd not done this kind of operation before, and it's going to be hard for him for a long time." He pauses, "All his life, really, but, well, I don't want to say anything now, but I will ask for you in the morning if you can have a look at him. Hopefully, the helpers will be in a better mood and maybe your friend is still asleep. He won't be great when he wakes up."

He gets up and yawns loudly, ignoring Macia who opens her mouth to ask more questions. "I need an early night," he says through the yawn. "If the boat arrives, it will be busy and there might not be much sleep for a few days." He walks to his room, leaving the girls to take the dishes to be cleaned.

Macia looks at Caecilia as they're cleaning the dishes. "What do you think Halit meant?" She glances around; they seem to be the last ones doing the dishes. "What kind of operation and what does he mean about his whole life being hard?"

Caecilia stares at the plate she is polishing. When she looks up, her eyes are filled with tears. "I thought... the thought I had..." She swallows hard, "I think they might have taken his leg off." Macia gasps and drops the cloth she is using. "The infection in his leg was very bad, and it was starting to spread as well, making him ill," Caecilia explains. "They might have thought that the only way to get him better was by taking his leg off."

Macia bites her lip and looks away. Gax with a missing leg? How will he manage, and how will they ever get back? There is no way he can hop back to Colchuyni, but will he be able to build a coracle and row them home instead? And how will Gax react when he realises his leg is gone? All to find her mother? What if her mother is as delighted to see her as Halit is? Will this be a wasted journey? Will Gax ever forgive her? "We really need to see him tomorrow," she whispers, "or maybe we should ignore what Halit said and go now?"

"It might be easier to see him if the new people arrive," Caecilia says softly. "They will all be busy, and less likely to notice us popping in to see Gax. Although we could try early in the morning, as they'll be getting ready for the people. We need to see him and find out."

Chapter 25

Breakfast is quiet; there is no sign of new arrivals yet. "It happens," Halit says, "Some people are weak or old and can't travel fast. Sometimes there are lots of babies and they need too much help. They will be here tomorrow. They have only been later than that once, so tomorrow is more likely." Halit looks tired. "I had to help the burial people. Three old people died, all on the same day, just before the new arrivals. Not great timing," he says, "although it does empty a few huts, so we might not need to build new huts for a while."

When Macia asks, he says, "Yes, we build huts for everyone. Normally we put two people in a small hut or one in a tiny hut. Most old people share with one young person, so they can be looked after. A few young people look after the babies, as it's a longer task. They have a larger hut as well, so there is space for the babies to play and walk. There is a large fenced-in area with a roof, where babies can be taken. Young children are assigned to older children, so they can learn a task, ready to take over. But many of the babies die, as they often get ill. There is no baby milk, so they get other foods mashed up and some of the babies can't handle it."

He looks at the girls. "You could try to see your friend. He might not make it through the day, and if too many people need the clinic, they might send him to the stream after all." Macia gasps, and he adds quickly, "I don't think they will, not after doing the operation." He finishes his drink and says, "Do you read your book every day?" When the girls nod Halit looks away. "I mentioned a book, but the old woman at the clinic just snorted and said books changed and are a waste of time."

Macia hesitates. Should she tell him more about the Book they brought along? "Not all books are a waste of time," she starts, "this one is special and like we said, it changes you. It's different from any other book."

Halit rolls his eyes and gets up. "Like people," he says, pulling his lip back. "People can be boring, but they'll always tell you how special they are and how they deserve to live longer. They have no regard for anyone but themselves, wanting food every day, and insisting the clinic keeps them alive with more herbs and more treatment. They add nothing to the village but trouble. Hopefully, your friend will be an exception and not a waster like those old people."

Macia clenches her hands under the table. Of all the people, Halit isn't the one to talk! She takes a deep breath, but before she can put her little brother in his place he has walked to his room to get his sandals. "See your friend, then stay out of sight," he warns over his shoulder before letting the door fall shut.

Macia releases a long, angry breath and Caecilia touches her arm. "He has no right," Macia says, resting her clenched fists on the table. "He took my mother away, and has been allowed to live all these years, simply because of my mother and the goodness of others." She takes another deep breath, her hands shaking. "I know he has made himself useful, but he would have needed so much help when he was little, so others would have had to care for him. When he is old, he will need caring as well."

Caecilia nods, and wonders out loud, "It is very odd though, the way these people from Elabi with their teachings rescue old people who might not live much longer. They go to great lengths to save people's lives, whereas they seem to have no problem with sending people to the stream or burying them. What makes them do it? They don't look at emotions the same way, and they don't follow the Book, but still, they save lives. Why?"

Macia nods, the anger having left. "Yes, I can understand rescuing the children, especially as my mother saved my brother, but why the old people? By the time people go Downstream, they are at the very end of their lives. So why prolong their days at such expense?"

They clear the table and clean the plates in silence. They can see Halit in the distance, walking quickly from one side of the village to another, collecting materials and food for the clinic, dropping things off... "No wonder he is tired," Macia smiles, feeling proud of her scowling brother.

"I don't think he sleeps very much either," says Caecilia softly, looking over her shoulder. At Macia's look, she explains, "I couldn't sleep, I was thinking of Gax when I heard Halit leave the hut. I was scared at first, as I thought somebody had come in. This morning, I woke up when he came back into the hut, not long before daybreak."

Macia frowns, kicking a small stone aside. "I wonder what he does at night. He doesn't strike me the type to visit friends, so what would he be doing?" She swallows, "Do you think he might go into the jungle at night? Like those we heard..." Her eyes sting as she imagines her little brother taking part in that horrible incident. "Maybe we should find out what he does at night?" She can feel her face warming up. "I'm not just being nosey," she says, not liking the sound of her voice, "but something is going on with Halit."

Caecilia nods, "He has helped us, but never with a happy attitude. But this is Elabi, or at least, the people were from Elabi. Nobody is going to be happy to help, so maybe we are reading more into this than there is."

"It was the way he stood when he first met us," Macia explains. "He wasn't happy to see us, but not surprised. But he looked…dark. And when walking to the camp, I felt he wasn't glad to have rescued us."

Caecilia sighs. "Nobody looks happy, there is no laughter, nobody chats and even the children are quiet."

Macia says it reminds her of her time beyond the hills. "It's the misery, the waiting for life to end or to go back to normal, with no hope," she says. "The Scitabi sounds like they have a bit more emotion, but are they just angry?"

"If Halit leaves again, I will follow him," Macia decides. "I know my mother will be back, but after her journey, she should sleep soundly. I want to know where we stand with Halit. Just in case he tries to double-cross us."

"I want to know," she continues as they get back to the hut. "He is my little brother, but I don't know anything about him. I don't know what he likes, I don't know what he is good at. I don't know if he is kind and safe or dangerous."

"I think you're right," Caecilia says, "and maybe we can hear him go out this night and follow him. It might be like you say, and he only does it when your mother is not here. But we can try." She smiles at Macia and swallows. "We better go and see Gax," she says, her voice wobbly.

The girls hesitate, and Macia says, "We better speak to God before we leave the hut."

The medical hut isn't far, but Macia is relieved when they get there. The door is open. "Do we just walk in?" Caecilia whispers and Macia peers into the darkness beyond. She can hear soft voices. She looks at Caecilia and taking a deep breath, nods and walks in.

The hut is dark, but small lights are burning, a pungent smell tickling her nose. Macia blinks and looks around at the doors around them, some open and some closed. Where would Gax be, and do they simply

CHAPTER 25

walk in, or should they call out to see if someone will come? Caecilia gives a nervous cough and the murmured voices stop. They can hear shuffling footsteps and the woman appears. She doesn't seem any happier to see them than she did before.

"You have come to see your friend," she says, and the girls nod. The woman turns around and they follow her. Gax's room is the last one in the hut, and the woman holds the door handle. "This is where he is. Don't go too close. He is very poorly, and if you make him ill with something else, there will be nothing we can do. He is still sleeping from the herbs we gave him, but there is a limit to how much we can give him. You start chattering to him, he might begin to wake up and he will probably die."

Macia shudders, and Caecilia's hand clutching hers is cold. They walk into the dark room. The smell of burning herbs makes them hold their nose. Macia pulls the top of her shirt over her mouth, struggling to breathe with the thick air hurting the back of her throat. The tiny glow of the light, a small flame flickering as they walk in, is all the light there is. They look at Gax. He's breathing. Fast and a bit raspy, but breathing. They see his legs, and hold each other tight. The leg that suffered in the attack is mostly gone. Bandages cover the end, just above where Gax's knee used to be. Caecilia sobs and Macia tries to catch her breath. "Air," she manages to gasp, "I need air." Caecilia nods and the girls leave the room. Caecilia closes the door gently, breathing a desperate, incoherent prayer as her hands push the wood into the doorframe.

Macia is sitting on the ground next to the clinic door, her face buried between her knees, shoulders shaking. Caecilia crouches next to her, her hand on Macia's shoulder. Halit walks past and his face turns dark as he scowls and hisses to Caecilia, "Get her away, quick. Get her to the hut, make her stop!" Caecilia nods, frightened by Halit's anger, and she helps Macia up.

Macia dries her face, looking desperately at Caecilia. "What are we going to do?" She gives another sob but catches her breath. She hadn't heard Halit clearly, but his anger had been plainly understood. She has to control her emotions, and quickly, before people see them. She holds her breath and closes her eyes as she smooths out her face like she has done so many times in the past. Her childhood training kicks in as she stands taller and only Caecilia can feel Macia's grip squeezing her hands. "I'm ok," she says, more to herself than to Caecilia but Caecilia nods anyway.

They walk back to the hut, Macia's eyes staring straight ahead, fully focused on taking one step at a time, standing tall, face blank, emotionless. Caecilia isn't sure what makes her feel worse, Gax's condition or Macia's struggle. "I don't know what overcame me," Macia says, as they're back inside the hut. "I have never reacted like that. It was the awful smell burning my throat and Gax's face."

She has some water and pours more out for Caecilia, her hands much calmer. "What are we going to do?" She repeats her earlier question. "Will he recover or not? I don't think they know what to do, do they?"

Caecilia drinks slowly, and says, "It seems they know what to do, or at least have an idea, as they're burning those herbs. They didn't want us to touch Gax, so they must understand about infections. I don't think they would have...would have operated if they didn't have some idea of what they were doing."

"There is nothing we can do," Caecilia says after a while. "We will need to wait and see. It will take a long time for Gax to recover," she warns, "and he will need to learn to walk again." Her voice trails off, and Caecilia gives a little sob. "How will we get back?" She suddenly cries and hides her face in her hands.

Macia sobs quietly, and although she tries to stop herself, fearing Halit will come in, or worse, her mother with the new arrivals, there

CHAPTER 25

is nothing she can do to stop the grief. "Gax is going to be so angry with me," she whispers in the end.

That makes Caecilia sit up and stop. "Why is this about you?" the girl hisses, making Macia stare. "Gax will be broken to find his leg gone, unable to join any other missions, if we ever get back that is. Why would you worry about yourself?"

Macia shakes her head, trying to make the words slow and calmer than they feel inside her. "Because it was to find my mother," she says, "all other missions, as you said, will be over and everything will be dreadful for him, just because I wanted to find my mother."

Caecilia takes a deep breath, and another and finally takes Macia's hands. "I'm sorry," she says, breathing deeply again, "I'm sorry. Don't think it's just about your mother though. Gax wanted to see Downstream, he wanted to stop Downstream from happening. I know he thought we would find a way to change Elabi, to stop people from going here. So yes, finding your mother was important, but Gax thought more about Downstream and the Message of the Book than your mother."

Macia isn't sure whether that makes her feel better, but she tries to smile at Caecilia. "I know it's not all about my mother, but if it wasn't for my mother, I might not have bothered, and Gax might not have gone without us." She looks away as she suddenly realises that Caecilia might have gone anyway, just to support Gax.

"Nothing is by chance," says Caecilia after a while. "We have to trust God. Maybe we should get the Book out and look at that. I don't know what to think or feel, apart from worry about ever getting back to Mataiox." Macia nods, but she is not keen to look at the Book. Her heart is still pounding and every time she thinks of Gax in that dark smelly room, she can feel hot tears burning in her eyes.

"It's important," Caecilia says, "as all I can think about is Gax, and I keep wondering why the Stream did this."

Chapter 26

Macia's head comes up with a snap. "The stream?" She stares at Caecilia. "The Stream? That's just water, there is no higher power in it. Gax didn't see the crocodile, that's all there is to the accident."

"I know that," says Caecilia, her face warming up, "I mean, things all went wrong, and I'm sure there was evil involved." She presses her lips together. "The elders believed in the Stream, and why wouldn't an evil power try to hinder us?"

Macia frowns. "Perhaps you're right," she says in the end, "and you're also right in saying we should read the Book."

The girls sit down, their notebooks open. "I don't know what we should read," Caecilia says, as she turns pages at random. "I know there is a lot about fighting against evil, but I don't want to think about fighting just now."

In the end, they use one of the poems in the middle of the Book, and Macia copies carefully into her notebook, "...Put Thou my tears into Thy bottle: are they not in Thy book?" She smiles through tears and says, "Here's another book mentioned; how special would it be to read that book? And to know that all our tears are recorded, although mine weren't particularly noteworthy today," she adds, making a face.

As they get ready for the night, Caecilia whispers, "Will you go if Halit goes out? I think we should both go."

CHAPTER 26

"Are you sure? Should you stay, in case something happens, you can then get help?" Caecilia shakes her head at the suggestion, and in the end, the girls decide they'd both follow Halit if he goes out. He has only come home for a moment to eat his dinner, but gone out again, explaining that they're getting things ready for the new arrivals.

Just as the girls are ready to turn in, Halit comes home. "Your friend is still alive," he says, "the staff say he's done as well as can be expected, so maybe he will survive after all." He opens his mouth, and the scowl is back in place, then he abruptly turns. "See you in the morning," he says and slams his door shut.

The girls look at each other. "I thought he was going to tell us how to control emotions," Macia whispers, and they both grin. "It's good to know Gax has survived." They blow out the little light, their darkest clothes handy to cover themselves if they need to go out.

They stay silent, and not long after, they hear the soft creak of Halit's door, followed by the click of the outside door. The girls get up as quietly as possible, pull on an extra layer and fumble with the new sandals Halit has organised for them. Their old, muddy, worn-out shoes have been donated to the shoe-making team, who were very interested to see the design.

Just as Macia is about to pull the door shut, Caecilia grabs her arm. She breathes in Macia's ear, "Halit is still there, look!" Macia looks, and Caecilia is right, Halit straightens up, just as she finds his dark shape. He must have had to adjust his sandals, but he hasn't heard the girls. He walks off, and Macia shuts the door quietly, and they follow him.

He walks through the dark, quiet village, girls not too far behind. No lights can be seen, and no sound is heard. Caecilia shudders. The village is quiet during the day, without chatter and laughter, but this dark silence is even worse. Halit slips through the gate and the girls follow more slowly, worried he might look back, and there will be no excuse outside the village.

Halit stands with his back towards them, listening, and the girls stop, holding their breath and clutching each other. Slowly, Macia eases the dark material of her tunic over her face, and Caecilia copies her. They move back a little into the bushes, keeping their eyes on Halit. Eventually, he rummages under his top, and brings out a small oil light. Caecilia is amazed at how much light one small lamp can give, and she releases her breath as Halit walks off.

The girls follow him through the jungle, the path seemingly endless. It is hard to walk quietly in the new sandals, and in the dark it's difficult to see uneven spots on the path. Macia suddenly stops and grabs Caecilia as the girls collide. She points ahead, and Caecilia gasps. There, many small lights are moving around the path. The girls step back a little and hide behind a tree, worried someone else might join, and come up from behind them. They can see Halit's little light going up to the others, then, all the lights move off. Not a sound can be heard from the group and the girls shiver.

They stand still for a little longer, aware of the darkness around them, and not just the jungle darkness. "Let's go back," whispers Caecilia, then she screams, smothering it as much as possible. "Something," she gasps, "something is on me!"

Macia grabs Caecilia, trying to figure out where and what until they hear a familiar chattering sound. The ferrets! The ferrets have found them here, in the jungle! Caecilia laughs and sobs at the same time as she kneels to gather up and hug the soft bodies and kiss the little heads in her relief, with Macia looking around, to see if anyone has heard the scream.

Eventually, Macia grins in the dark, touching the lithe bodies. "They seem fine," she says softly, "not too skinny, so they must have found food. I have missed them. I wonder if they will come back with us?"

Caecilia shrugs and says, "As long as Halit doesn't know we found

CHAPTER 26

them while following him through the jungle at night, it should be fine."

Macia is still restless. The scream hadn't been very loud but sounds carry in the night. Those people will be used to the jungle sounds and they will be listening out for anything unusual. Especially after what happened a few days ago.

They walk back towards the village. "We have to make sure to stay on the path," Caecilia whispers and shudders. She bites her lip, "I know it was one long path, but coming this way, there might be other paths branching off." She stops herself from going on, then giggles. "Your brother would not be happy, as I am having emotional thoughts. I had forgotten about the rules."

Macia nods in the dark, then says, "Yes, although the Book tells us not to worry. Also, in the part of the Book I had in Elabi, it said about self control being the fruit of the Spirit of God, so I wonder if there is a place for fewer emotions. Oh no, you are right, there is a different path here!"

The girls stop and hesitate. Macia lowers herself to have a better look. "I can see the difference," she says in the end. "This smaller path has more leaves and is narrower. I think we stay on this main path, as it seems wider." She is right, for soon the village walls loom up in the darkness. They are glad to get through the gate, past the sleeping village and into their hut.

"Would it be safe to light a lamp?" Caecilia asks, looking around in the dark, trying to think if there is somewhere to keep the ferrets. Macia lights the little lamp, and together they work to create somewhere for the ferrets to stay.

"It's not very secure," Caecilia says, "but it will keep them safe for now. We can try to get something better in the morning." She yawns, then adds softly, "I wonder who those people are. Do you think they were the ones attacking the elders?"

Macia swallows. "It looks like it. I hope it isn't the same group. Halit… I can't stand the thought of Halit being involved." Macia pulls a face. "I want to see my mother, but when I look at the village and Halit… It makes me wonder if we haven't made a mistake. And then there is Gax. Maybe we were wrong to come." Her voice wobbles, and tears are suddenly unstoppable.

"I know what you mean," says Caecilia, putting an arm around Macia. "I don't think it's wrong of us to come though." She stares at the tiny flame, "I think…I think we did right. We prayed about it, and it is still right that we went to check the radio chatter Linu heard. We might never know, I mean, we can never know what people think about us."

They turn the little flame down and try to get some sleep. Neither of them hear Halit's return, or their door being opened. Halit glances in, but when he hears their steady breathing, he closes the door again. He frowns. There was something or someone behind him in the jungle, he is sure of that. He doesn't see the ferret's house, and soon, Halit is fast asleep as well.

Macia is the first to wake up in the morning. Will she see her mother today? And how will her mother react? She smiles a little to herself, as she can still see her mother's beautiful face, and she imagines her mother's smile, her eyes warm and kind, thrilled to see her long-lost daughter again. Then Macia's smile slips away. What if her mother reacts like Halit? They can't leave the village yet, not with Gax unconscious. They will be stuck in here for weeks. Will they have to live with her mother and Halit all that time? Hiding the Book, and feeling unwanted.

She sighs but tries to smile as Caecilia sits up. "Is it time to get up yet?" Caecilia straightens her blanket as Macia dries her face quickly. "We don't want to get up later than we have done so far, otherwise Halit could get suspicious," she says. "I wonder…if he goes out again, should we follow him?"

CHAPTER 26

Macia hesitates, "I don't know. Maybe we could bring something to help us, so we could follow him for longer. I don't know if I want to get close to that group though. What if they spot us? It's hard to move without making a noise." She pauses, then changes the conversation, "I'm not sure if I'm looking forward to the new arrivals and my mother."

Caecilia nods, "I understand. I'm not sure I'm looking forward to it either. We don't know how the others will react, and we don't know how your mother will react to us reading the Book. Halit is bound to tell her. And what if she is part of the night outings?"

That makes Macia smile. "I can't imagine my mother on a killing spree," she says in the end. "And then there is that man Halit mentioned. The one in charge of Downstream. It sounds like Halit knows the man." She frowns, "There is so much we don't know, and it's hard to think, and even harder to know what to pray. Gax..." she swallows, "with Gax like that, it's hard to think ahead or to know what to look for. I don't even know what Gax hoped to do once we got here, or Downstream."

"We'll have to see how it goes. It might be clearer once your mother is here," Caecilia smiles and together they walk into the main room for breakfast. It's hard not to yawn with Halit, but both girls manage to stifle their yawns and try to look as rested and awake as possible. Halit scowls more than ever, and Caecilia is sure he keeps looking at them more than he usually does. Does he suspect something? She wonders if they should tell him about the ferrets. Maybe later in the day, so it might look like the soft creatures only just arrived that afternoon.

"We'll visit our friend, and after that, is there something we can do to help?" Macia looks at her younger brother, trying to feel something for him, trying to remember the soft little toddler he once was.

Halit grunts something about not having the time to explain everything. "Maybe when Mother is back, as there will be more work, and she might have time to show you what to do," he says as Macia simply looks at him. Macia nods and collects the bowls, wondering if her mother will be more keen or less busy to allow them to join in.

They walk to the clinic in silence, looking forward to seeing Gax, if he is still alive. Surely, they would have told them if Gax had died in the night? The door is open again, and they walk in, not bothering to call out this time. "I'd rather avoid the woman if I can," Caecilia mutters to Macia as they walk through the corridor, past various doors. "She's not very encouraging, and I don't want her to send us away."

Gax's door is slightly ajar as they get there, and Macia can smell the herbs and she shivers. Pulling her top over her mouth, she pushes the door further open, and the girls walk in.

To their joy, Gax has his eyes open, and he moves his head as they come in. His eyes fill with tears as he sees the girls. "Where were you," he whispers, but it doesn't sound like a question. He closes his eyes, letting a few tears roll down his face, without bothering to wipe them away. "Where were you?" he asks this time and he looks at them, his lips trembling. "My leg…" His voice melts into a sob and the girls shuffle closer to each other.

Chapter 27

Macia clasps Caecilia's hand and steps forward a little. "I'm glad to see you awake," she starts brightly, making her mouth form a smile. "When we came yesterday, you were still unconscious, so this is more than we hoped for." Her smile isn't reflected by Gax, and Macia can feel the corners of her mouth starting to sag, but she forces them back up. "I'm sorry, we're sorry about your leg," she starts again, but Gax squeezes his eyes shut, his shoulders heaving with quiet sobs.

"I never expected," he sobs, "I never expected this to happen. I felt so ill, just before we got to the village, and everything reminded me of Elabi, and my head felt so strange. I wanted to just lie down and sleep, and then I woke up, and this room..." He sobs, turning his face into the lumpy pillow. In the dim light, Macia can see the dark stains on the pillow, showing it's not the first tearful session of the day.

She realises there isn't much left of her nails, and she pushes her hand into her side. Should they let Gax cry like this? What will the villagers think? "Gax," she says, trying to sound gentle, but she hears Caecilia's soft gasp. "Gax," she carries on, as Gax moans and cries. "I'm so sorry, but Gax, we also need your help."

Gax's head whips around, and he opens his mouth to complain but instead, he tries to dry his face. He looks at Macia's face, then Caecilia's. Caecilia moves closer to the bed and taps his arm. "It must be hard, waking up to…to all this," she says, and Gax nods, fresh tears rolling.

Macia frowns. They do need Gax's help. The new arrivals will get to the village sooner rather than later, her mother will be with them, and they need to know what their plan is going to be. Gax has been out of it for more than a day, he can fall apart some other time, but not in this village, with Elabi citizens watching.

She moves closer to the bed as well, and taps Gax's leg, leaning forward a little. "I know, it is hard, and we have been praying for you, but Gax…" That's as far as she gets, as there is a sharp gasp and loud tut at the door. The old woman.

"What are you talking about?" She glares at Macia, making an effort to keep her face free of all emotion. "This man needs rest," she continues. "The last thing he needs is people demanding things from him or allowing him to lose all control," she adds, looking at Gax's pillow case, her face no longer blank. Macia notices that the corners of the woman's mouth really cannot go any lower. So much for the Book's influence in reaching this village.

"He needs rest," the woman repeats, "and you two better do something more useful than talking to recovering patients. If they recover, that is. Filling someone's mind with emotions and questions isn't going to help. Considering facts and using your will is what makes people ready to recover and be productive. It's people who feel there is something they can still add to society that we take on. Without a will to live, there isn't much chance of life continuing, and why pour valuable resources into someone unwilling to live?"

She glares at them as if they have contradicted her out loud, and Macia is about to do so when Caecilia steps towards the woman. "We simply came to see our friend," she says softly, "and we're thankful for what you have done for him. In just a few days, he has come a long way. It's been a hard road, and his mind will need to adjust as well as

CHAPTER 27

his body. Surely, he should be granted time and support to make that adjustment." She makes sure that her voice makes the last sentence a statement, not a question. Macia pulls a face, and quickly covers it up with her hand, pretending to sneeze. Caecilia looks back at Gax. "We will see you later," she says with a kind, soft smile, and she briefly squeezes his fingers. Gax nods, no longer crying, his face hot.

Macia nods at Gax as well, and smiles as encouragingly as she can, then follows Caecilia out of the room, past the glaring woman. They walk straight out of the medical hut, not looking back, although Macia can feel the woman's eyes drilling into their backs. She walks as calmly as she can, making sure to show they're not rushing.

"That was awkward," she says, releasing a long breath as soon as they're outside, out of the woman's sight.

Caecilia turns, her face red, her eyes blazing. "Why did you lay into Gax like that?" Macia stares and Caecilia continues in the same hissing voice, "Can't you see how upset he is? He's just woken up, found out he's lost a limb, and you tell him he needs to forget all that and help us? We don't need his help, he needs ours, to overcome all this."

Macia takes a deep breath and speaks as slowly as she can, as she can feel her anger welling up. "Gax is upset and I get that. But he can't lie there crying all the time. These people are from Elabi. If they think he's weak and emotional, they will not help him, but will concentrate all their efforts on the new arrivals. Also, people's attitude towards us isn't great. Do you want to spend months in this village?"

Her face feels hot and she forces her fists to come off her hips and relax her stance as Caecilia's eyes fill with tears. "I don't want to be here either, but Gax...He's had such a shock. We can't put demands on him now," she sniffs.

"Sometimes it's the only thing that works. We have been kind and patient with him on the journey, even though he wasn't helping much, but he has to work hard on getting well, it's the only way. This is still not the healthiest place, it's hot and humid, and there are insects and everything, so he could still get an infection on top of it all and die. He has to get better sooner rather than later."

Caecilia nods slowly. "I know you are right and Gax probably knows it too. It's just that… He's had such a shock and the people here aren't kind, so it's important he knows we are on his side and we support him."

Macia agrees although she feels Gax has had a lot of support in the last week and should start pulling his weight a little. She doesn't say so, as she can see Caecilia is very emotional about it all. "It's also our witness," she points out, knowing that Caecilia places a lot of importance on that. "Gax crying and all of us being ruled by emotions… It will be hard to share the Book with people if they don't accept us because of how we act and react."

Caecilia's face flushes again, but she has to agree. "We'll have to pray for strength and protection," she says in the end, and Macia looks away to hide a smirk. As much as she is, was, looking forward to meeting her mother again, she feels uncomfortable in the village, the stares of the people around them making her shiver.

Walking back to the hut, she says, "I wonder how people here deal with those that hold to beliefs and everything else they don't like. It's too far for the hills, and there isn't much point sending people back to the Downstream facilities. Whoever they sent back would tell them about the village, and that would put everybody at risk. So what would they do?"

They look at each other and Caecilia turns pale. "The Scitabi," she whispers and glances over her shoulder. "Maybe they take you out into the jungle and that's what the Scitabi are for?"

Macia frowns. "Would they still do it if they'd known someone for a long time? What if it's one of the young people?" The girls are quiet as they enter the hut and put the Book on the table.

CHAPTER 27

Just as they finish the reading of the Book with a prayer for protection, healing and more courage to speak up, there is a commotion outside. More voices can be heard, crying voices and commanding ones. The new arrivals. "Should we go and see?" Caecilia doesn't sound like she wants to, but having just asked for more courage, should this be a good time to practise what they hold to?

Macia opens her mouth, but before she can say anything the door flies open. It's Halit. "Don't come out," he growls. "Now is not the time for family reunions or other emotional displays." He sneers at them. "You're getting yourself known at the medical clinic and not in a good way. I should have left you in the jungle," he suddenly hisses with a surge of emotions, "and I don't know what Mother will say to you later."

The door slams shut behind him, leaving the girls in stunned silence. "So much for our plan to go out boldly," Macia manages in the end. "Unless you think we should ignore Halit and his commands?"

As cries and commotion goes on outside, they tidy away the books and do a little cleaning around the house and the ferret enclosure, and by the time they finish all is quiet. "They settled everyone in quickly," Caecilia says, "I suppose those babies we could hear have been fed and cleaned and are probably asleep now." She smiles.

"Maybe we could help with the children," Macia suggests, "Demonstrate the love of God to them."

Caecilia thinks about it. "Maybe," she says in the end, "Or will the other staff members turn on us? Will they notice the difference, and will the village see the difference if there is a whole batch of kids with feelings and faith?"

Macia smiles, her eyes bright. "Imagine that! A whole load of kids following the teachings of the Book, loving God and living for Him and with Him!"

The door slams shut. "That would be the worst thing to happen to this village," Halit stands there, eyes blazing. "Don't even dream of changing us or our village. We have lived like this for many years and it's what works. There have been one or two people in the past that mention fith…fath…" He scowls as Macia fixes the word for him. "Yes, faith. That word. It caused a lot of trouble, as they talked to others around them, making people restless and emotional."

He turns to them, his face full of anguish, "They stopped the village from dealing with…from functioning and staying safe. It's a place where people die quietly, and where children might live. We're not against Requipacem, it's not meant as a punishment. They come here to live a little longer, not to have faith interfere with their emotions and to cause unrest in the village."

He takes a deep breath, and Macia isn't sure what to say to that speech. He is right. Faith in God changes everything. She smiles as she thinks of those people Halit mentioned, the ones who loved God and managed to share this with others around them, clearly with some results. She hesitates, then says, "What do you mean by dealing with? How would faith change how you deal with things in the village?"

Halit looks away, his face warm. When he looks back, his eyes don't look straight at Macia, and she shivers a little. Where is the soft little boy he once was? "Some people change their mind about Requipacem," he says, "but we can't keep feeding people for years who cannot and never will be able to look after themselves. We are limited, in resources and space. The faith people didn't like it, saying something about image. I don't know what they meant, but it seemed to apply to everyone, even senile old ones who just lay on their mats."

Caecilia smiles, "Image bearers," she says softly, "everyone is an image bearer, all made in God's image."

Halit glares at her. "Exactly," he growls, his lips pulled back, "that's exactly it. It stopped some of the helpers from doing what they needed to do to protect all of us. And it's also what caused the Scitabi to start.

CHAPTER 27

Talk about image and being made free. Nobody is free, we all have to work together and think of the outcomes. You can't do what you want; you can't be free unless you live by yourself in the jungle away from everyone, but even then you're not free as the jungle is divided up. Felix and the masked people have agreements, so no freedom for anyone."

"It's not that kind of freedom," Macia says shortly, wanting to say a lot more to her little brother, but instead she asks, "How well do you know Felix? And how come he is involved? Why doesn't he have a problem with the village?"

Halit shows his teeth again, like the ferrets when they're feeling cornered. Macia struggles to keep her face from scowling back at him, and she can feel her fingernails digging into the palms of her hands. "Nobody says anything about Felix liking the village or even knowing the village. He knows the headman from the mountain village. They have an agreement. We aren't like that headman," Halit hesitates for a second, then turns to the door. "Stay here and keep your ideas to yourself," he growls, slamming the door shut again.

Chapter 28

The girls look at each other. "It sounds like we won't be the first ones," Macia says, trying to smile.

Caecilia swallows. "I don't know what to think," she says softly, "his ideas about freedom sound right, I mean, nobody is really free, are they?"

Macia shakes her head. "It's not that kind of freedom," she explains. "I wasn't free before coming to Mataiox, was I? But in a way I was, because I was with God, and God was in me. He made me free, even though I couldn't walk anywhere without permission. Even when I was locked up, I was still free in a way. I don't know how well the people before us have explained freedom, and it sounds like the Scitabi got things mixed up as well."

Before Caecilia can respond, the door opens again, but it isn't Halit. "Macia. Halit said you'd come."

Macia stares at her mother, and feels her face go cold, then very warm, her head feeling light all of a sudden. She tries to speak, but can only give a small gasp. She takes a few deep breaths, her eyes glued on the beautiful tall woman standing in front of her. Her hair has grey streaks in it, but she still stands straight, her eyes dark as ever. Darker, Macia thinks, before getting any words out. Darker and without any softness.

"Mother," she manages to bring out, but stops at the cutting hand

CHAPTER 28

movement by the tall woman.

"Don't call me that. That's long past. I assume your father had a new woman? I am simply Amara." and Macia nods and swallows.

"Mother... Amara," she tries again, choking on the word. She knew her mother's name, of course, but never has that name felt like this. "I... we have come. We were on a mission to find Downstream, but instead, we found the village. I mean, Halit found us and brought us to the village. I did hope and pray to see you." She sees the hot flame flashing through her mother's eyes at the mention of prayer, but the words are out.

"Pray?" Her mother hisses, and her face contorts like Halit's instantly. "Don't use that word in my village," she continues, "we don't need prayer, we don't want prayer, and the same counts for you two. Three, I heard," she corrects herself. "The weeping one, flopped in a bed that is needed. Who has no desire to live, but is made to live, and who is too weak to face Requipacem with dignity."

Both girls feel their faces warm up, and Caecilia stares at the ground. Suddenly, Amara points at her with her chin. "You look like someone I know," she says, "Mollis. You're Mollis' daughter? Timaya? Tima? Or another, younger one?" Caecilia squeaks out her name and Amara nods. "Yes, I'm sure they had their three children as well."

Amara stares at the girls, and they can see the older woman thinking. A small smile grows on her face, making Macia shiver. "There is a nice surprise in the clinic," Amara says, "A surprise for all of us. I didn't want two surprises in a week. But there we are, we hardly ever get what we want. Not here, anyway." She looks at the door, then back at the two girls. "I need help in the clinic," she says. "There are a lot of very ill people this time. People who are weaker than they thought when we set off. People that maybe shouldn't be here like your friend and...and the surprise guest. You can help. You can look after your friend and the surprise guest. It will help you to think before setting off on a journey you haven't thought about." She holds up her hand to stop the girls from arguing. She states pointedly, "You had no idea what you were going to find or what you would do when you found it. Now we have to help you to come to a decision. You will want choices, leaving us without choices. This is on you, and your over-emotional friend. You better try to contribute to the village while you decide, to make up for us feeding you and caring for you."

Amara strides out of the door, but just as she is about to close it, she catches the girls' eyes, saying, "I better see you at the clinic straight after lunch. Go and get the food for us four."

The girls release their breath simultaneously. Caecilia looks away, unsure what to say. "We better get the lunches," she says in the end, her voice not as steady as it should have been.

Macia looks at the ceiling, eyes closed with tears slowly escaping. "I have thought of this moment for so long, especially since we started. Seeing my mother was my greatest dream." She sniffs, wiping her eyes.

At lunch, Halit switches between scowling and sneering. Amara doesn't say anything but glares at Halit when he drops his fork and simply nods when he asks permission to go back to work. Soon after, Amara gets up. "Clean the plates and get to the medical hut," she says, her eyes at the door already. The girls jump up and almost get into each other's way, collecting the plates and cutlery.

They walk faster to the washing-up hut than usual, and once inside, by themselves, they can talk. "Why would she not look at us, or even say anything?" Macia tries to make her voice sound steady, "Even in Elabi that would be seen as rude and therefore emotional." She wipes the wooden plate as dry as possible. "She hasn't even asked us why we came."

They return to the clinic as soon as they can, trying to look as blank as the other helpers. There is no sign of Amara, but the old woman is there. "You have come to help," she says, the corners of her mouth further down than usual. "Not just to cause trouble with the young man, but to help others to suffer as well."

She turns around and the girls follow her, glancing at each other. Caecilia is nearly in tears but Macia rolls her eyes, and Caecilia stifles a nervous giggle. This time, they go through one of the open doors, leading to a short corridor. There are a few doors, all closed. "The people here don't have long," the woman explains, "and sometimes they demand Requipacem after all, which is a private matter, not be overheard by others who are struggling facing up to facts." She makes it sound as if Requipacem should be faced up to by all, and Macia gives a tiny shiver. Poor Gax, being cared for by this woman, although cared might not be the right word.

The woman opens a door, and with a strange grin, bids them enter. "He might not live long. I am not even sure he is here by choice; it might have been decided for him," she says and walks away, her one hand leaning on the walls.

Macia watches her go, and steps into the room. As soon as she sees the figure lying still and pale in the bed, she gasps. Caecilia stands behind, her hands clasped over her mouth. Macia gives a small sob as she staggers closer to the bed so she can hold onto the wooden sides. The man has his eyes closed, but his chest goes up and down in a regular pattern; restless but regular.

Macia turns her back on the bed, holding her cheeks with her hands, willing some warmth and colour back into them. She looks at Caecilia, "Tell me I'm seeing things," she begs, her voice filled with tears that have to be kept in. "Tell me this is just a very strange dream and soon we'll wake up in Mataiox or even Colchuyni."

Caecilia groans softly, "No, you're not seeing things." She pulls a face and sighs, "Sometimes the road feels too hard, but God is in the hard things as well as the enjoyable ones. We have to find a way to be carried by Him when it's too hard to walk, even to walk by faith."

Macia smiles a little, wiping her tears away. "I can do a thousand mudflats, but I don't think I can do the next few hours, let alone days," she moans. Taking a few deep breaths, she says, "I can't do this," and her lips struggle to cooperate, "but He can and I can't do this crossing by myself, I have to trust Him whether I feel like it or not."

She turns back toward the figure in the bed, fingers the sheet, tugs the thin blankets straighter and tries her best not to cry. The man is thin and pale and his face a soft yellow. His hands lie on top of the blanket, but they're the hands of a very old man. There are no special rings, no sign of good skin care balm on the back of his hands, his nails brittle and a few look broken, jagged at the edges.

"What is man, that Thou art mindful of him," she breathes softly, then blinks, and stops herself from biting her nail. The last intact nail on her hand. The room is silent, except for the man's breathing. As the girls watch, he moves his head restlessly from side to side. One side of his mouth is moving, and the other side hangs limp, making his face look twisted, disgruntled. His one hand judders on the blanket, fingers twisting into the material. He gives a few low moans, without moving his mouth; moans that seem to come from deep within.

His eyes open, slowly, repeatedly. He stares at the ceiling for a long time. Macia wonders if they should make a noise, and let him know they are here. Before she can decide, his eyes wander around the room, falling on the two girls. He stills, all movement gone. He moans again, almost as if trying to say something, then he sees Macia. As she leans forward a little, smiling, his eyes reach her.

His face twists and contorts, the one hand is gripping and banging the thin blanket and his mouth drools as his throat makes the most awful bellowing noises. The girls step back in shock, staring at the man in horror. They have no idea what the man is saying, shouting, but the message is clear. It's against Macia, the hatred and fury written

CHAPTER 28

all over the man's scrunched-up face with the limp half-mouth staying neutral in this battle.

As the girls remain, the man's agitation grows and his voice becomes shriller. Caecilia grabs Macia and tugs at her. "We're upsetting him," she murmurs, hoping the man won't hear. "We're better off out of sight, so he can calm down, otherwise he will have another stroke." Macia nods and allows her friend to pull her out of the room. Caecilia pulls the door but doesn't shut it. That way, they can hear the man and just about see him through the crack.

"What are we to do?" hisses Macia, her face wet again. "We can't look after him if he goes like that every time he sees me!"

Caecilia holds her friend's stone-cold hands and swallows. "Maybe I can help him, and you come in when he is asleep. He will sleep a lot, and also, we don't know what else is affected, it might be his memory, so next time, he might not mind seeing you. You can look after Gax," her voice catches, "just be gentle," she grimaces, trying to soften the anxiety in her voice, "and urge him to get better. I will stay here. He's gone quieter, you go to Gax, and I'll go in."

It is true, the loud voice has turned into soft moans, and Caecilia pushes Macia towards the main corridor. "Go, see if he is awake and needs anything." She frowns, "You might know what he needs physically to get stronger and better. He will need a lot of moving, otherwise he will get sore on his back, and that can cause dreadful infections." She bites her lip.

Macia squeezes her hands as if she knows exactly what Caecilia is thinking. "I will be kind," she says, trying to smile, but giving a small sob instead. Caecilia glances around, then quickly hugs her friend, touches her hands once more, then steps calmly towards the door. Macia walks away, not rushing, but with purpose.

She walks past the old woman who is smirking whilst folding clothes. Macia ignores her, merely raises her chin automatically, and walks towards Gax's room. He is awake; unhappy but not crying. She smiles at him. "You came back," he whispers, and his voice wobbles a little.

Macia smiles brightly, "Of course, and I'm here to help you. They had a load of new arrivals, so we were told to help you and…" her voice catches, so she steadies herself, back turned towards Gax as she rearranges his water jug on the small end table. "There is someone else who needs a lot of care." She quickly swallows the 'as well' she was going to attach, but decides against it. Yes, Gax will need a lot of care, but he also will need a lot of stamina and willpower. Equating him with the helpless man in the other bed isn't helpful. "Caecilia has gone to help him, and I'm here to see what you need."

"I need my leg back, I need my family, I need," he starts but Macia holds up her hand. She manages to slip the frown, remembering her promise to Caecilia and instead pulls the corners of her mouth up.

"We're talking needs as in, what you really need, like clean sheets and drink and sitting up," she says smiling, but with a firm voice. "Gax, nothing happens by accident. It might be a dreadful road you're taking, but it's still the correct road. You have no map, no plan, but that's because you have a Guide. We had no map of the mudflats, we simply relied on the guide. You need to trust again the best Guide. I know it's impossible, but this Guide makes all things possible, every day of the year, not just the one lowest spring tide of the year."

Gax closes his eyes, his face intense. Macia rolls her eyes as her back is turned. When she looks back at him, her face under control once more, Gax is looking at her, his eyes clearer than they have been for the last few days. "Thank you," he whispers. His eyes fill with tears again as he says, "I needed that. I'm so sorry that you had to tell me that. I should have known, shouldn't I?"

Macia shakes her head. "We can all feel lost without a map and a compass," she smiles. "I only realised this afternoon, and only because Caecilia told me off!" Gax's eyes fly open wide in surprise and Macia

CHAPTER 28

giggles. "Yes, who knew? But Caecilia explained it all to me and made it so clear. I was ashamed, but it also felt good to rely on God once more. It's so easy to follow Him when there's a path, a waymarked path and a map and everything you need along the way. It's different out on the mudflats."

Gax sighs a long, content sigh. "You are right," he says softly, "although I might need reminding again in an hour or so." Macia laughs softly and she looks at him, his bed, and the room, her hands on her hips, surveying the scene and the materials available.

"We need a plan," she says, satisfaction making her face glow. "I like a good plan," she admits with a grin, "but we do need to think carefully. If you lie down too long, you will get sores. They can be hard to heal and might prove dangerous. You will also need to get stronger and better at balancing. It will take time for your body to adjust, but we don't want you to get a sore back or injure your other leg. So we need to look at what we can do, and what we have to work with. And we need to think about building a boat," she adds, her voice less steady than a moment ago. Can they leave? What about the man in the other room?

Felix frowns at the short letter, ignoring the noises coming down the corridor. His workers will handle that. "We were killed," he reads out loud. "Killed? But he's writing to me. Many of our people. Ah, the other elders."

He sighs, putting the letter down. Amara had said something about jungle attacks. It looks like the elders have been dealt with. Felix rubs his forehead. He doesn't feel bad; they should have stayed in Colchuyni. And they should have kept the strangers from entering the jungle. Hopefully, it doesn't affect him or the woman. Thinking of her makes him smile. He looks at the large calendar. It won't be long before he will see her again.

He puts the letter away, and stands up, stretching. It is late, and tomorrow will be a busy day.

Chapter 29

Caecilia steps back into the quiet room. The man hasn't moved on the bed, but his breathing is now laboured and raspy. His eyes narrow as he glares at her, and his mouth is making sounds, but they're unclear. She smiles a little at him, not wanting to look callous or too happy.

"I'm just going to check what needs sorting out," she says briskly, and walks around the bed, checking what is available in the room. There are fresh sheets and another blanket on a small table in the corner, the table's shaped legs a health hazard in itself. There is an envelope on the edge, half tucked under the bedding. The envelope is clearly from Elabi, its recycled thick paper instantly recognisable. She hesitates, stops herself from glancing over her shoulder, and simply moves a little in front of the table, blocking the man's view. She gently pulls out the envelope and peeks inside. The sheet has the man's name; seeing it confirmed makes her eyes sting.

Caecilia takes a deep breath, her lips moving silently, and then she looks at the man again, standing where he can see her without having to move. His eyes glare at her but she ignores that. "Hello Brutus," she says softly, watching his eyes lose some of the anger. Instead, tears start to well up, and he looks away, his face scrunching up, and his cheeks turning red once again. Even now, any display of emotion is unwelcome.

CHAPTER 29

Brutus grunts, making a moaning sound. Caecilia can see him getting more agitated, his one hand banging the sheet again. She touches his arm, and makes shushing noises, watching Brutus go dark red in the face. She stands still, till he has calmed down again, and watches his eyes drift shut. A soft snoring tells her he has fallen asleep. She stands straighter with a sigh. How can she ever help Macia's father? Who thought it a good idea to bring this man to the village? There is no way Brutus could have requested this himself, as he is unable to communicate. He is immobile, and she doesn't think he will recover from his stroke, which was just over a week ago, according to the paper in the envelope.

Caecilia gently moves the man a little, to check his sheet. Everything looks clean. Caecilia is relieved, as she doesn't fancy changing the man's sheet by herself, nor does she want to ask the older woman to help her. What is she supposed to do now? There isn't anything to tidy or sort out, and Brutus is asleep. She looks at the tall chair. Should she simply sit for a while, watching him sleep?

Just as she takes a step to the chair, Brutus chokes, his eyes fly open and bulge. Caecilia gasps and moves to roll him over onto his side, banging his back for good measure. He drools, but his breathing becomes more normal. Caecilia settles him in as well as she can, arranging his pillows, tugging his blanket straight. He looks at her, but soon, his eyes droop shut once more. Caecilia lowers herself onto the chair, understanding why she might have to stay and watch Brutus, even when he's asleep, or maybe because he is asleep.

Sitting in the quiet room, her thoughts wander. They will need to build a boat, as there is no way Gax could walk back to Colchuyni and across the mudflat. That leaves only the main route open, but will it take them to Elabi? If only they had a better map. Will Macia want to leave when her father is here, as well as her mother and brother, however hostile? Caecilia sighs, struggling to breathe in the dark room. She can feel her face warming up. A short time ago, she had been lecturing Macia about spiritual mudflats, only to find herself stuck and floundering.

She leans back in the chair, her eyes closed. She can feel herself drifting off, vaguely aware of soft noises from outside the room. Footsteps, voices, some sharper than others, doors closing, someone crying out, moans... It takes her a while to realise the moans come from Brutus. Caecilia jumps to her feet, ashamed that she has drifted off, forgetting her task as well as her promise to Macia.

She uses a soft cloth on a stick to moisten Brutus' mouth and clean his face. He glares at her, and she gives a small shake. "You're not beholden to me," she says softly. "I chose to be here today, I am here to help, and there is no judgment involved. Everything in Elabi is in the past for both of us, and we can only focus on the present, as we don't know what the future holds. I know Who holds the future, but..." She stops as Brutus instantly becomes agitated again. She sighs quietly, and simply stares at him, waiting for the storm to pass.

Oddly enough, he seems to find that amusing, and he calms down and mutters something, his eyes glinting with a sense of humour. Caecilia tucks that one away to share with the others. She wonders what Gax will think of Brutus being here. "Thank you," she says, with a straight face, "now, where were we." She rolls her eyes at him, and continues, "It is my job that I was asked to do, and I'm happy to help." She cleans his hands which feel sweaty and decides to go and change the water and rinse the cloth. She hesitates. Can she leave him for a moment?

She steps out of the door with the small bowl of water and used cloths. The older woman is standing nearby, talking to a young lad. She spots Caecilia and frowns.

Caecilia takes a deep breath and starts, "I used all the water, and need to rinse the cloth as well. What would be the best place?" The

CHAPTER 29

woman signals to follow her. She shows Caecilia a larger room where there are plenty of wooden buckets with water as well as casks with special water taps. The buckets come in different shapes and sizes.

"That is for drinking," she points at two large casks, "and those buckets are for rinsing and cleaning." The buckets are small, and several young children are walking with freshly filled buckets to replace the ones that are taken to be emptied. The room is silent, apart from the quick little footsteps of the children. Only one little girl peeks at her, the others keep their eyes firmly fixed on the mud floor. Caecilia smiles at the little girl, trying not to notice that her dress is tattered and her feet bare. The girl walks with a hardly noticeable limp, but it would have been enough to get her sent away from Elabi.

Caecilia rinses the cloth, and thanks the little boy who takes the bucket away. "What is your name?" she asks him as he picks up the round bucket. He glances at her, shrugs his shoulder and walks away. Caecilia frowns. She refills the bowl from the large cask and returns to Brutus' room.

He wakes up as she walks in, and she helps him to sit up. She bites her lip. "We will have to get you moving and rolling over," she explains to Brutus, "otherwise you will get sores. Especially where you have lost some feeling." He grunts and blinks moisture away from his eyes. "Can you blink twice if you understand that bit?" Caecilia asks, having a sudden idea. Brutus grunts, but blinks twice. Caecilia beams, "Now blink once if you mean no," she instructs, and he does a deliberate blink. Caecilia nods, pleased with the opportunity to communicate. "That's good, that way I can ask you, and you can let me know what you need."

The afternoon crawls by, with Brutus drifting in and out of sleep, and Caecilia's trips to the washroom to rinse the cloth and get clean water. The same young children are there all afternoon, trundling up and down with the little buckets. She tries to smile at them each time she comes in, but only the little girl will glance her way, and it takes Caecilia the entire afternoon before the girl gives the slightest glimmer of a smile. To then glance around, worry all over her little face.

Caecilia looks up when the older woman comes in, with a young man. "He will watch in the night. Go home and in the morning, be sure to get back, you and your friend."

She walks out before Caecilia can say anything, and the young man shrugs as she looks at him. "She never says much, that one," he says, his voice deep. One eye is different, and Caecilia struggles to keep her eyes from straying to the white-looking eye. "She is always in a hurry to go, and only her age makes her slow down," he adds and clicks his tongue. He turns his face towards Brutus, and says, "Has he been hard to look after?"

Caecilia can feel her face warming up, especially as Brutus' eyes fly open, and his face goes dark. His mouth trembles and guttural noises come out, but no clear sounds. His fingers scrunch up the blanket, and his face glistens. Caecilia sighs. So much for tact. "It's been a privilege to support Brutus," she says, slowing her words down and keeping her voice low, to stop any anger or sharpness from entering into her voice. "We worked on a communication system, so double blink is yes, one blink is no. That way, I can ask Brutus if he needs anything." The young man stares at her, a small sneer forming. "None of us like to rely on others or to struggle with limits in our life," she says quietly, and, although it makes her blush a little, she stares rather pointedly at the young man's eye.

It is his turn to go red. "I didn't think," he says, and his humbleness warms Caecilia.

"I'm not telling you off," she smiles, "Anyway, I better go, I will be back in the morning," she tells Brutus, "and I'm hoping to see you more rested." His face looks tired, sagging on the one side, but grey and

CHAPTER 29

wrinkled. He blinks twice, and then his eyes fill with tears. Caecilia pats his good arm once and turns away, as she can see his frustration building in his emotional response.

She hesitates, should she wait for Macia? In the end, she decides to go to Gax's room, as she would like to see her friend for a moment. She can hear their voices and has to swallow. She can imagine their afternoon, Macia encouraging Gax, helping him to overcome his sadness and grief, discussing the Book, their memories together, and all that time she has been looking after Brutus. Her feet ache and not once has Macia stopped by to ask her how she is or how her father is. It's time for dinner, and still, Macia and Gax are simply chatting. Caecilia can feel the tears and she tells herself it's mainly tiredness and grief for all things lost, but surely Gax is her friend as well?

She takes a few deep breaths, holding the air until she can feel her face cool down and her eyes dry up. She pushes the door open, trying to smile but having to give up. Gax is sitting up in bed, looking exhausted, but less filled with self-pity than before. Macia looks ready to fall asleep while standing up, and Caecilia finds smiling at them a lot easier than she expected. Macia smiles at her, and says, "How is my father? I'm sorry I can't look after him instead." Gax looks outraged, and she giggles, "Not that I mind helping Gax, but I should be the one looking after my father."

Caecilia explains about the communication system they set up and what she has done all afternoon. "He choked a few times; he could do with sitting up more to sleep," she says, and Macia nods.

"They have given me a foam block to go under my pillow, so I can sit up," Gax says. "Maybe that will work for Brutus?"

They say goodbye to Gax as the same young man comes in, explaining he will be looking after people on this side of the corridor as well. "You are the youngest person, and better off than most others this end," the man says, "so if you hear us in the night, it could be bad news for a person. I might not be able to come and see you as much as I would like to either," he warns, "but if you call out, I'm bound to hear you." Gax nods and assures the man he'll be fine.

The young man leaves, and Gax whispers, "I'm quite glad to be alone for most of the night. That woman made me shiver, and I didn't want to fall asleep with her in my room! She reminded me too much of the Elders." The girls shudder and he continues, "And she kept checking on me, which I understand, but I look forward to being able to sleep in peace."

Chapter 30

Dinner is quiet, the atmosphere grim, although Amara isn't as hostile as before. She looks at Caecilia, "I heard what you did this afternoon," she says, and Caecilia inclines her head, wondering which bit of the long afternoon Amara is referring to. Has her interaction with the little girl been noticed? "The cloths have been rinsed a lot, and it seems Brutus," her voice hitches a little, "…Brutus seems calmer as well."

Caecilia inclines her head again, as a gesture of thanks. "Yes, we found a way to communicate, which has made him feel less out of control." She hesitates. Should she ask why he is here?

"I can see you wondering why he is here," Amara says, "and the answer is that I recognised him. My leaving for Downstream had nothing to do with Brutus," she glances at Halit, "or my daughters. I have no reason not to help Brutus. I know he probably won't live long, he could have another stroke any day or simply die from the effects of this one, but I somehow didn't like the idea of Requipacem for him, without trying to give him more time."

Macia stares at her plate and Halit scowls. Caecilia takes a breath to say something, but Amara continues, "I don't think he wants to be here, I don't know if he was happy to face Requipacem, but there we are. It was maybe an emotional decision, and I might have felt some regret as soon as we took him," she pulls a face and swallows. "That in itself would have made him unhappy, I suppose."

Halit glares at his plate, refusing to look at his mother. Macia looks up from her plate, "I don't think letting someone live longer is something to regret," she says softly. "Life is precious, all life," and she looks at her little brother, "but you were right, it did give me a shock. Sadly, Brutus," Macia pulls a face, "Brutus wasn't too happy to see me. We hadn't parted on good terms, and to see me here upset him. At least he recognised me," she says, trying to sound bright.

Amara nods, "To return with Brutus and to find you here, well, it wasn't what I expected."

Macia's fingers are clasped tightly together under the table, "I wasn't sure what to expect," she says softly. "You haven't changed much from the photograph," she tries to smile at her mother. "You left a large hole in our lives when you left, but I am proud of what you have achieved here. It's wonderful to see so many young people and we're grateful for the care we have been given, especially our friend Gax."

Her mother's face turns red when Macia mentions her leaving, but softens at Macia's praise for the village. "I had to go," she says softly, "it was an emotional decision, I know, and Brutus would never have agreed to it. But Halit was so small and so ill, and you girls were doing well. I knew Brutus would come back from the disgrace and I found myself on the boat before I knew it."

Macia nods briefly. "It was a shock," she says, trying to smile, her lips trembling. "We lost some standing, at least father did. But because of his books and his contacts, he worked himself up again. We had help for a long time, and then father remarried again, to show stability and how he had moved on, putting Elabi first. We managed to keep the house, only had to leave it for a few weeks."

Amara pushes her empty plate away. "I'm a little surprised to see him with a stroke at his age. And the way he wasn't happy to see you, what happened?"

CHAPTER 30

Macia sighs. "I was sent beyond the hills, he had to bear a lot of that, and when I escaped from the Hills, avoiding Requipacem, they must have gone for him again, I assume."

The hut goes quiet. Caecilia peeks at Amara and Halit. Halit is no longer scowling but gapes at Macia. Amara's eyes are wide with shock. It is Halit who speaks. "Fith. Faith," he corrects himself, and Macia grins and nods. "Was it such a problem, that they had to send you beyond the hills?" His eyes are wide with shock, and he wrinkles his nose.

Amara snorts. "You'd get sent there for a lot less than having faith, but yes, faith would get you there quickly. I have never heard of anybody escaping though. Where did you go afterwards?" She tries to look away, but Caecilia has seen the interest in the woman's eyes. She might not want Macia here, or Brutus for that matter, but she is interested.

"I got to Mataiox, where Gax is from. He was there, with Caecilia."

Amara nods, "Yes, Mollis' daughter. Did your parents know about you leaving? Also for faith, I presume?"

Caecilia nods. "Yes, it was. I don't know what happened to my parents. My little sister returned to school after a while, and Macia saw her there. But we don't know what happened to my parents. Macia didn't see them beyond the hills, so maybe they were returned already." She swallows, trying to keep the hope deep in her heart alive, praying for her parents, hoping they returned to Elabi and their peaceful lives.

It goes quiet in the hut. Amara looks at Caecilia, and her eyes go softer. "They might have returned to Elabi before Macia got there," she says softly. Caecilia nods, feeling her eyes sting, fighting against the tears as she doesn't think Amara would be impressed with any signs of emotion. Amara continues, "Don't worry about emotion. We have relaxed the rules and ideas about never showing emotion. When

I first fled into the jungle with Halit and two other younger people, I couldn't stop my emotions from taking over now and then, and I soon realised that my secret tears were both healing and a release from the tension and fear. We didn't want to be found, so we travelled further into the jungle and found this open space. It wasn't very open then, but there weren't many large trees for us to sort out. We built a hut, made a fence around it, and started living off the jungle. Once Halit was a little older, I started to think about others coming on the boat, who might want to live longer. So two of us returned to the Requipacem clinic and waited for the boat to arrive. Once everyone was inside, bedded down in the large clinic, we sneaked in during the night and spoke to almost everybody. Three people said they wanted to live longer, so they came with us. We extended the village, built a spare hut, and we went back after a few months. That is how it started." She sighs but doesn't look unhappy. "It keeps me busy, but I have become an emotional person since going on the boat with Halit." She frowns a little, "Not as emotional as some people I know," she adds quickly.

The girls feel their faces warm up, and Macia shrugs. "In Mataiox, where we live now, people don't have a problem with showing emotions. It's probably gone the other way," she adds.

Amara nods and gets up. "I need to go," she says, looking at Halit who gets up to go as well. "You girls sort out the plates, and I will see you in the morning."

Macia takes a deep breath as she dries the plates, glancing at Caecilia. "I need to think about what she said. Sending Halit off by himself to die would have been terrible for our family, but I was abandoned by her, whichever way you look at it. She doesn't seem to feel the same way. And then my father is so angry with me." Her breath catches, "What shall I do about him?" She gives a small sob. "As my mother said, I'm probably the cause of his stroke. I know I did the right thing, but it's like my mother, I might have done the right thing, but it still

CHAPTER 30

caused trouble for him and now he's dying."

The girls walk back from the washing up place, silently, controlling their emotions. The village seems busier, and slightly noisier. It reminds Caecilia of the little water girl. "She will be so tired," she says out loud, making Macia raise her eyebrows. "The little girl," she explains, "the one that had to carry the water. Those little children will be so tired!"

"It's great to involve children in tasks," Macia says slowly, "but it sounds like they were working very hard."

"And they don't teach them to read or write," Caecilia adds, "What future is there in this village?"

They are glad to get into bed. It is dark when they hear Amara and Halit come in, and Macia whispers," We'll find out if Halit leaves the house, even when my mother is home. Shall we follow him?"

"I think we should," Caecilia whispers back, "although we need to be extra careful. Your mother might not have a problem with Halit leaving the village at night, but she might object to us following him."

The girls stay still, and just as Macia is about to give up and give in to sleep, they can hear Halit moving around, closing the outer door. The girls rise and grab their black clothes. The ferrets make little noises, and Macia opens the little door they have made for them. The walls of the hut are thin and she has made a little door in the wall, keeping the hut protected against unwanted creatures, but allowing the ferrets to get out during most of the night. They didn't want Halit to hear or see the ferrets, so they release the two furry creatures before moving to their door.

"We need to go," Caecilia urges, her voice as quiet as possible. She feels a moment of panic, as she can imagine Halit out of the village already, and they will struggle to find him in the jungle. Just as the girls are about to open their door, there is another noise in the main room. A creaking noise, shuffling. Quick as a flash, the girls dive back into bed, pulling the blankets high up, to hide their black clothes. Just in time, as Macia sees the door handle move. She glances at their little window. It lets in enough light to see the door, as well as the furniture. The person coming in will be able to see their shapes, but won't be able to see clearly. The girls stay quiet, forcing themselves to breathe calmly and deeply as if they were asleep.

After a few moments, the door closes again, but the girls don't move. Not until they hear the outer door click shut for the second time that night. They move swiftly through the dark hut, and carefully open the door, not wanting to surprise Halit or Amara if they're nearby. The village is deserted and silent. Both girls slip through the door and click it shut. The click sounds louder than it should in the night air. They stay near the shadows as they walk through the village. Soon, the gate looms up, looking like the last safety point before the dark jungle. Nighttime noises make Caecilia shudder, the memories still fresh in her mind. They manage to shut the gate without any noise, and for a moment, they stand still, their backs against the rough door. Where are Halit and Amara, and are they together, or is Amara following her son?

The small pinprick lights are barely visible, but Caecilia spots them. Quickly, the girls walk along the jungle path. The moon helps them to see where they're going, and soon, the lights are closer. Until one of the lights disappears. The girls stop, and Macia grabs Caecilia's hand. "Do you think they noticed us?" she breathes. Caecilia shrugs and the girls remain still for what feels like ages. Then one of the lights shines between the trees, far to their right. The other one is still visible ahead. "They have gone separate ways," Macia continues, still not speaking above the merest whisper. "Why have they done that?"

Caecilia shrugs again and bites her lip. "Do you think they heard us and are trying to get behind us?" Macia hesitates, but as the little light to the right is getting further and further away, she shakes her head.

CHAPTER 30

"It's getting too far away," she says, "maybe we should stay on the main path, going the way we went last time, and keep a good lookout for the one on the right. We don't want to lose the one in front, as I want to know what my brother is doing."

The girls walk slowly, more cautious, and soon, they spot other lights, like last time. This time, they move closer, as quietly as they can.

They follow the group, glad of the noise made by so many feet, staying in the shelter of trees as much as possible. Caecilia shudders as her sandals don't give her much protection, and leaves, soil and slime gets in between her toes and the soles of her feet. The group keeps their voices low, but the girls can hear the constant low muttering.

They walk longer and further than the girls were hoping for, and Macia is sure they're going towards the stream. She doesn't want to tell Caecilia, knowing her odd comments about the stream and its power.

Caecilia shivers and touches Macia's arm. "I know we're getting closer to the stream," she breathes, and Macia nods, and gives her hand an encouraging squeeze. "How much longer do we follow them?" Caecilia asks, and Macia shrugs.

"No idea," she whispers back, "I suppose we haven't got much choice but to stick with them. Otherwise, we'd get back to the village and still know nothing about what goes on." She hesitates and whispers again, "You're right, we do have a long day tomorrow."

Caecilia suddenly gasps and clutches Macia. "We're near the shelter where we left the elders," she hisses in her ear, her voice wobbling, "and I don't want to get any closer."

Macia agrees, and she is sure the air is starting to smell foul as well. Time to return to the village and their warm beds.

The girls turn around, and both try to smother the scream that's leaving them, as they're confronted by a tall person, carrying a little light.

Chapter 31

The figure steps closer. It's Amara, looking even less pleased to see them than that morning. Macia swallows, not sure what to say, and whether it's best to stay quiet. "Why are you here?" the woman hisses in the end, her face moving in the flickering light she holds in her hand. "You have no business leaving the village, following us through the jungle. Why did you do this?"

Macia takes a breath, but before she can think of an appropriate answer, Caecilia grabs her arm with a small sob. "They're coming as well," she whispers in Macia's ear. It is true, the larger group is closer, the many little lights shining on the scene. Macia shudders and looks back at Amara, not wanting to see the menacing-looking group or the shelter where the elders are buried.

"You!" It's Halit, standing in front of the girls, his face twisted in fury. "I knew someone was behind me the other night, and I felt it tonight as well."

"You mean you led these people to us?" Another boy comes to stand next to Halit. He is shorter than Halit but looks about the same age. "Nobody is going to be happy about this," he says to Halit, then looks back at the girls. "Who were these girls anyway, and why did you bring them to us?"

Halit stares at the boy, his mouth open. "Bring? I did not bring anyone," he growls, making himself stand taller so he towers over the boy. "They sneaked out, and I double-checked yesterday, but they were asleep when I got back." The short boy sneers and Halit continues, "These girls came to us, they were looking for us. Not us as a group," he adds hastily as he sees the boy's reaction. "They were looking for our family, I meant, and that is how I found them. I ended up taking them to our village as my mother wasn't back from…back yet."

An older man comes forward, dragging his leg behind him. "We need to get rid of these girls," he says, his voice thin, as if he is much older than he looks. The man looks at Amara. "Surely you agree?" he asks, but Macia doesn't think he's expecting Amara to disagree. Macia doesn't expect her to either, and neither is Caecilia, judging by the way she is clutching her arm.

"It depends," Amara says slowly, glaring at the girls, but Macia wonders about the droop of her mother's shoulders. "One of them is my daughter," she tells the man, and there is a surprise rumble through the group.

"Your daughter?" The man repeats, his voice high. "Why is your daughter here, and how did she get here? Who else knows your daughter is here? And you know the agreement there is between our group and everybody else in this dreadful jungle," he says, looking pointedly at the shelter in the dark shadows.

Macia shudders. It is quite clear that the man wants to deal with them the way the elders were handled. She doesn't dare look at the rest of the group and tries to stand tall and calm, not wanting to appear weak or emotional.

"They've been trouble from the start," Halit hisses, waving his little light. "Talking about strange topics and carrying things with them nobody in the village has ever seen, and speaking about fith."

"Fith?" The man asks, staring at Halit, his mouth in a sneer.

"Something like that," Halit raises his chin, standing with one leg forward a little. Macia nearly laughs with shock. Is he taunting the

CHAPTER 31

man with his two healthy legs compared to the man's one withered leg? "Fith, faith, same thing. It's talking about something and...and reading a book, writing little shapes in another book."

The old man gasps, and so does Amara. The younger people in the group simply stare, but there is another young woman, who gasps out loud. "Book?" she hisses, "They have a book? What kind of book?"

Halit looks pleased with the attention, and Macia is relieved to be out of the spotlight for a moment.

"It's several books," Halit states, his light nearly extinguished as he waves his hand around. "There is a book with pictures. Pictures of plants and trees and animals we see in the jungle." The group gasps, and Amara sniffs, some of the hostility draining out of her face. "Then there is a book with just lots and lots of little symbols in it. That is the one that makes them write symbols as well."

"Letters," the old man coughs, and keeps coughing till he suddenly loses his balance. Macia dashes forward and grabs him, catching his little light with her other hand. He shakes her off. "I don't need to go..." He stops and laughs a wild laugh, which ends in a long, wobbly sob. "There," he says after he has wiped his face, "I almost said I don't need to go Downstream, having been here for more years than I can remember." He laughs again, and Macia can feel Caecilia shiver. A laugh like that would be enough to get you sent Downstream, she thinks by herself.

"Anyway, child," he says, his face back in its sneer, "those symbols are called letters. You make words and sentences with them. And there is a difference between a book and a notebook." Halit glares and the man shrugs. "Who needs books anyway," he says, waving his hand. "What is more important is the question of what to do with these girls."

He looks at Amara, who sighs. "I know, there is the agreement," she says, sounding tired, "but I have just been to see Felix." The group mutters and she shakes her head. "Don't be like that. You know he's not like the others, and we need him. We need him on our side. He had a message." She glares at the girls. "It all started about a week ago. Some people from the mountain village left. They were strangers, which doesn't make sense."

Halit snorts. "They probably meant them," he says, flapping his hands towards the two girls. "They stayed in the village, didn't they? And those masked ones followed them. We didn't realise in time what exactly was going on, and before we found out, it was all over and I found them with one of the dead masked ones."

Amara gasps, "They killed the masked ones?" She stares at the girls in horror, and Macia's eyes fly open!

"No," Halit says, looking up at the sky for a moment, "They didn't kill them. They were putting one of the dead ones in the ground." The group gasps again, and Macia bizarrely realises they are providing more entertainment than the young people have ever had. "I was about to sort them all out, then she," and he points at Macia, "she said my name. Then she asked about you."

Amara inclines her head, her face no longer looking angry. "So who killed the masked ones, the Elutera?" She looks around the group, then back at the old man. "Felix said the head elder sent another message, saying they were attacked, killed. He escaped?" She makes it sound like a question, and Macia nods her head. Her mother turns to her. "You saw him?"

Macia nods again, and trying to sound calmer than she is, she says, "We saw him running past us, without his mask, and covered in blood. Later, we found his mask, with all the other bodies." Her voice trembles then, and she desperately fights the tears. She mustn't break down in front of this group, not if they want to stay alive. "We had been followed by them for a long time, and we knew they were ahead of us. We heard the noise, the screams and sounds of the attack, but we

CHAPTER 31

didn't know what had happened until we saw the bodies. Not all of them were elders," she adds, and looks at the group, wondering how many of their group had been killed.

The old man shakes his head as she looks at him. "Not us," he says and coughs again. "Not us, not our style," he says, "although we have an agreement with Felix, it's clear that we're the only ones sticking to what we promised," he glares at Amara.

Amara scowls at him, "Felix is concerned about the letters. It sounds like the elder is angry and desperate to have his people revenged. There have been many questions in the mountain village, and there is much unrest. He says that the attack was wrong and needs to be paid for to appease the villagers. They also need help now that so many of their men are killed."

The old man stares. "Felix wants to have more doings with the mountain village?" His voice is higher than ever, and he coughs for a long time as if struck by the shock. "And why us? It wasn't us that did it," he says and stares at the girls again. "How many were they with? Just two girls, coming all the way down from the mountain, on the wrong side of the stream and all the while pursued by masked ones?" He laughs again, but Amara shakes her head.

"There is another one in our clinic," she says, "with a leg missing after being attacked by the stream."

"By a crocodile," Macia corrects, feeling Caecilia's shudder at the mention of the stream. Amara glares at her, and the group steps back a little.

"Do. Not. Speak. Their. Name," Amara hisses, her face more contorted than ever. Each word is a loud hiss of breath, and the group seems to shrink away a little further with each word. Macia feels herself shiver, or is that Caecilia, clinging onto her?

Amara stands up straight, her eyes narrowed. "Feed them to the Stream," she orders. "That will placate the mountain elder, calm the stream and cheer up Felix. We cannot have more trouble coming our way. We then can see who was responsible for this," and she waves towards the shelter with buried elders. "The masked ones will need to be revenged, so the head elder can control the villagers. There is too much trouble in the jungle, and we need to have our peace back."

The group mumbles and looks at each other, until the old man nods slowly. "Nothing against you," he says, sneering at Macia, "but like Amara says, we need our peace."

The girls step back in horror, and one very quick glance tells Macia that there is no hope of escape. Amara hasn't moved but is certainly not going to help them. Halit seems to be hesitant, but there is no way he will come to their rescue either. The group is determined to feed them to the crocodiles and nobody will know they're gone. Gax…what will happen to Gax? Brutus… Thoughts flit through her mind as she shuffles back, desperately.

Just as the group steps out to take them, Caecilia screams out, "Lord Jesus, help us!"

The effect could not be more astounding. There is a thundering noise, and young, lithe bodies appear from every corner of the dark jungle, roaring words that Macia can't make out, pushing the group back with a ferocity that scares her. At the same time, the group jumps back from the girls and the old man screams in horror, hiding his face, stopping his ears, his light extinguished on the jungle floor.

Strong hands grab the girls from behind, and Macia struggles for her life, until she hears the words in her ears, "In Jesus' Name, be still and let us help you." The words are so shocking and unexpected that she feels all the blood draining from her face. She feels light headed all of a sudden, but the strong hands are still there, carrying her off into the jungle. She can hear Caecilia sobbing and tries to look around, half twisting her ankle as she tries to look back, but the voice hisses, "She is fine, we're just taking different paths, to make sure nobody

CHAPTER 31

follows us later. We don't want anyone to get hurt, not even the foolish, dangerous villagers with their stubborn old man and devious leader."

Macia's head spins as she is half-carried through the jungle at top speed. Branches slap into her face, she is sure that her feet are bleeding on the top and she wouldn't be surprised if she finds herself minus several toes by the time they get to their destination.

They reach a more open space in the jungle and the dark shapes of other youngsters appear in the night gloom. "We stopped the leader, and most of the group is safe as well," one of the young people reports. Macia realises it's a young girl. The girl smiles at her briefly, then continues to the person behind her, who is still holding her, "The woman tried several times to escape. The old man did, but only for a moment. One little kid did escape, but he ran the wrong way. We will look for him when it's light, as he might need some help to get back to the path and their village." Several of the youngsters chuckle, including the young man holding her, but it doesn't sound unkind.

They walk most of the night, and Macia is hardly able to move by the time they get to their destination. There is no sign of Caecilia. Macia fights against the tears, swallowing, holding her breath, blinking, and looking at the sky, but she can feel her face getting wet.

"Everything will be alright," the voice says in her ears, "just trust and stay close to God." She blinks, the tears forgotten as well as gone, and she tries to look around at her captor, but he chuckles. "Not yet," he says softly. "Let's get to the main hut first, and hopefully Caecilia will be there as well."

He knows their names? Macia gasps as she goes through what looks like a more open place with low structures, hiding amongst the jungle greenery. She doesn't try to look around anymore, too exhausted to care where she is going. It's hard enough to walk. In the semi-darkness, she can see other shapes moving, just ahead of her. She can hear a high shriek, as one of the shapes seems to tumble. Caecilia.

Macia smiles to think they're nearly together again.

A dark shape appears between trees, a much larger hut than the small ones they have passed. Macia is guided to the door, entering the hut after Caecilia. A small light appears, and soon, several oil lamps are burning. Macia takes a deep breath. She moves closer to Caecilia, and the hands that have been clamped around her upper arms all this time finally let go. Her shoulders sag a little. The hands had been strong, warm, comforting and confident, and she misses the feel of the rough fingers.

She turns around to finally see the young man who has rescued her. Her mouth drops as she stammers his name, her cheeks glowing with instant heat. "Riu..!"

Chapter 32

"Riu!" she repeats, and suddenly her eyes fill with tears again. "Your father... I'm so sorry." She takes a deep breath and looks at Riu.

He nods. "Thank you. I heard from my friends, the Levato," he adds softly, indicating the other young people around them with his chin. "They also told me what you did. That was kind. And brave," he smiles, his own eyes filled with tears.

Macia inclines her head and takes a deep breath. "So...where are we and what just happened?"

Riu nods. "My father knew something was going on in the jungle," he starts, then sighs. "This could go on a while," he says softly, "and you might want the entire story. But it's the middle of the night, and we're all exhausted. Maybe we should rest first. Let's just say that this is another village in the jungle, with mostly young people. We call ourselves the Levato. They're the ones that got away from the woman, the leader of the village." His face grows dark, and Macia shivers. Is her mother the 'devious woman' mentioned before by the other young girl? She glances around, but can't see the girl in the large hut.

"I will show you where you can sleep," Riu says and the girls follow him outside. Soon, they reach one of the small huts. "There isn't much space," Riu shrugs apologetically, "but it's dry inside and comfy. Do you need anything, like food?"

The girls shake their heads, and Macia says, "What will happen to Gax, do you think? Will they kill him?"

Riu hesitates. "I don't think so," he says, "as Amara won't be there to give that kind of order. None of the others would kill him just like that. I don't know what they will think of her disappearance; they probably assume she has gone Downstream for something else. Your brother not being there will be strange as well, so hopefully, this can be resolved soon, as we don't want chaos to land in the village." He pulls a face, "All that to say that I think Gax is safe."

The girls nod and thank him, crawling into the booth. It's more spacious inside than they expected, and finally, they can sit down. There are two mattresses on the floor, similar to the ones on their beds in the village. Macia looks at Caecilia, and suddenly, they are both crying and hugging each other. When they calm down a little, Caecilia sobs, "When they started towards us... I was so scared. I shouldn't have been, but I was, and so I cried out, and then..." She laughs between her sobs, "I thought a load of angels had appeared from heaven to help us, and I was so confused when the angel spoke to me and started pulling me through the jungle. It took me a long time to realise that they weren't angels!"

Macia giggles. "It was very confusing. I hadn't heard them coming at all, but in a way they were angels, doing what they needed to do to rescue us." She takes a deep breath and wipes her wet face. "I didn't recognise Riu's voice at all, and I still don't understand how he is here. He seems to be in charge of these young people, the Levato. Anyway, my eyes won't stay open any longer, I need sleep. I also need another shower, so I hope this village has a shower hut as well," she says, her voice trailing off as she lies down on one of the beds.

Caecilia lies down on the other one, "My feet are cut to shreds, I think," she says, with a small giggle turning into a sob. "Goodnight." And as the girls settle down to sleep, their minds whirling, trying to

CHAPTER 32

understand what has happened.

After a while, Macia whispers, "Are you still awake?" She's sure that Caecilia is awake, as she can hear her sobbing quietly.

"I'm sorry," whispers Caecilia, "I didn't mean to keep you awake."

"I couldn't sleep after all," Macia whispers back, then a little louder, "I wonder if it's morning yet? I'm sure I heard voices. I'm too tired to get up, but I just can't sleep. Not after last night."

"I keep seeing the old man, and... and your mother. They wanted to kill us and feed us to the stream," Caecilia says, crying. "Why would they do that?" She gives a strange laugh, "I mean, I know why they wanted to do it, I just can't accept that they were prepared to do that to us. We'd stayed with them, eaten with them, and then they want to kill us."

"I know," Macia sighs, "it was too dreadful. But one of the girls seemed interested in books, did you notice that?" She doesn't know why that comes to mind, but it suddenly makes her think about the different people in the group. "We shouldn't think about last night," she says in the end, "for that way we will never sleep. Maybe we should think of nice, happy things." Her voice trails off as she struggles to conjure up any nice, pleasant images that aren't attached to something else. Mataiox and the soft beach, but the grief of being so far away spoils the image. The views from Colchuyni, but again, so much grief and sadness attached to that memory.

Caecilia gives a half laugh, having come to the same conclusion. "There is always grief attached to whatever nice thing I think about," she says, "even the best things, like people and beautiful places. Even the Book, there are memories when I read the Book that make me sad, and there are still parts in the Book that are so hard."

Both girls are quiet for a while, trying to think of good things, and Macia finds herself returning to the Book in her mind. "There are some beautiful things in the Book," she says quietly, "things to calm you and hold you safely, to envelop you in comfort."

Caecilia nods, although it's too dark to see. "Yes, I know what you mean. There was something about being written on the palm of God's hand like we did in class when we needed to make sure to remember something. But it wasn't written, it was engraved, never to be erased again." She smiles in the darkness, "Maybe I can fall asleep now."

Macia grunts something that she hopes Caecilia takes as a yes. She can hear Caecilia's contented sigh and steady breathing, and she buries her head in her pillow so Caecilia won't hear her. She knew the words Caecilia mentioned, but she knows what comes before those lovely words. She knows she is blessed to be engraved, but why can't she have both? Have her mother's love as well? Or not even her mother's love, but to not be forgotten by her mother, as the words before the promise say. "Dearest," she groans silently, "Dearest, she didn't not love me, she didn't just forget me, she tried to have me killed. She set up the group to kill me. I know I'm loved, but why can't I have my mother's love too? My father losing his temper and nearly killing himself as soon as he sees me, and my mother hating me just as much." She rubs her face against the rough cloth of the pillow. She thinks of Gax, in his bed at the clinic, and fresh tears wet the pillow. "How will we ever get out of here," she wonders again, "and what will Gax's parents say when they see him? If they see him."

She doesn't realise she is no longer writing in her head until Caecilia whispers, "What do you mean? You mean we go without Gax and simply tell his parents?" She sits up, her voice high and shrill, and Macia shakes her head.

"No, I mean, we will bring him home. But it will be hard to get him out of the village."

Macia sits up. "I'm getting up," she says, hugging herself, folding her fingers in, as most are red raw already. "I can't sleep. I want to find out what's going on."

CHAPTER 32

Caecilia follows slowly. "I'm sore," she groans as she tries to stretch her arms and legs without punching Macia. "My feet are sore, and even here in the dark, I can tell they're covered in cuts! I hope I won't get some infection in them," she pulls a face. "We could do with my book on plants, to see what we can use to stop our cuts from going bad." She looks up with a start, "The ferrets! We need to get the ferrets! Good thing they were let out, otherwise that would be very hard, but what if somebody in the village sees them and thinks they're rats and tries to hurt them?"

Macia chews the last remaining bit of her thumbnail, "We could go into the village, as nobody would know anything," she says slowly. "The others have disappeared, but the villagers won't know how or why, and they won't know our part in the disappearance. We should go soon though, before too many people are awake."

Caecilia stares at her, but hesitates. "What if they suspect anything?" She shudders, "You have seen how nasty they can turn."

Macia shrugs, "We'll have to look as if it's more than normal. We could bring that basket Halit used to gather plants in the jungle. Line the bottom with our books, and leave the village that way. I saw another one, so we could take a basket each. It might be hard to get everything out that way, but we could get most things out, and we will be able to rest another time. Depending on what happens to Halit and my mother," she adds, frowning. "That would make it hard if they're there, but we just have to pray it goes well." Or simply find a way, she thinks, then feels her face warm up. When has God let them down on this trip? She licks her sore thumb, finding the question repeating itself in her head, over and over, taking on more of a bitter edge with each repetition.

"We better go," Caecilia says, glad they have a plan.

They crawl out of the booth, and Caecilia is relieved to find morning hasn't arrived yet. That way, it will be easier to get in and out of the village. As they pass the hut, they see the girl who helped with the rescue in the night. She smiles at them, but her face shows answers are needed. "We need to get to the village," Macia explains. "All our belongings are there and our pets." The girl raises her eyebrows at the mention of animals but nods.

"It's still dark, you should be able to get in and out before too much trouble wakes," she smiles. "Let me take you to the gate, as it's hard to find."

They follow the girl through the jungle. Fortunately, she sticks to reasonable paths. They make good progress, but the girls are glad when the gate looms up in the darkness. They thank the girl, who whispers, "I will wait for you here, but be quick, as we want to get back to base before it's light."

The girls slip through the gate, and walking quickly through the village, close the door of the hut behind them. Macia leans against the door, breathing out a huge breath she didn't know she'd been holding in. "We better pack," she says, and her voice shakes and so do her hands as she lights a little lamp.

They dash into their room and look around. What to take, what to leave for later? "The books," Caecilia says, and they start making a pile of things on the bed. "We can still take our bags, as it's dark." It takes them a few minutes, but then the bed is filled with needed items. Shoving it all into two bags doesn't take long, and the last thing they need to do is get the ferrets ready to travel again.

The ferrets' smart little eyes stare at Macia in disgust as she wakes them up to transfer them into their basket. She tickles their tummies and they wriggle against her. She nuzzles them, her eyes pricking. "We're on the move again, little ones," she whispers against their soft fur, the soft cream hairs hardly visible in the semi-darkness, "but hopefully, this is the last rushed move you need to make."

They take one last look around the room and close the door.

CHAPTER 32

Nothing is theirs in the large room, and soon, they shut the door to the hut behind them. Macia hesitates a moment, listening, looking around, to see if anybody else is awake. It stays quiet, and the girls walk softly through the village.

As they pass the last hut, there is movement. They peer through the darkness and suddenly a little girl stands in front of them, her eyes wide with shock. She opens her mouth to call out, but Caecilia recognises the little face. She dashes forward and gently places her fingers on the girl's lips, smiling at her. "Sh," she smiles, "it's only me. You remember me, don't you?" The girl nods, and her shoulders sag with relief. Caecilia smiles at the little girl and kneels before her. "What is your name?"

The girl stares at her, then shrugs, "Just girl. Or you. Or water girl," she says softly. Then she smiles, her little serious face glowing in the first glimmer of dawn, the morning sky no longer opal but charcoal grey.

"Alright," Caecilia manages to keep her smile in place, despite the little wobble when she finds the girl has no name, "well, my little water girl, I hope we'll see you again soon. Take care, and I will..." she hesitates, then turns it into, "I will think of you, and hope and pray you're alright until we meet again." A thought strikes her, "Why were you awake already?"

"I needed the toilet hut," the girl says, "so I went, but I have a little time to sleep before I need to go to the food hut." She smiles again, and carefully touches Caecilia's face. "I want to see you again," she whispers, "and I hope too. I hope nobody knows you are not here, and I hope they will all be like you," she wipes her eyes, and turns around. Soon, she disappears in the shadows of the huts.

Caecilia struggles back onto her feet, and the girls rush to the gate and out before others appear. They walk to where they saw the girl from Riu's camp last, and she is there, waiting for them. "I'm glad you're here," she grins, "we better get going, the light is about to appear."

Chapter 33

The walk through the jungle seems quicker, maybe because it's not as dark. Soon, the little booths dotted around the jungle appear, followed by the larger hut. The girls are relieved as their guide takes them to their booth. They would never have found it back by themselves. "My name is Siate," she says, just before she turns round. "I will see you later in the hut when it's light," she adds with a smile.

The girls thank her and crawl into their booth with bags and ferrets. Macia looks around the minute space and pushes the ferret's basket into the corner. "Hopefully they won't mind staying in their basket during the day," she says and struggles out of her backpack.

Caecilia takes her sandals off and drops onto her bed. "This bed feels even better now," she grins, and she takes a breath as the tears are close once more. "I am suddenly really tired, I think I might sleep this time," she says with a yawn.

Macia nods, and soon, the little booth is quiet. Outside, life is starting in the camp. Figures can be seen crawling out of different booths, but voices are kept low, and the girls don't hear anything. The ferrets prick up their little ears but as nobody comes near their booth, they soon curl up together in the basket and join the girls in snoring softly.

Caecilia is the first to wake up, and she stares at the woven rafters just above her bed. It takes her a few seconds, but then the events of the night come flooding back. So do the tears. "Gax," she moans quietly, "Gax, will we ever see you again? I just want to go home. I wished we had never started this journey."

She wipes her face and looks across at Macia. Macia is frowning in her sleep, her head moving restlessly on the pillow. Caecilia hesitates. Should she wake her friend? She doesn't seem to be happy just now, so waking up might be better. Macia groans, and suddenly she opens her eyes and stares at Caecilia. Caecilia has to giggle, and says, "I was about to wake you; you weren't having a good dream, I think."

Macia sits up, rubbing her eyes. "I was dreaming of masked crocodiles," she says, then laughs a little. "Glad I'm awake. I'm hungry," she carries on, patting her hair into some order.

The girls get up, "I think this booth was only designed for one person," Caecilia laughs as they keep knocking into each other while dressing and clearing up.

"Hopefully there is food," Macia says again, and Caecilia rolls her eyes. "When I'm stressed, I need food," Macia grins, and they get out of their booth into the jungle sunshine.

They get to the big hut, and Siate is there, smiling at them. "I was wondering about getting you," she says, "as I thought you might be hungry after last night. You did a lot of walking," she adds, looking at their scratched and bruised feet. "Let me show you inside, and get you something to eat and drink," she continues, and the girls follow her into the hut. Long tables are placed in the middle with benches around them, while torches hang from the walls. There are a few young people still eating, but they are nearly finished.

"Looks like we're just in time," says Macia, and Siate nods.

"We start quite early," she says, "as we need time in the day for other activities, and we want to rest when it's hot, to save our energy. And most nights we go out, so we all need to catch up on sleep as well," she

CHAPTER 33

shrugs as the girls look at her. "We don't raid, like...like others," she pulls a face.

The girls nod. Food first, Macia decides, and they slide in next to some young lads. The boys nod at them and continue their conversation. "He said it's the God of all good things," one slim boy says. The boy opposite him nods but the little boy continues, "But there is so much bad, even when good things happen. Is that the same God? He says it isn't, but sometimes bad things happen to a good person. And good comes to the bad as well."

Macia forces her eyes away from the boys. Should she explain about the one good God? But then, the question still stands, doesn't it? Why is Gax in a bed, having lost his leg? Why did the evil head elder make it safely back to the village? Suddenly she stills. Are the boys talking about God? Are they referring to Riu? Riu, who whispered the name of Jesus last night?

Macia sighs and smiles at Siate, as she puts steaming bowls of food in front of the girls. "Thank you," she smiles and hesitates between starting with all the questions or simply eating. Food wins out in the end, and Macia swallows sweet, hot mouthfuls of some kind of grain.

Caecilia puts down the wooden spoon. "That was delicious. I can't believe how hungry I was," she giggles and sighs deeply, "I can't remember eating so much for quite a while," she adds, and her face grows more serious. "I wonder how Gax is," she says quietly, and Macia nods as she finally lays down her spoon as well. "We better be quick," Caecilia says, looking at the young people moving the tables and benches around. She doesn't move though, her whole body is tired and aching, and her heart feels too heavy for anything.

Macia gets up and smiles at Caecilia. "We better help, it will do our aching muscles good," she says as she helps Caecilia up. "Come on, the quicker this hut is tidy, the quicker we can get some answers."

"I'm not sure it's answers I want," Caecilia says, rolling her eyes like the young people in Mataiox do, "but you're right, we better help after all they have done for us."

Once the hut is tidy and the floor swept, Siate reappears, smiling as always. "Glad to see everything done," she says, "it's an art coming in at the right time," she jokes, winking at Caecilia, who laughs.

"My younger sister was pretty good at it," she says and looks away. She misses her little sister Savisia. She misses her parents. Gax… She sniffs and smiles as much as she can. "What do you want us to do now?" She hopes it's something interesting, without too much need of thinking about the past.

"Riu will be here in a minute. We will set up benches and we can talk and see what needs doing. He has many questions, and he is sure you have some as well. We also need to decide what to do with the captives, as it takes a lot to feed and guard them."

The girls nod, and Macia looks down. Does Riu expect her to sit in judgment against her mother and brother? She doesn't even know what they have been up to, and how involved they are. Riu must know more and so does Siate, she is sure. She was the one who called her mother the devious woman, so what has she missed?

They follow Siate to a corner of the hut where they set up benches in a kind of circle around a low table. A young boy comes in carrying a large pitcher of water, followed by two boys with clay cups. The design is a little similar to what they have seen in Colchuyni, and Macia wonders again about the relationship between the mountain village and the Levato camp.

Riu comes in and the girls are pleased to see him. "I have many questions; many, many questions," he grins, "and I think you have questions?" They nod and he waves at the benches. "We sit here, and we find answers. Then, when we have answers, I have more questions. Questions about your Book. Those are important questions, but they still need to wait. The Book is what we need most, but first we need

CHAPTER 33

to handle life. You can help."

The girls are stunned and look at each other. In all this, Riu is interested in the Book? If only Gax was here…

Riu sighs. "My father," he swallows, and the girls see the tears in his eyes, "my father, you know what happens to him, yes?" They nod and he continues. "I don't know, my mother doesn't know, and then the Head elder is back in the village. He looks bad, he is hurt, and dirty and he says strange things. He says the Stream turned against them, and the Stream is angry. Angry with everyone. I know he is bad, the elder. And he is back. My father, I believe my father is good, and he is not back. The Stream only likes what is bad, he will destroy good." Riu sighs and takes a few deep breaths. He pours himself some water.

"When my father comes not back and my mother is sad, I think about you. I know they all followed you. They want you. The Head elder even says so although people in the village know not what he says. I know. My mother knows. That evening, my mother tells me to go. To find you, to learn about my father. She tells me about the Levato. She tells me to go and to protect us from the Stream and to bring another God to the Stream, to destroy the stream forever." He takes a sip. "She says, the God who breathes life, bring the life breath to the Stream. The breath will destroy the Stream and give life to all those that the Stream does not love."

Macia's eyes fill with tears at the reminder of that day when Riu's little nephew was given CPR and lived. She nods and Riu continues. "I leave the village, follow the path, I was afraid," and he shudders. The girls pull a face as yes, they were afraid too.

"I find a crossing. I know it is a crossing, but the path is this side. I do not know what to do, but my heart, there is a strong breath in my heart, and it pulls me towards the stream, telling me to cross, to leave everything behind, to breathe a new way. I go across, and I feel new breath in me. I do not look back. I can feel everything new. The air is new, the ground, the colours, my eyes, everything is new. I walk in the light, not the darkness, and when I see the stream, it is just water, slow, powerless, filled with evil and darkness, but I breathe the light." He stops, and the girls can feel their shoulders relaxing as Riu takes deep breaths, his face glowing, his hands on his heart, as if holding the new breaths in his lungs in both hands.

"I walk, and then I feel the evil again," he says, and his voice shakes a little. "I see the shelter, but my father is not there. There is only a young boy, standing between the trees, watching me as I come out of the hut. He watches my tears and he waits. Then he talks to me, and I have no breath, good or bad," he suddenly grins, "and he asks who I seek. I tell him, and he shows me the grave. He tells me girls and a sick man buried my father. He said there were tears then. He also tells me about the young man coming to take you. But the boy takes me here, and I meet young people. Siate. She knows my father. There are tears in the camp. Many tears. I knew my father was good, and they knew. But there is evil in the jungle. And it sometimes swallows the good. That, I do not understand. Sometimes, maybe, there is nobody to breathe life, is there? Sometimes you need a person who holds the breath of life to pass it to others."

The girls are quiet and all that can be heard in the hut are the voices and noises from outside. Caecilia wipes at her eyes and Macia has to swallow. A small breath, is that all it takes to overcome evil? Macia isn't sure, as it feels so much more is needed when seeing so much grief and destruction.

"Tell me, please," Riu says softly, "and then I will tell you where we are here, now. I am leading the Levato. Not because I want to, but because of my father. I didn't really know my father, but I am getting to know him more every day. But we will come to now later. First, tell me about your journey. You are here, in that village. Where is your friend? You said he is needing medical help?"

CHAPTER 33

Macia nods and takes a deep breath, holding it for a moment, and then she shares their story. She makes sure to include the little bottle of oil, dropped by Riu's father, and he glows. "Your father was with them, but not part of them," she says softly. "We do not know what happened in the end. We saw different groups at different times. Then there was the attack. We hid. We saw the head elder, running past in terror, covered in blood, without his mask." She shivers, "We found them the next day. We pulled them all in the shelter. Then we found your father. He was still alive. He said," her voice trembles, and emotions make her pause for a moment. Not all her training in Elabi can contain her grief and the horror of that memory. "He didn't say much, only 'sorry, tell Riu, evil'. Does that mean anything to you? I know it's not much, but maybe it will help you?"

The hut is quiet, as Riu cries softly, and Caecilia struggles to keep her sobs as quiet as possible, not wanting to take away from Riu's grief.

When Riu is calm again, Macia continues to explain how they got to the village with her brother, Halit, and how Gax had to go into the medical hut and how he lost a leg. She explains that her mother returned from Downstream with the new arrivals and that one of those was her father, who'd had a stroke. She struggles to tell Riu how angry her father was, and that he is still angry, even after the stroke. "We knew Halit went out in the night, and we followed him. We couldn't follow him very far the first time, as there were lots of them, and we were worried about being discovered. We were amazed when my mother went out as well, and we saw her light going off to the side. We tried to keep a close watch on her light as well as follow Halit and the group. Somehow, she did come up behind us. We never heard her coming, and suddenly, we were confronted by her and then the whole group. There was an older man, who seemed to be the leader." Riu nods with a frown, and Macia continues, "In the end, my mother and this old man decided to feed us to the crocodiles, and the group started moving towards us. Caecilia," she smiles at her friend, "Caecilia cried out, and suddenly, you were there."

"Thank you," says Caecilia, smiling at Riu, "I didn't know what to do, but God heard me and you were there, overcoming evil with good, it seems," she adds, and Riu's eyes light up.

"Yes," he says, "yes, that is one way of breathing life into something bad and making it alive and whole." He looks at the floor, thinking hard. "But there is still a lot of evil we need to face," he says softly. "Some of the evil you might be aware of, some of it might be new to you, as it was to me."

Chapter 34

"I came to the Levato and found my father had been here many times. He was very fit and he would walk and walk, or use a narrow boat on the stream, but that was only after my nephew was saved," he smiles at the girls. "Nobody knows my father had a boat. Young people from the Levato made the boat. They go on boats often."

The girls look at each other, and Macia sits up a bit more. A boat! The Levato have boats? There is a way out? She takes a deep breath. They have to stay in the here and now, in this conversation with Riu.

"I came to the Levato. The Levato knows my father is no longer here, and now I am here in place of my father. I am needed here. I am not needed in Colchuyni, and it will be hard in the village, as the Head Elder might suspect me. I suspect him and know he is an evil man," Riu continues. "I learn what life is like in the camp. There is a bit of a book, it's a special book. It is in a bad state, pages fall out, and it got wet in the camp and the jungle air is not good for books," he shrugs and smiles at the girls. "The book looks like the book you have. The big book with the many words."

Caecilia gasps and leans forward. "Is it like a small pack of pages?" she asks, her eyes wide, her face leaning forward. Macia's eyes have gone bright as well. Another bit of Gax's old Book?

"There was another man in Elabi," Caecilia explains, "he got ill, well, yellow, but he had one of Gax's packs," she grins at Macia. "I think he said he lost it. Gax was upset and worried, and I don't think he ever saw the man again. I thought he had died?"

Riu shrugs. "I do not know how the book got here," he says. "There were a few older people to start with in the Levato. One of them had the book pages, and they could read. They taught some of the young people to read, but not all. Life is very busy, but the young people want to read the pages and my father wants to read the pages. Now my father is gone, and I need to read the book, to answer the questions and to help the young people."

Macia nods and grins. "That is wonderful," she says, "do you know what the portion of the Book is?"

Riu shakes his head. "They are stories about Jesus, and the stories are incredible. We learn a lot, but we need to learn more. Many things about the jungle we know, but we don't know much about the Book."

Riu continues, "I read the story about the man being no longer alive but buried. And Jesus calls him, and he comes out, alive. Like my nephew," he smiles, "but that was the breath of God, not the voice. We need to learn about the voice of God, and we need His breath to help us against the evil in the jungle."

They drink some of their water, and Macia tries to rearrange her shirt. The hut is warming up in the daytime. "There is great evil in the place," Riu says, and his face looks sad and serious. "The village…not all is well in the village. Downstream, it is not very far. The woman goes, a day, two days before the boat comes. She stays, makes arrangements, then she returns taking some people with her and some babies that might live and can help in the village. Some of the young people we rescue, so she needs new youngsters. Then, in a short time, she will go Downstream again, for a few days. To check the place, to see if anybody is still in need of rescue, she says, but it is to live well and have a good time. Felix is her man now," Riu says, and he sighs. "I am

CHAPTER 34

very sorry," he looks at Macia, and then looks away. "Felix is not a very nice man. He is maybe not completely evil. He does his job and he has now a woman, a wife. Your mother, she knows what goes on. Many people die, but she will take their money. With the money, she makes a nice house for Felix and for her. Your brother, he is doing things in the village. He is not very bad; he just does not know what is good and what is wrong."

Riu inclines his head. "I am sad for you. You came to find your mother, but she is a bad woman. She only takes people that give money and that won't need very much help. She will take babies that have maybe a problem, but are quite strong, and can work. The others, she will let die. Then she and Felix live in the house. The boat brings things for Felix. He buys with the money."

Macia frowns, "Won't the people on the other end of the boat think it strange that he wants all these things?"

Riu shakes his head. "He says to them it is for the clinic, for people resting and waiting. He also buys many, many good things from the Head Elder. The Head Elder might get special things from the mainland when it's the crossing."

The girls are stunned. Amara is living a strange, double life? "I suppose life in the village isn't very good," Caecilia says softly, and Riu shakes his head.

"She likes life in the village. The work, the busyness, the challenge. But it is busy and not very comfortable after a while, so she goes back to Felix and lives in the nice house."

"Why did she bring my father?" Macia asks, her voice strained.

"I think she knows him," Riu says, "and she wants him away from Felix maybe, and perhaps in the village to watch him and show him how good her life is?"

Macia nods. "What about Halit? Does he know about Felix and her special house?" She feels her face warming up at the bitterness in her voice, but can't change it.

"He knows nothing about the house," Riu says. "He knows Felix is a good friend, but he knows not that Downstream is not far. He thinks it is a long way. And she makes him believe that. They placed some people who died a long way in the jungle, and Halit had to walk and bury them with her, so he thinks it is a long way. He has many duties, and I don't think he likes life. He goes out in the night, to hunt in the jungle. They look for the small group of people that are hiding in the jungle," he swallows, "the ones killing my father. The Elutera."

"There is a small group living in the jungle. They must be people from Colchuyni," Riu continues, "We think maybe people were sent away or even sent for a reason to live in the jungle. The Head Elder might not like Felix, or might not trust Felix. Maybe the group doesn't like the Head elder because they killed all the elders. Some of the group is young. Maybe young people from the boat escaped. They ran into the jungle and joined the others. They sometimes attack the village. One day they attacked the village and killed many people. All old people," he says softly. "All old people that were beginning to need more help."

Macia gasps, "So the group, the Elutera…you don't mean… You think she would…"

Riu inclines his head. "We are not completely certain," he says softly, "maybe it is not true, but some say she does know them, or Halit knows them, or even Felix. I do not know. I hope it is not true. But they killed only in some huts, not all huts."

Macia's eyes sting. Caecilia sniffs a few times, "This is so hard to hear," she says softly. "We came full of hope and looking forward to something good, only to find evil."

"You found death," Riu says, equally softly, "now you are here, to breathe life into death, to bring hope and peace and to defeat evil because you follow Jesus. He needs to live in us; He needs to rule the

CHAPTER 34

Levato, the village and Downstream. This jungle needs to be filled with Him, so there is no place for evil."

"Where is my mother," Macia asks, licking a speck of blood from her finger, "and where are the others now? Are they safe where they are?"

Riu nods. "We have a special place, further away from our camp. It's safe and sheltered, and won't compromise the Levato. It's easy to guard for a short time." He sighs, "We will need to decide what to do with them."

The girls have to agree. "What will you do with them? Are they all from the Scitabi?"

"Yes, the younger people go there and those that want more out of life, except for Halit. The old man is in charge of the Scitabi, and they meet up at night. They say they check the jungle, but they check each other. The woman doesn't want the Scitabi to know too much. The Scitabi doesn't want to lose the freedom they have. She makes Halit deal with them."

Macia groans, "What a mess. So are there children with the Scitabi?"

"No children. No very old and sick," Riu says, "just young people like Halit, or older people who are doing well. They must be still good for life."

"What do you want us to do," Caecilia asks.

"I do not know," Riu sighs. "I really do not know. Maybe God will know, and He can breathe life into the situation?"

The girls nod and Macia says, "Of course, we will pray about it. Maybe Caecilia and I should return to the village and try to keep it going? It might not work..." Her voice trails off as she thinks of the old woman. Will she even listen to them?

"You can tell her you are Amara's daughter, that Amara is not able to return and you have been left in charge?" Caecilia bites her lip, but there doesn't seem to be another option.

Riu agrees. "Maybe it works, maybe it doesn't work," he shrugs, "You can try. If it works not, we think of another plan. But if it works, the village will be good for a while longer. The problem is the Scitabi. It has young people, there must still be ten people left, maybe more. We don't know. We can find out," he says, "then we can plan for them. I don't like the idea of a jungle war."

"Maybe I should go to the Scitabi, tell them I'm Amara's daughter, and that I'm now in charge. Choose a young person that looks sensible, and make them overseer or something. They can come and report every day or every other day?"

Riu grins, "That is a good plan. They like feeling busy. Having a plan and aim is good."

"The villagers should learn to read," Caecilia says, "that will keep the children busy. The young people can come and carry the water and do the heavy work, rather than the small children." She thinks of the sweet little girl, the water girl. "It's good for the older ones to have jobs and maybe there is a way we can reward them. Is there something they might want?"

Riu shrugs, "I do not know. It might have to wait longer," he sighs, "until the jungle is better, safer. Then we can ask for the breath of Life to go amongst the Scitabi and change the people from the inside."

Macia stands up. "Maybe we could start? Start going to the village now? We need to look after Gax and my father, then see what we can do in the village. Should we speak to many people in the village or just to the medical people? The rest probably runs by itself?"

They think about it for a while, and in the end, Riu says, "Maybe see how it works. Is the village happy with you, then change. If the village is waiting for the woman or wanting the woman, maybe wait. Maybe they are tired of the woman. She took their money and belongings, so maybe they do not love her. But she gave them a hut, so maybe they do want her back."

CHAPTER 34

"Would the villagers not tell Halit that the journey was very short?" Caecilia frowns. "You only need one villager to say how close to Downstream the village is, and the whole plan would fall apart."

"She says they will go back and face Requipacem the same day," Riu says quietly.

"Will my mother's hut be safe for us to stay in?" Macia looks at Riu as well as Caecilia. Caecilia shudders but Riu nods.

"I think it will be safe. The village will fear her. Felix would not come to the village. The Elutera? I do not know what they will do. But the hut is large and strong, and it is her hut. The village will like that."

In the end, they decide to walk back into the village and sort things out. In the night, Riu's people will bring their belongings to the gate, including the ferrets. Caecilia shows Siate how to carry the ferrets. "I have never seen animals like this," Siate says, not sure what to think of them. "Having animals live with you can be nice, I think," she adds, sounding a little doubtful.

The girls pack their bags, so everything is ready for the night and then set off for the village with Siate, who points out the small paths between booths. "That is the path to the Scitabi, the one with young people," she points out. She turns around, "That is the path to the stream where we found you, and there is the village path."

The girls turn with her and nod, but they know there is no way they will find their way by themselves. "When will you come in the night?" Macia asks.

"We will come to the hut," Siate says, "rather than the gate. It is too dangerous for us to wait at the gate in the dark. We can come in and come to the hut. We will knock on the wall at the back. You have the extra room?" Macia nods, wondering how they all know so much about the village. Siate grins at Macia's face. "Many of us lived in the village when we were little. We were the ones helping, and working but also asking questions. It is why we were not happy in the village anymore. So we know the inside of many huts, many of the places. We think some of the Elutera might come from the village, too, as they know their way around as well. Do not open the door if you hear not the knock on the wall.

Caecilia looks at Siate, "You mean the Elutera can come into the village to kill us?" She has to swallow, to stop her lips from trembling, especially when Siate nods. "What can we do?" Caecilia whispers.

"Stay in the hut in the dark, and lock the door. Maybe block your door as well," Siate says, "and be ready to move."

They can see the village gate and Siate touches their shoulder. "Ask for the breath of Life; ask God to walk with you and to be your Light." Another quick touch and Siate has gone, leaving the girls to enter the gate by themselves.

Chapter 35

The girls look at each other, nod, and stride towards the gate. Macia opens the gate, and they walk through, shutting the gate quite deliberately. The village is quiet, but they can see a few people around. They stare at them, as always, but the girls walk straight to the clinic. Macia looks around, and seeing the old woman, walks straight up to her.

"My mother has been hindered from coming back today," she says, "so I will be there if you have any questions." She nods at the woman and walks towards Gax's room. Caecilia nods as well, and at the corridor, turns off towards Brutus' room.

Brutus is asleep when she walks in. Caecilia looks at him and frowns. His mouth seems to be drooping more, and he looks smaller in the bed than he did last night. She blinks. Was it only yesterday that she said goodnight to Macia's father? It feels like a lifetime ago. She looks at Brutus again. He looks older and sicker than last night.

She hears a noise behind her, and the old woman inclines her head when Caecilia looks around. "He had another attack last night," she says, not looking too upset. "He might have more. Maybe has had more. Hard to tell. He won't live long." She hesitates, looks at Caecilia, glances over her shoulder, licks her lips, and leans forward a little. "I don't know why Amara brought him here," she whispers, "nobody comes here that won't live, if you know what I mean."

Caecilia nods, and says, "He was her husband, so maybe she wanted him with her a little longer?" The woman looks, then cackles with laughter.

"To taunt him, you mean? I wouldn't be surprised." She looks at the sleeping man. "She'd better come quickly though, otherwise he'll be beyond teasing. I don't think even now he'll be bothered by her wonderful free life," and she walks away, mumbling and chuckling.

Caecilia sighs and straightens the thin blanket under the man's arms. "I don't think it's funny," she whispers, "I think this village is sad and cruel. It needs…" She stops and bites her lip. Yes, it needs the breath of God, the breath of Life, to change. Simply caring for one man in a dark room won't change the village, she knows.

Macia is glad to see Gax awake. His eyes fill with tears when she walks in. "Nobody has been to see me," he says, his voice shaking, "I had breakfast, but she didn't say anything. What is going on? I need the toilet, but there was nobody to help me."

Macia smiles as brightly as she can. "We got delayed," she says lightly, "I will tell you about it in a minute. Let's help you to the bathroom first." Together they manage to move Gax from his bed onto a chair with wheels attached. This is pushed to a small bathroom designed for the wheeled chair. Macia waits outside until Gax calls her in.

"I don't think I will get used to this," he says, in the same trembling voice. "I can't rely on others all my life." His eyes fill with tears and Macia looks away, making sure the sigh that escaped stays as quiet as possible.

"I will tell you what happened last night," she says softly when Gax is back in his bed. She checks the door, to make sure there is nobody in the corridor listening. "So, we followed Halit and my mother," she starts, and the entire tale follows. Gax's eyes are bulging by the end and he leans back in his pillows, exhausted. "So there we are," she concludes, "we will have to see what happens from here. I don't know

CHAPTER 35

what Riu will do to my mother and Halit. I think Halit might be set free, but I'm not sure about my mother."

She closes her eyes, her head against the backrest of the large chair. She concentrates on breathing deeply, slowly, until her eyes no longer sting. Gax's voice sounds a little more steady, "At least, if there is a boat, we can get away. We won't have to build a boat, and we can leave this nightmare behind. When do you think I will be able to travel?"

Macia looks at him. "I don't know," she says, and swallows. "My father is here as well, so I don't know. I will need to find out what happens to my mother and Halit, and then we can see what Riu has in mind. He might need our help, and we can't just leave the village like it is."

Gax stares at her. "But we found your mother," he says, his voice rising a little, colour appearing on his face. "We found Downstream, we can't do much about it, it seems, and we can't fix this village within a few days. Your mother will probably come back soon, and she will sort it out. It's not our problem. We didn't make this problem, and there is nothing we can do to fix it. We need to get back home, as my parents will be expecting us by the time the year is up. You have a course to do and so does Caecilia. At least we know what happened to your mother, we have found Downstream, so we can report back to Linu, and that's the end of a very dark, costly chapter of our lives," he says, glancing at his folded-up trouser leg, his voice wobbling.

Macia stares at him. "We can't leave Riu in the lurch," she says. "They risked their lives to rescue us, and they need our help. For one thing, he and the other Levato want to learn more about the Book and about God. We can't just walk away."

"What a horrible thing to say," Gax says, sitting bolt upright, tears suddenly on his flushed cheeks. "Don't you realise, I will never walk again, just because we were given the chance to find Downstream? If it wasn't for that radio chatter making everyone think they'd found

Downstream, and the fact that your mother might still be there, we would never have left Mataiox. Why should we risk and give up even more? We have done enough. The Mission School can send specially trained people to help Riu. They can send teachers for the children, with books and paper, and they can send medical personnel to help in the clinic. They can even send someone with leadership qualifications to run the village if your mother doesn't return before then."

Macia's mouth drops, but before she can say something, there is a noise at the door. It's Caecilia, and she looks troubled. She tries to smile at Gax, but he looks away, drying his face. "Macia," Caecilia says softly, "your father looks very unwell. He had another stroke or a couple of strokes overnight, and he still looks unwell. I think, maybe, if you want to…" She swallows and sighs, "Maybe you should come and see him, just in case he has another stroke. I don't think he is well at all."

Macia glances at Gax and feels her face warming up, but manages a small smile. "I'll come and see you in a while," she says to him. He nods, and whispers, "I'm sorry, Macia," but she simply nods once, and walks out of the room without looking at Gax, her back straight, and for a moment, she looks exactly like Amara.

The girls hurry through the large hut, and Macia stops outside Brutus' door. She takes a deep breath and opens the door. Brutus is still asleep, but like Caecilia, Macia is shocked at how much he has changed overnight. She slips in quietly, not wanting to wake him. She lowers herself onto the chair and swallows. "I'm sorry, Father," she says quietly, "I don't know what I could have changed, but it's been hard for you. If only you knew what I know, and how much love God has towards us, and how He has changed me…" She wipes her eyes and sniffs softly. Should she tell her father more, can he even hear her?

Caecilia spends the morning looking after Gax and identifying what

CHAPTER 35

needs to be done in the medical hut. She wants to help the little water carriers, who are busy again. Macia is looking after Brutus, but Caecilia does the walking up and down with the clean cloths and fresh water. The little girl isn't there. "She helps with the food making," the little boy says, without looking at Caecilia.

Caecilia smiles at him, but the boy refuses to look at her. A few times he tries to walk past her, but she blocks his way. "Do you work in different places each day?" She wants to know, to find out how the village is operated.

The little boy nods. "Most days, although not some days," he says, making Caecilia smile. "This day is hard," he adds, quietly, as he glances up for a moment. "The hut is warm and there is water needed all day. And working here is…difficult," his voice nearly a whisper, he looks over her shoulder, glances behind and looks at her, wanting to go. Caecilia nods and thanks him, then returns to Brutus' room.

The afternoon slides by and just as Macia wants to suggest they see Gax, Brutus moves a little in the bed. She stands up immediately, then hesitates. Should he see her if he wakes up? He's been asleep all day, his breathing noisy, and now his hand is moving restlessly, gripping the blanket. She turns towards the door to see what Caecilia thinks, but the gasping, rattling noise makes her move back round. Brutus' eyes are open, staring at her, but Macia doesn't think he can see her. He shudders, and suddenly, the room has gone silent.

Macia rushes forward, "Father? Father!" she calls out to him, but Brutus is no longer breathing, his hands still, his face pale grey. Macia holds her face, feeling the tears roll over her hands, as she sobs. Her father is gone, no matter that he had left her life a long time ago. There is no way to apologise to him, to see if he will forgive her eventually, no time to tell him anything. She sobs for a long time, but when she is finally done, Caecilia touches her shoulder.

"I am sorry," she says softly, and the girls hug.

"We better let the old woman know," Macia says in the end, and she strokes her father's face one last time. They find the woman in the main space and she nods as Macia tells her.

"I was thinking it could happen," she says, her face less hard. Maybe she has some feelings after all. "We will deal with him," she says, not unkindly, and she walks towards another room.

"Should we find out what they do?" Macia asks, "After all, we do need to know how the village works, in case my mother is gone for a long time."

Caecilia nods slowly. "Maybe not when it's your father," she suggests, "I'm sure there will be other deaths. I found out from one of the water carriers that they work in different places. They're never sure where they will be."

Macia frowns. "That's a good way to keep people on their toes," she says, "as nobody knows what needs to be done apart from a few. I wonder who organises it all." She sighs, "Maybe we should make a list, to see what we need to find out and what can wait?"

They decide to see Gax. Gax is sitting upright, and as soon as he sees their faces, his eyes fill with tears. "Your father died?" He whispers.

Macia nods, shivering at the word. It was one of the things she found hard to get used to in Mataiox, the open talk about someone no longer alive. "It looked like another stroke," she says, her voice wobbling slightly. "The old lady will do everything, but the next time someone goes, we will need to find out what they do."

Caecilia moves closer to Gax and smiles a little. "It sounds like we might have a boat to get us back. The Levato have a boat, so I hope we can use it." Gax nods, drying his eyes. "We might have to stay a little longer," Caecilia says, her voice calm and slow. Macia busies herself folding a blanket and picking some dust off the floor. She doesn't want Gax to see her face. "Riu rescued us, did Macia tell you about last night?" Caecilia knows she did, but smiles when Gax nods. "Good.

CHAPTER 35

The Levato risked a lot for us; we can't simply walk away right now. Riu has so much to deal with already, and he has been kind to us. We won't have to stay very long, but your leg needs healing more anyway, so hopefully, by the time you're well enough to travel, we can go."

Gax nods, "It won't take me long to get better," he says with a smile," I feel better each day, especially if I know there is a way home. I had been so worried about getting back, getting all of us back," he corrects quickly.

"I still think there is no rush," Macia says, holding her one throbbing finger where the nail as well as a tiny corner of her skin has gone. "Riu asked for our help with the Book, so we need to find a way of helping him. Maybe he can have our Book when we leave, and we can take notes in the next weeks so he can understand the Book with our help."

"Weeks?" Gax's mouth is wide open, his cheeks flushed. The girls both glance at the door and he lowers his voice. "Weeks? I think by next week we'll be able to leave, especially as your father…your father is no longer here," he adds. "There is nothing left for us here. You have seen your mother and your brother, but that's no longer a reason to stay here, and we know about Downstream. I don't think we can do anything about that, either, so we need to get back home. I will need better medical care and better food, and you both have studies lined up. Like you said, in the next few days we can make notes for Riu and he can have the Book as we go. Once we're back, I can speak to the Mission School about sending a team out here."

Macia's head is hurting, and she pushes her fingertips against her temples. She unclenches her jaws to answer Gax, but Caecilia puts a calming hand on her arm. "Again, this is not the time to make decisions," she says softly. "We will need to find out how the village is run, we need to speak with Riu to see what he needs and there is the judgment Riu has been talking about. There are still a lot of things to look into, but Gax is right, it might only take a few days. And to send a specially trained team from the Mission School might be better as well. They can send someone who has a lot of medical skills, as well as teaching staff. That would be much better than the three of us muddling along."

She tugs at Macia's sleeve, "We better go, as it's nearly time for dinner. We need to make that list with things to sort out. Gax will need some rest, and maybe you could start working on what kinds of notes we could draw up for Riu?" She asks Gax with a smile and nudges Macia closer to the door at the same time.

Gax nods, calmer. "Yes, I'll think about that. Do you know what portion they have? I wonder how it got here." His mind drifts back to Elabi, and he shudders. "I can't remember what I gave out," he sighs, "but it would help if we knew what they had exactly."

"It sounded like one of the Gospels," Caecilia says, "as they knew about Jesus' life and teachings. It sounded like it was quite complete, but I will see if we can find out more." One last bright smile and Caecilia has finally gotten Macia out of the room.

In the corridor, her smile disappears. "What were you thinking?" She hisses, her face flushed. "We know it can take a while; it will take longer than we think, I'm sure, looking at the rest of this trip. But Gax is getting really upset by it all, and he is helpless, stuck in his bed. He must stay calm, so he can heal quicker. We all want to get back as soon as possible, so why make it sound like we're here as long as possible?"

Macia glares back, "Who says I'm keen to return? I don't like to leave Riu with a mess, it's not fair on him. He has landed in this, and he is eager to follow Jesus along with the rest of the Levato. What is more important than that? What if that had been the main reason for us getting here in the first place?"

Chapter 36

The girls walk back in silence, and the meal is eaten quietly. "My eyes are falling shut by themselves," Caecilia sighs after they return from the washing up. "I could sleep for a week."

The girls sit around the table, notebooks open. "Should we start making notes for Riu?" Macia wonders as she looks at the Book. "We could see what they ought to read next, maybe, and make notes? Or should we wait for Riu, and show him the Book first? Maybe he knows what his people need or want?"

Caecilia nods and yawns, "Maybe we should just read something, and go to bed early? I have let the ferrets out already, so they can have a good night's hunting."

Macia agrees, and lighting the little lamp, she sits down again. "We'll carry on from where we got to last time," she says and carefully turns the pages in the Book. "These pages are feeling a little damp, just like Riu was saying about his Book," she struggles to separate two pages, and just as she manages to open them up to the right place, there is a noise.

The girls sit upright to listen, mouths open with concentration. "There," whispers Caecilia and the noise is repeated, sounding far away. A scream? Followed by shouting, more screams, roars, yelling... The girls edge towards the door, and Macia hesitates, hand on the handle.

"Should we lock the door, open it, hide?" Caecilia shakes her head, she has no idea. In the end, Macia opens the door a little. The screams have mostly stopped, and one roar breaks off midway. The girls look at each other, faces pale, and Macia's hand on the door handle is wet and shaking. Just as she is about to shut the door, she can hear running footsteps coming their way, groans and soft wailing cries. The dark shape is coming their way and just as Macia is about to slam the door shut and lock it, she recognises the running, limping figure. Halit.

"Help," the boy sobs, "Somebody, help, where are you?" He is sobbing and stumbling, and Macia calls out softly, not wanting to invite any pursuers at the same time.

"Halit, quick, this way!"

He looks up and tries to limp faster. Macia pulls him in, then snatches her hand back. Halit is wet and sticky, his face covered in blood, clothes ripped. "Halit! What happened? Are you badly hurt? Where is Mother?"

The boy shakes his head and sobs, cradling his arm in his other hand. The girls help him to a chair and Caecilia looks around the hut. They have some water left, but not much. "Halit will need a lot of water to clean up, but is it safe to go and get water?" She looks at Macia, and the girl bites her lip.

"Maybe I will quickly get some from the washing-up hut," Macia says, "I will take a bowl with me." She grabs a deep dish and opens the door, peeks out and listens for any noises, but the jungle is back to its normal nocturnal noises. She slips out, and staying in the shadows, dashes to the washing-up hut, praying the water is still hot. It is, and the bowl is quickly filled. As she is about to leave, she spots one of the large buckets the water carriers use, and after another quick look and listen, Macia fills that up as well.

She rushes back, slopping water, and after a glance around, slips through the door. Halit is still sobbing, and Caecilia has found some rags to clean him up with. She breathes out a long breath as Macia

CHAPTER 36

walks in. "So glad you're back," she says, "and with lots of water." She smiles, but her lips tremble.

Macia kneels before Halit. "I need to clean you up, Halit," she says softly, but as Halit carries on crying she stands up, and speaks a little louder, "Halit! We need to clean you up and see where you are hurt. I will clean your face first, then we'll do the rest."

She looks at Caecilia, "Maybe you could get him some clean clothes from his room? This top needs to go, and so do his trousers." Caecilia nods and quickly leaves the room. Macia starts to clean Halit's face. The smell makes her gag, but she tries taking shallow breaths through her mouth, looking at Halit's eyes, rather than the dark streaks on his face. One of his eyes is nearly swollen shut, and turning a purple shade already. She cleans that eye carefully, and Halit whimpers.

By the time Caecilia returns with clean clothes, Halit's face is clean enough. Next is his arm, and he reluctantly withdraws his other hand enough for the girls to have a look. Caecilia leans over and nods. "It's a large cut," she says, "and might need sewing up. But we could try to bandage it tightly instead? It might be less risky, I suppose, as the needles would have to be sterile." Macia looks at the ceiling, willing her stomach to settle down and Halit moans and cries. Caecilia sighs at him, and gently nudges Macia out of the way. "How about you check outside," she says softly, "and I will clean the boy."

Macia chuckles at that and nods, relieved to get away from the smell and the tears. All is quiet outside. Not one of the other villagers can be seen. Did they not hear anything? Or does this happen more often and they have gotten used to it? Or are they too scared to look out? Whatever it is, Macia is grateful for the quietness, and after a last look, closes the door again, locking it this time.

Halit has calmed down a little, and Caecilia has finished his arm as Macia walks over. "Does it look alright?" She whispers, and Halit stares at Caecilia as well.

Caecilia nods, "He has a gash on his arm, but apart from the black eye, I think he is alright. There is a lot of blood on him though, not sure where from."

Halit scrunches up his face and starts to shake as well as cry. "It was awful. They suddenly came in, and they went straight for…for the leaders, and then the rest of us. The guards tried to protect us, but by then it was too late. I got hurt but managed to…to stop the boy fighting me, and I ran away. I hurt my leg when I fell over something, but I just kept running. I thought the village would be safer and I was going to hide in the hut till the morning, then go back and help." He sticks his chin out, tears gone. "I was! I was going to go back and help," he says and his face flushes red.

The girls look at each other. "It must be the Elutera," says Caecilia, and Halit nods.

"They're a danger to everyone, but it's hard to stop them. They suddenly appear and attack, and then they hide again for ages. Nobody knows where their camp is, and maybe they don't have a camp. We don't know who they are either. I don't know why they attacked us, especially the older ones." He starts crying again. "I heard mother, then it stopped," he sobs, "I'm sure they killed her. But why? And what am I going to do?"

Macia sits down, her legs shaking. Will she have lost her mother today as well? Tears fill her eyes, and Caecilia touches her arm. "Don't give up hope yet," she whispers. Just then, there is a knock on the wall near their room. They all freeze, and the knocking is repeated.

"Siate!"

Macia dashes to the door, her heart racing. She had forgotten the girl was going to come. Would Siate bring more bad news? Could she handle more trouble?

She peeks through the door, and soon, Siate appears. The girl smiles, but it doesn't make it to her eyes or the rest of her face.

CHAPTER 36

"My brother is here," Macia whispers, as soon as Siate is close enough to hear. "He was hurt, but he's alright. We have cleaned him up." She swallows and slows herself down. "He said they were attacked. It is bad? He says, my mother..." Her voice trembles, and Macia stops.

Siate shuts the door and looks at the others, taking in the water bowls and messy clothes lying on the floor. She nods. "It was bad," she says softly and inclines her head towards Macia. "I am really sorry. The guards tried, but couldn't stop the first part of the attack. In the end, they overcame the attackers, and not all the group was killed. Like your brother, some managed to get to safety, and a few overpowered their attackers. One attacker managed to survive, so she is locked up. We will deal with her another time. She is badly injured, but will live, I think. Hopefully, she will tell us more about the group. There were a lot of them, and I wouldn't be surprised if that was all of the Elutera. The guards were there, and some of our people had arrived to change shifts, so we had double guards. There were a few young people from the Scitabi who put up a good fight, so it wasn't the disaster they were hoping it to be."

She takes a deep breath. "It will change some of the plans," she says, looking at Macia. "The woman is no longer here, so someone has to lead the village. The village needs to be told the woman is no longer here. Felix needs to be told his woman is no longer here, and things might change, as we don't think the Elutera are here either. There will be more safety, more peace, more time to learn other things than fighting." She smiles at this, her face lighting up. She looks at the table and gasps.

"The Book? Is that the Book, all of the Book? And you will read it to us and tell us? That is good, a good thing to come out of all this dreadful evil. We will be free to read, free to speak and live with Jesus' Life in us." Her face is glowing, and the smile only dims a little as she sees Halit scowling. "It is no good scowling," she says, looking at the boy. "You are very fortunate to be alive. You still have breath in you, but you will need the breath of Life as well. Things will change, especially for you. Be glad you are alive and that you have your sister to help you," she says, nodding at Macia. Halit scowls even more and shrugs, and then his eyes fill with tears again.

Siate looks around. "Maybe stay here tonight," she decides. "The boy will need sleep, and you will be tired as well. Your father?" Macia shakes her head and looks away. Both parents, gone, just like that. How is she going to bear it?

"I am sorry," Siate says and touches Macia's shoulder. Macia nods but doesn't turn round. "We will come in the morning," Siate says, "in the morning Riu, and some of us, will come. We will need to work together, as that's the only way for all of us to have a good life in the jungle."

Macia turns round, wiping her eyes. "Yes," she admits, "it's the only way forward. Everyone has been doing things in little groups, with too many secrets and too much control in the wrong hands." She looks at Halit, "Like changing jobs around all the time or going through the jungle at night. Someone will need to tell Felix as well. Is there a need to hurry the message to him?"

Siate thinks about this. "I don't know," she says in the end, "I will ask Riu. I don't think it matters before the next boat, but he will need to know about his woman. And maybe we can work with him if he is willing to spare people's lives. We don't know him. He is a greedy man, but I don't think he is evil. He seems happy to let people live, so maybe he can be bought, I don't know. We will decide on him tomorrow."

Halit sneers. "Why would somebody walk for days just to tell Felix? Why not end it all, keep the village like this, and simply live here? We don't need Felix or more people."

Macia frowns at him, and says, "You realise Felix lives very close by? It's not days of walking. That was a lie, to stop you and others from

CHAPTER 36

going towards Downstream."

Halit flushes and his non-injured hand makes a fist. "I know exactly where it is, and it will take three days at least to get there." Flecks of spittle come off his lips and Macia takes a step back, pulling a face to show him her feelings.

"They lied to you," she says matter of fact, "We will show you when we have time. Many things might not be what you thought. As it is, we all need sleep. Siate is right, we need rest. Father died this afternoon, and mother now as well," her voice shakes, "and we need to deal with a lot tomorrow. Thank you," she says to Siate, "we will wait for you tomorrow. We'll probably be at the medical hut, as Gax is still there and those people seem to know a lot of what goes on. When you arrive, we can find out everything we need to know. We will keep the boy with us," she says, with a glare at Halit, who mirrors her anger. "The old woman at the clinic was fine today, so hopefully, tomorrow will go well. We can see who in the village can be included in the plans."

Siate wishes them good night and is soon gone. Macia locks the door and indicates with her head for Halit to go to bed. "Try to sleep, your arm needs healing," she says, trying not to frown. "Tomorrow, they can have a look at it in the clinic, if you need to. There will be changes, but they'll make things better, I promise," she says, softer, seeing the tears in the boy's eyes.

He shrugs, "I know mother wasn't good to you and there were problems," he says, "but she was my mother and she did everything to look after me. And now she is gone, and I don't know what to do without her. Why would I stay in the village or even in the jungle? Why make life hard, without a reason to be here?"

Macia touches his good arm. "It's hard. We will talk tomorrow, and we will tell you all we know and you can be part of making decisions, I promise. Maybe there is still a job that you're needed for. Anyway, there aren't many other options. There's Mataiox, where we're going back to, and there's Elabi, although you wouldn't get to live very long, I think." His head comes up with a snap, and she giggles, "Stop being difficult, it's too late. Go to bed and get some sleep. Tomorrow you'll find out more, now rest."

The girls clean up the mess left behind by Halit. "I'll take the water back in the morning," Macia whispers. "I don't fancy walking through the village in the dark." She checks on the little door they made in the wall of the hut and is thrilled to see the ferrets. "So glad you've come back," she whispers as she buries her nose in their fur. She strokes their long backs, giving a gentle scratch just behind their little round ears, before putting them in their basket.

Her pillow is wet that night, but Macia manages to sleep a little. She keeps waking up, thinking of the attacks, her sister and Ignava, Brutus' wife, before drifting off to sleep again, fresh tears rolling off her cheeks.

Chapter 37

Breakfast over, the three hurry towards the medical hut. Halit stays with the girls, and with his one eye shut, his face bruised and his arm wrapped up, he looks a state, as his sister points out. "You better stay with us. First, we need to see Gax, our friend," she says to him and he nods.

The old woman can be heard but not seen, so all three walk into Gax's room. He smiles but the smile slips when Macia tells him what happened the night before. "I am so sorry," he says, looking at Macia and briefly at Halit, "I really am. She might not have been what you expected or wanted, but still, she was your mother. How dreadful," he says, and his voice shakes. Looking at Halit, he says, "I'm grateful you're alive. Hopefully, your cuts and bruises will heal soon, even if other things will take longer to heal. What will happen?" he asks the girls.

"Riu and some of the others are coming to the village in a while," Caecilia says. "We will need to discuss and make plans, as there will be changes in the jungle. The Elutera seem to have all been killed last night, except for one girl."

"They have someone staying with their belongings," Halit says, "and I don't know how many. Usually, only a few, and this was a large raid, so maybe one or two. They're usually the ones who are weak or injured." Macia thinks of the young boy who was killed when the group attacked the elders and nods.

"Maybe everyone can now live in one village," Caecilia says, "it would make it easier to share resources. Those booths they use at the Levato can be made anywhere, so young people could sleep in them, dotted around the village. The larger huts in the village can be used for other things, and there will be more people free to help with the tasks. Will they still save people from Downstream?"

Halit shrugged. "They might. My mother was determined to save people, but sometimes it made no sense in who she brought to the village."

"It was to do with money," Macia says softly, and when she sees Halit's face, she explains, "She has…had a nice house with Felix. They used people's money to buy things for the house. Some things might have been bought for the village," she adds, "as there are large buckets and other things you wouldn't be able to make or buy from Colchuyni. She would promise life to people with money, and rescue them from Requipacem. She rescued children that looked strong and who would be useful."

She struggles to keep her voice even, as she can feel anger and bitterness inside, where it has to stay for now. She has to remember that her mother did save people's lives, even though others weren't rescued.

Halit looks sad. "I didn't know," he says, and he doesn't look as tall as he did earlier. "Maybe we can help others, as it's a good thing to let people live who want to live longer, right?" Macia nods and smiles at her little brother.

Caecilia goes out of the room, as she can hear a noise. It's Riu, with Siate and some of the other Levato she recognises from the other night. "We're this way," she says after greeting them. "We're in Gax's room. Do you think we could do the meeting in there? That way, Gax gets to be involved as well. Halit is with us," she adds, "and he has just

CHAPTER 37

found out about his mother and all the money she and Felix spent." She sighs, "Anyway, welcome to the village." She watches them all piling into Gax's room and looks down the corridor. When will they get back to Mataiox? Like Gax, she'd love to go yesterday, but how much longer will they need to wait?

"I am so sorry," Riu says, touching Macia's arms. "We did what we could, but the attack was such a surprise. Your mother, the old man and a few others were killed before anyone realised where the attack came from. The guards rallied, the relief guards who were on their way raced in, and some of the Scitabi fought well. They captured one girl from the Elutera. She was hurt badly, very badly and she might not live, we don't know. We need to ask her questions. Maybe she can tell us more about the Elutera. But four Scitabi lived, and Halit," he adds, and inclines his head towards Halit who lowers his head.

Siate leans forward a little. "You have the Book," she says, "the whole book. We need to rebuild everything. The village, the Scitabi, Downstream…and we need the Book and the Breath of Life to do so. We need help, as we only know a tiny part of the Book. The Book will guide us, won't it?" She looks around, and they all nod, except for Halit, who glares at his sandals.

Gax gives a little cough, "I would like to go home, to my parents, and well, I have things I need to see to at home," he ends, his face flushed. "I will need more medical care," he says as the others don't react straight away, "but the Book can stay, that's not a problem. Also, it will be a few days at least before I can travel."

Macia digs her fingernails into the palms of her hands, and slows her voice down, "Has anyone seen Felix' house? We will need to tell him my mother has gone," she adds, softly.

"I have never seen the house, but I'd like to," Riu says, "it sounds very special." Siate nods and a few others raise their hands to show they'd like to see the house as well.

"We will need to find a way to combine the village, the Scitabi and Levato, as well as the few people from the Elutera," Riu says. "It might not be easy, as they're all different, used to doing things their way. What do you think about the Scitabi, Halit? The old man is gone, so who will be in charge?"

Halit swallows. "Nobody, I think. It was just the old man, telling everyone what to do. They have their food hut, so I'm sure that is still carrying on. They might have stopped everything. I can go and see what needs doing?" For the first time, the scowl has left his face, making him look younger. Macia feels her shoulders relaxing a little.

"That would be great," Riu says, "check what they need, tell them a little of what happened, and that we're all one village, one people. We need each other. We can't be like this anymore. We will have to think about how we do it. Maybe you have an idea?" He looks at the boy with a slight smile.

Halit shrugs. "The Scitabi village is not very big; the huts are not very good. There aren't many of us. The food is not like here either. There is nothing to do." He traces patterns with his sandal, "We need something to do. I like the book they have, the book with the pictures," and he indicates the girls. "We have no knowledge," he adds, "and many of the old people laugh at us. They're always telling us what we should do. There are lots of us, so we could build better huts, and make nice things. We have time, we have materials, there is no need to live like this," and he gestures over his shoulder towards the door.

"That is a good point," Riu says, and he grins at Halit. "If we're going to be staying here, in the jungle, we should make ourselves comfortable. Colchuyni has some lovely, comfortable houses, we should have that here as well. I don't think Felix or anyone else is coming to look for us, there are no more Elutera."

"What about the head elder?," Caecilia breaks in and Riu shrugs.

"I don't think he will come this way again. When we see Felix, maybe

CHAPTER 37

he can send word to the Head Elder to stay out of the jungle." He thinks for a moment. "Maybe we can have better links with Colchuyni. The evil has gone, it's all exposed and there is no longer a reason to live in fear of each other." He smiles at the others, "And they need the Book, and the Breath of Life from God as well."

Gax has his eyes closed, and Caecilia leans closer, "Are you alright?" she whispers, "Are you getting too tired?"

He opens his eyes and tries to blink the tears away. "I just want to go home," he breathes, "It's far too much for us to handle, we're tired and we need a lot more resources. This is a massive undertaking." Caecilia nods. Just hearing Riu talk about the different plans makes her feel exhausted.

Macia says, "We need a list of priorities, so we know what to do first, what is most important, and then what we like to do, as there are so many options! I think we need to see Felix first, or second, as the village should be sorted out first. But it could be different people doing things at the same time," she says. "We need a large board of some kind, so we can write down the list."

"Yes, the village here first," Riu says and they all agree it will have to be Riu, Siate, Macia and Caecilia sorting it out. "Halit can sort out the Scitabi," Riu continues, "and then some of us will go to Felix and see what we can do that end."

He takes a breath to continue, but Macia raises her hand. "Let's do those two things," she grins, "otherwise, we'll be making the list again. Is there time to get to the Downstream clinic after we have met people in the village?" Riu nods, so Macia says, "Let's meet with people here first. Who will go with Halit to the Scitabi?" Three volunteers step forward and Macia grins at her little brother. "Do you know what you need to say and do?" she checks, and he nods.

"I will tell them what they need to know, set things up, and maybe start looking around the Scitabi village to see what we will need," he says, and he looks at the three young people coming with him. They agree, and one of them points out that comfy huts are important as well as food. "And we need to find a way to be closer to this village," Halit adds.

"Maybe the booths we have in our camp could work," one of the helpers suggests, "They're easy to make but comfortable. We could use the old huts for storage and working in, or something like that."

Macia asks, "Is it just the old woman we need to speak to, or are there others in charge of things?"

Halit nods, "There is the woman in charge of cooking and a few older people who do the hut building and repairing. The woman builder is not very easy, but the other two builders are fine. There is the man in charge of finding food and wood as well. But that's it, I think."

They decide to let Gax rest and meet with the others in Amara's hut. Riu, Siate and the other helpers go to the hut, whilst Caecilia and Macia go around the village telling those in charge to come to the hut for a meeting. The old woman from the medical hut snorts and scowls, but shuffles off towards the exit. Like Halit predicted, the woman doing the building work isn't happy with the interruption. "I was told to sort out this hut. How will I sort it out if I'm being sent all over the village? We haven't got endless hours in a day, and there is only so much we can do at our ages."

Macia inclines her head in understanding. "It is not helpful, I agree, but it's necessary. We will try to keep the meeting as short as we can. It is important for everyone, and especially for those involved with housing everybody." That catches the woman's attention and she grunts as she puts down the tool she had been holding. "That's a nice hammer," Macia says, "not too heavy, but well-built."

The woman looks at her, eyes narrowed. "We need good tools. Without the right tools, we were struggling to do the work. Tools

CHAPTER 37

were lying around Downstream, so when your mother rescued the people, she raided the stores as well. That is how we get some foods as well as certain tools and essentials." Macia nods, not sure how true that is, and as she doesn't know how much the others in the village know, she leaves it at that.

When they finally make it to the hut, Riu smiles at the girls, indicating some seats. "Well done," he grins, "nearly everyone is here already. We got the chairs and those benches sorted out, so we could all sit down. We will have a long day, so we will need to rest when possible."

Macia looks at the people sat around her, then smiles at Riu and he inclines his head. She gives a small nod, and leans forward a little. "My name is Macia," she says, "and I'm Amara's daughter. As you know, my mother rescued many people. There were some wrong choices. You know that, I don't have to go through all of the bad decisions she made. She and my brother were being held by the Levato. Last night, the holding camp was attacked. My mother, the old man from the Scitabi and several others were killed. A few youngsters, including my brother, survived. There will have to be changes. My mother has gone, so have the leaders of the Scitabi and most of the Elutera."

The builder woman looks at Macia and clamps her lips together, then says. "Amara is gone, and so are the Elutera. Like you say, there was good and bad. We're alive, which feels good. That we got here, and how, and all those who didn't, maybe it was bad. It's in the past though, so no need to keep digging up the dirt." She nods a few times, to emphasise her point or to stop anyone from disagreeing, Macia isn't sure.

The other villagers mumble, rubbing their sandals into the hard dirt floor, and glance at each other. The woman from the clinic scowls, her arms crossed, and Macia holds her breath, wondering who will speak next. One of the other builders sniffs and shrugs his shoulder, breaking the tension.

"Thank you," Macia says, with a slight smile, seizing the small window of opportunity offered, as none of the others say anything, "so yes, things will change. You can help with this. We want to combine the villages, so the Scitabi can help out, they will need to learn, like in school and they can build better and more comfortable huts. We will be here for a long time, the villagers, I mean," she stutters, as she can feel Caecilia jerking sideways at her words. "You have come here to live, so why not live in more comfort? Riu will start helping the Scitabi to make better furniture, better huts, that kind of thing." The old people nod, beginning to look pleased, so she continues, "We might need your help with passing on knowledge and supporting the young people. We want the younger children to enjoy being young as well."

There are a few frowns, but Macia is determined. "We want them to laugh and play, to learn to help each other and be kind."

"Kind," one of the old builders snorts, "That's a word I haven't heard in a long time. My gram used to say it to us, until, well, until they took her away. My father never let us use the word again. See what comes from being kind, he would warn us, every time we forgot and slipped up."

Chapter 38

"From now on, kindness will be a common word," Macia states, "along with peace, joy, and gentleness."

Riu sits up straighter. "Is it from the Book?" he asks, his eyes shining.

"It's in one of the letters, near the end of the Book," Macia smiles, "it talks about…" She hesitates. How do you explain the Spirit of God working in a person? There is so much they need to share with Riu and the others. She can feel her heartbeat speeding up, as she tries to think how to even start. "It's living out having the Breath of Life in you," she says and looks at Caecilia, who nods. If only Gax could be here, he would be much better at explaining it all.

Riu looks pleased as he rolls his shoulders and looks around the group. "Yes, we will need to change the way we behave towards each other, and how we work together," he says. "The children need to be allowed to play and enjoy their days, younger people need to be kept busy," he grins, and the older people chuckle, "and older people should be allowed to slow down and share their knowledge and skills."

The old woman sniffs, and Riu smiles at her. "Who will do the work?" she demands, and before Riu can answer, she continues, "I know what to do, but who is there to help? I would need a lot of helpers, and they would need training."

Riu nods again, "Yes, that is where the Scitabi come in," he explains.

"There are lots of young people in the Levato as well. They can be trained, and we can have different roles within the clinic. The first round of training will be harder, but after that, the young people can pass on their knowledge. We also need to learn from the Book," he says, looking at the girls. It goes very quiet in the hut, and Macia can hear voices in the village in the sudden silence.

"The Book," one of the builders says, his voice cautious. "The Book, as in the faith book? The one that is banned and gets you sent beyond the Hills quicker than you can say Lighthouse?"

Caecilia smiles a little at the mention of Elabi Lighthouse, but her smile slips away. Her father used to man the lighthouse, but who will be doing that now? "Yes, that Book," she says, pushing the thought of her parents away for now. "The Book is with us, and it's important," she starts, not sure how to best put this to the group.

"We learned a little," Riu says, "I saw the breath of life given to my nephew, bringing him back from the dead, and I knew they followed God. A God who gave life, not just to our bodies, so I was interested. When I came to the Levato, it turned out there was a small portion of the Book, but nobody to read it. I can read a little and we have been given His breath of Life. The girls have the complete Book, and they will help us to follow Jesus and to live through the Breath of Life in us."

The girls nod, wishing again that Gax was here. "Gax will help as well," Macia says. "He will make notes to go with the Book, so when…when nobody is here to teach, the Book can still be read," she ends, not wanting to talk about leaving just yet.

"We need to find out what needs doing and who can do what," Riu says. He looks at the old woman, "How many young people would you like every day and every night? Who is there at night in the clinic?"

The woman looks around and sighs. "In the day it's me and usually three or more others. In the night, it's only one or two. If we have

CHAPTER 38

someone about to…to go, they're usually dealt with before it's dark, and otherwise, we might pop in a few times during the night. I don't sleep very well. Often, I come early in the morning, and have a rest later in the day."

Riu decides they will need more people to keep an eye out at night. "We will have a few young people to care for those that are ill in the night as well," he says, "and plenty of helpers in the daytime. How many would you need in the daytime?"

Caecilia chips in with her knowledge, "Can you have different groups in the day? Some to look after the people, some for cleaning the clinic and some to look at medicine and medical help for people?"

The old woman looks at her, "Like you would get in the clinic in Elabi, you mean?" she asks, and Caecilia nods. The woman sighs, "That would be good. At the moment, we're trying to do it all, but it's too much. Different teams would be great." She thinks for a moment, "We would need about two or three per team, a cleaning team, a caring team and a medical team. That would be nine young people. Plus about two or three at night. Twelve youngsters?" She looks at Riu with a small sneer on her face, but he nods.

"Twelve people is fine. It might be hard at first, but it's a great aim." He looks at the ground, and Caecilia is sure that he's counting people in his head. "We have probably eight people free right now to help you. We will need people to build and cook as well," he looks at the other old people and they nod. "So maybe start with eight, and train those first?"

The old woman nods, looking pleased, and somehow younger. "It will be interesting to see what they're like," she says, sucking her breath in sharply, "I will check them out first, see who will be better at which task, then assign them their roles after a while. Maybe we don't need three cleaners. One or two might do, and they can help with cleaning up after the cooking mess as well," she says, with a sudden grin at the woman in charge of making the village dinners.

Soon, the numbers of young people are allocated, and Caecilia and Macia will take on the young children, to teach them to read. "The young people will need to learn as well, but their lessons can be in between or after their jobs," Riu decides. "We have a few very young people, maybe they can help with the children as well, and some young ones can be taught to look after the babies." He sighs, "How will we remember all this?"

Macia jumps up. "Let's use one of our wipe-out boards," she suggests. She gets the sheet and pen and starts making a list. "Clinic, eight," she points, "cooking hut, three; builders, seven or more, especially at the beginning and four young people for general help, tidying and helping around the village." She pauses. "They might need to be slightly older and know what to do," she writes again, "Babies, three or four, young children, probably two." Then waves the pen across the numbers, "That makes twenty-nine young people. Do we have that many across the villages and Levato?"

Riu thinks for a moment. "Yes, I think so. The Scitabi lost a lot of young people last night," he swallows, "but not all of them had gone into the jungle with the old man. They must have at least another ten people, plus the five that survived. Halit will know what to do around the village," he points at the chart, "so maybe put him in charge of the four people working round the village and wherever there is a need. Then there is the one young girl that we captured. If she is still alive." He hesitates, "Maybe she can come to the clinic?" The girls both nod straight away and the old woman scowls. "We need to care for her," he continues, softer, "she needs the Breath of Life more than any of us."

They all get up to go to their various tasks. "We will start tomorrow," Riu says, "so we can find the right people for each job, and let the young people know they'll be working hard from now on." He chuckles and Macia laughs. She's sure the young ones will enjoy it. Not doing

CHAPTER 38

anything becomes hard after a while.

They wait till the old people have left. "Shall we quickly go Downstream now?" Riu looks at the girls and they nod, but not enthusiastically. "It's better to get it over and done," he says softly. "I don't know what Felix is like, but we will have all afternoon to get there and back, that will be plenty of time. I don't want to stay in the forest once it's dark, as we don't know how many of the Elutera are out there. I don't think they're a threat anymore, but we don't want to get it wrong."

They get some food from the cooking hut and grab a bag with drinking water for on the way. "Do you think there will be a path?" Macia asks, and Riu explains that there is one, used by Amara as well as the people from the boat each month.

Soon after they leave the village, a path veers off towards the right, and the stream is in view once more. Caecilia shudders. "I don't like to see the stream," she says, and Riu smiles kindly.

"I understand," he says, "but tell yourself it's just water, and God's breath can stop the water flow if He wants to."

Caecilia looks surprised, "Yes. Yes, I'm sure you're right," she says, "I know you're right," she corrects herself, "but it's easy to forget when it's dark and there are so many noises, and the stream looks so…evil."

"That's when remembering is most important," Riu says softly, "when all the evil is there, and death seems to have won. Then you tell yourself again about the Breath of Life and how everything changes where the Life is."

They walk in silence for a while, and suddenly, the path is wider and more accessible, and the vegetation is thinner. Light shines through, and the jungle feels hotter, but soon, Macia can feel a slight breeze as well. Shallow steps appear, made of rough planks, and as they round a corner, the bay opens out before them. Macia gasps. "Downstream," she whispers, and her eyes sting. "Gax should have seen this," she whispers and is surprised when Riu touches her hand.

"It's nice how you think of him, and make him feel part of all this," he says softly. "In the hospital room, you made sure that he felt part of the meeting and decision-making. He must find it hard, missing out and having so much to overcome. But Jesus will walk with him, won't He?" Macia smiles through her tears and wipes her eyes.

The bay is wide, but calm, with palm trees lining the shore like she has seen in travel brochures in Mataiox. There are flowering bushes near the edges, and the clinic itself is white with red roof tiles. It's a large place, she realises, and when she points it out, Riu nods. "People don't all die as soon as they arrive," he says, pointing out the deck chairs at the side of the building. "Maybe it's one or two people a day, so it can be almost the entire month before the clinic is empty again."

The girls shudder. "Imagine, sitting in the deckchairs each day, waiting your turn," Caecilia whispers. "No wonder so many people want to go with Amara." They look at the peaceful scene below, the soft rippling water, the dark green fronds of the tall palm trees barely moving in the breeze, the bright pink flowers... "The place of death," Caecilia carries on, her voice shaking. "I wonder what people expect when they arrive. A last resting place, where they will be looked after? Or do they know it will be Requipacem sooner or later?"

"They will only know if somebody tells them," Macia is sure of that. "I'm sure most people think it's a last resting home, as you can tell by the cards people send you just before you go. The people are quite hopeful, looking forward to well-deserved rest. I wonder when they tell them, and if they ever tell them."

Slowly, they make their way down to the bay, the white building dipping in and out of sight. Just before the last bend, there is another path, veering off, and Macia looks down the path as far as she can. Between the trees, set back, but with gorgeous views, is another building. It is white as well, with the same red roof tiles, but elegantly

CHAPTER 38

shaped, its large windows looking out over the bay and the soft pink beach. "That must be Felix's house," Riu says softly, and she nods, without taking her eyes off the building. To call it a house is doing it an injustice, as it's the most beautiful building she has ever seen. It isn't very high, but seems to have wings, with red arches, contrasting with the white walls.

"Should we go to the house or the clinic," Caecilia asks, and after a last look at the gorgeous mansion, Macia turns towards the clinic.

"He's more likely to be at the clinic in the afternoon," she sighs, and they carry on downwards. The clinic looks deserted. No old, frail people lounge in the deckchairs, no babies can be heard crying, and no voices are heard. Just the palm trees and gentle waves. "Such a beautiful place for so much sadness," Macia says, and Riu squeezes her hand briefly, before heading for the doors.

The doors look like the entrance of a large, fancy hotel, like the ones the girls have seen in the nice areas in Mataiox. Inviting, luxurious, welcoming you inside for a pleasant stay. Except this place will eat you up once you're inside. Riu pushes the door open and walks up to a registration desk. They stop near the desk, to look around. It's well-decorated, with some beautiful sculptures in the corners, and a large vase with what Macia suspects to be fake flowers. They edge closer to the desk, looking around for any sign of life.

Riu looks left and right, and calls out, "Hello? Felix? Anyone?" He grins at the girls and shrugs, pulling a face, and making them giggle nervously. Macia spots the bell on the counter, and after hesitating for a second – does she really want to meet Felix? – she presses the bell. Echoes can be heard all through the building, and they wait, hearts drumming away in their throats.

Chapter 39

A door closes, and footsteps can be heard. Sandals slapping against the marble floor. The man looks surprised to see the young people near the reception desk, and he hesitates. "Who are you?" He looks at them one by one, his eyes staying on Macia a little longer, a frown appearing. "Who are you?" he repeats and he takes a step forward.

Macia steps towards him, trying to smile. "My name is Macia," she says, her voice not as steady as she hoped, "I am Amara's daughter. Are you Felix?"

Felix simply stares at her, glancing at the others, his eyes narrowed as they return to Macia. "You are Amara's daughter? I know she has a son, but never heard of a daughter."

Macia feels unexpectedly hurt that her mother has never shared with Felix about the family she left behind. "Two daughters, actually, but my sister is still in Elabi. Well, she was, the last time I saw her," she adds with a shiver. "My mother left to go with my little brother, as you probably know," and Felix nods. "We met my brother when we got to the village in the jungle," she explains, "and later, my mother arrived."

Macia looks at Riu. Should she tell Felix what happened? Riu steps forward. "There was an incident between the Scitabi with Amara and Halit. The girls were in danger, so we, the Levato, stepped in and

CHAPTER 39

rescued them. Later, the Elutera attacked the holding place and they killed most people before we could stop them. Amara was one of the first, I'm sad to say."

Felix gasps and wobbles. Macia and Riu jump forward and grabbing his arms, they round the desk and lower him into an opulent-looking desk chair. Felix's hands are shaking and he wrings them together. "You mean Amara has been killed?" He looks at them, his lips trembling. Looking at him from close by, Macia realises he must be her parents' age, or a little older even. He is tanned, and judging by the roots of his hair, the dark auburn colour comes from a bottle.

Macia nods, "I'm afraid so." Felix gives a shuddering sob, his nervous hand wringing making Macia's heart ache. "We have come especially to tell you," she adds, "and there are questions as well, mainly about the future."

Felix doesn't seem to have heard. "Where is her body now?" he asks in the end, looking at Macia.

Macia hesitates and looks at Riu. "We dealt with all the bodies according to protocol," he says, and Felix nods and sighs. "We have decided to combine all groups. The Elutera are mostly killed, apart from one girl, and there might be a few who stayed behind." Felix nods again, and Macia is sure he knows a lot about the different groups in the jungle. "The Scitabi will be merged with the main village," Riu continues, "and all young people are given jobs and responsibilities. They will all learn to read, and the younger children will have schooling as well. The younger children will have time to play with less work."

Felix stops his hand wringing and stares at the young people. "They are big changes," he says slowly, licking his lips. "What about the old people? And what will happen here? The next boat, I mean..." his voice trails off as he is visibly processing the changes. "And without Amara," he adds in a whisper, his eyes filling with tears. He looks away, and composes himself, stiffening his shoulders, and pressing his lips together. "What does Halit think of it all? Does he know…does he know about his mother and this, I mean?"

"The changes will be for the better," Caecilia says, stepping forward a little. As it was Macia's mother and Riu's people involved, she had stayed out of the conversation. "It will be better, so this place will be better for it as well," she says, her voice resolute. "We will look at what happens here and how we can help you. Do you work alone?" She can't imagine Felix doing all the work, including administering Requipacem to desperate people.

Felix shakes his head. "I have three men and two women to help. They came here as children when it turned out their minds weren't… weren't suitable for Elabi. They are good workers though and they wouldn't ever ask questions." He glances around the lobby, "They do most of the work. I'm running the place. Some of the older people like to help in the garden, but most are here to rest."

He sighs. "It will be different without Amara," he says, and his shoulders droop. "I don't know what will happen now to those she would have taken with her to the village." He glances around, his hands sliding over the desk, nervously, lost. He stands up. "Let's go to the lounge so you can sit. I will ask one of the staff to bring us a drink and you can tell me what you want from me."

They follow him along one of the corridors. The marble is shiny and the walls are covered with beautiful art. Macia recognises some of the scenes in the paintings, and she points them out to Caecilia, who smiles. "Nice to see those places," Caecilia whispers.

The lounge is light and the warm colours make it seem permanently sunny. "What a lovely place," Caecilia says, smiling at Felix. He looks at her but doesn't react, so Caecilia pretends to be busy studying another painting, this one including her father's lighthouse. Felix waves at a few seats together and walks over to a telephone on the wall. After

CHAPTER 39

ordering the drinks, he joins them, frowning at Caecilia who isn't in a rush to sit down. She looks at him as she leaves the last painting to sit down. Something has changed about Felix in the last few minutes, she thinks.

"What do you need from me?" Felix asks again, looking at Riu.

Riu chews his lips, not saying anything for a while. Macia shuffles in her seat, wondering if she should start, but Riu takes a deep breath and says, "I don't know yet," he looks at Felix and leans forward a little. "We don't know enough of what happens here and what kind of facilities you have here. You say you have five people based here, working for you. The place looks empty, so what do they do when there is no boat? And how large a part of a month would that be?" He looks at the ground, "We need to know about what happens and how we can work together to save lives. How is the saving of lives determined? Also, we need to speak about talking to those who will face death."

Felix sucks in an audible breath, "We don't usually talk about it in those terms," he says, his lips tight, his eyelids lowered almost shut, making Macia shudder involuntarily.

Riu snorts, "Let's be straight," he says, his tone firm, "We're all adults here, we know why people come Downstream. You are here to end their lives, we just need to know how it's done, at what kind of time scale, I mean, and we need to know what options there are. Amara must have had a chance to see people before taking them off to the village, and there must have been time for preparations as well. Clearly, people don't die on the day of arrival." Riu ignores Felix's narrowed eyes and flushed face. "From now on, one of the changes we want to make is that we will speak to those who will die here. We want to tell them about the Breath of Life and the special Book that tells them of the life that is forever."

Felix gasps in horror. "I have no idea what you are talking about," he says, his voice shrill, "and this is not the conversation we should be having. I can tell people about your villages, and before the week is over, you would have to survive like those Elutera."

Riu grins, "And what about your beautiful home?" His voice is soft, and his face calm and open, "would they sort that out too? Would you be replaced if they heard about the scheme you and Amara had set in place?" He watches Felix for a moment, then continues, "Of course, we don't mind you being here. We do have questions and concerns. We want to hear what you have to say first before we say anything about this place. We will hear you, then you will hear us. We are in this jungle together. We have some of the people that came from you, you will need us as well, as you want to continue your lifestyle, even without Amara."

He sits back and inclines his head to Felix, inviting him to answer. Felix takes a few deep breaths, his hands balled on the armrests of his chair. Slowly, his face returns to its normal tanned hue, and taking another deep breath, Felix says, "I see. Yes, I want to stay here. I don't have anything against people in the jungle. I don't mind many of my clients disappearing into the jungle," he smirks, "there is compensation for that to happen, and if they want to die in the jungle, that is not my concern."

Macia can feel her face warming up, and she leans forward before the man can carry on. "It's not really about your feelings on the changes we were discussing," she fights to keep her voice soft, and pulls the corners of her mouth up, "it's good to hear you don't bear a grudge against the people that leave this place, but at the moment, it's more important that we hear your side of the happenings in this place, the schedule you have and how you handle each new boat load of people."

Felix's face grows dark red again, and he glances over his shoulder at the door, before he hisses, "I can't see how it can matter to you what we do here. Let's keep our communities separate. You tell me how

CHAPTER 39

many people you want each month and for how much, and I will tell you how many will be suitable and who will be able to come with you."

"Was that the arrangement with Amara?" Riu asks, his smile gone.

Felix shakes his head. "No, only for maybe the first few months. Then we decided between ourselves what we wanted each month, and how much we would need. Amara would work out how much the village could handle each month and we would look at the people and arrange it." He glances at the door again, "Some months, we could see it was going to be hard to fulfil our wishes, but most months, we managed just fine. Without Amara, my needs will be limited. We have, had, a beautiful home, and I'm comfortable there. I still have my wages from Elabi. My workers don't need very much and even get some income from the clinic as well as…tips," he smirks and when he sees the young people's faces he explains, "Some people come with some valuables stored away. They won't tell us and they don't want to live in the jungle. When they have gone through Requipacem, the valuables return to Elabi, although some might not make it," he chuckles, "after all, things do go missing in transit, it's a lot to sort out when someone is no longer here."

Caecilia avoids looking at Macia, as she watches the woman coming in with their drinks. Felix hardly acknowledges the woman, so Caecilia helps her to place the drinks on the table. Felix looks at the door, even after the woman quickly leaves the room, shutting the door louder than expected. Caecilia takes her time sitting down, unable to look at Felix as he leans back in his chair, slurping from the tall glass of cool drink.

Riu picks up his drink, stands, and casually wanders around the room, studying a painting, looking out of the windows. He leans against the window frame, then slowly makes his way back to the others. Macia leans forward to get her drink, her eyes on Felix. "Can you tell us your schedule?" Macia asks, her voice flat.

Felix shrugs. "The boat always arrives the same day, at the beginning of the month. For the first week, we allow people to settle in, and only administer Requipacem where necessary. Babies and very young children are usually first, as they need a lot of looking after by the staff." At the mention of staff he looks at his watch, then the door again, and shuffles his feet. "They also make a lot of noise, and it upsets some of the older people to hear them. They will be kept separate if dedicated to the village," he adds. "We usually keep them in our house, where Amara and whoever came with her looks after them. After that week, we know who wants to go to the village, and everything is sorted for them. Amara will leave with them, and we make a list of Requipacem that the workers can follow. Some people aren't ready yet, and occasionally we have someone trying to be difficult. We space it out, so the work isn't too hard for our staff and people often don't realise what is going on till it's their turn. The medication we give is very good," he presses his lips together, "and we are told by Elabi what to do. This is how society works, and everyone benefits from it. Life is simply like this. Those people are unable to contribute to society, and drain all resources, without any hope of improvement."

The door opens quietly, but Felix's head whips around, and a large smile breaks through as he jumps up. Two men enter the room, fists dangling by their sides. They nod at Felix, who has moved to the side. The three young people stand up as well, and Caecilia can feel her heart banging away in her chest. What is going on? Nothing good, that's clear, and all doubts are gone as the men whip out large batons from behind their backs at the same time, making Caecilia gasp in horror. Felix's laugh hardly registers, as she watches the men slowly advance.

Riu touches her elbow, breaking the spell, and he hisses, "To the window, it's open, but don't stand in front of it." They shuffle backwards, Riu in the middle. When they get to the window, he

CHAPTER 39

makes the girls stand just to the side of the window. Macia glances through the window. She realises that Riu must have had a plan, as the window is definitely ajar. That is why he went to look out of the window, she realises, and looking back at the slowly advancing men with their batons, she can feel the numb fear beginning to be replaced by a relieved expectation.

The men's blank faces begin to grow smiles, and Felix is rubbing his hands, still laughing. "Too much trouble," he cackles, "too many questions. We don't like trouble and we don't like questions. They're the top of our list; they always make the top of our list. First to cause trouble, first to go," his voice is shrill, and he bounces on the balls of his feet, his sandals making a loud flapping noise against the marble floor. Despite the threat, Caecilia finds this noise more irritating than anything else, and she can feel herself moving a little towards Felix, wanting to stop him, to silence him, and to stop his feet from creating the noise.

Before she is even outside Riu's reach, everything changes. The men with their twisted grins find themselves staring open-mouthed. Felix's maniacal chuckle turns into furious shrieks as one young person after another dash through the now wide-open window. Siate is the first to enter, flashing the girls a quick grin, before concentrating on the two men with their batons. The room fills with noise and confusion, but all is quiet within a minute, as batons hit the ground, followed by a screaming Felix. The two workers find their hands tied behind their backs before they understand who they are up against.

Riu sighs, a large smile on his face as he turns to Siate. "Great timing, and I'm glad you found us. I'm relieved they took that long, as I worried Felix might pull something on us before you were here."

He turns to Macia, "I didn't want to say they were following us, just in case you girls looked for them, and I didn't know what Felix was going to be like, so I didn't want to sound unkind." He shrugs, "I hope you will forgive me?"

Macia smiles and nods, "Good thinking," she chuckles, "I must admit, I would have been looking at the window every time Felix looked at that door. I'm glad he didn't call them as soon as he saw us at the reception desk!"

"I should have," Felix screams, his face red and his eyes bulging, "I should have seen you were trouble, but I was curious. My feelings were given a place, and Amara had warned me it would happen one day. She said my feelings would be my downfall. She was right, she always was and now she is gone," and suddenly he is sobbing, rocking himself with his hands bound behind his back.

Chapter 40

The two workers are taken away to another room, and soon they are left with Felix. "You have told us your views and your schedule," Riu says, his face hard. "You have told us the kind of person you are, and that is all we needed to know. We don't have a problem with you being here and doing your work, but things will have to change."

He walks around and looks at the girls. "I can't agree with Requipacem," he says softly. "I believe in the Breath of Life, and how can we take that breath away? I know it happens," he adds quickly, "like we saw those Elutera die as they attacked us, but to take a person's breath away just because they're not useful to you... I can't agree."

He turns back to Felix, "It will have to stop. People can come here off the boat, nothing will change that way. Do the people working the boats ever come here?"

Felix has stopped crying, and he nods. "The captain comes to reception to sign the acceptance papers, and take back the death papers as well as the box with valuables for Elabi."

Riu nods slowly. "Without Requipacem, how many people would still be alive when the captain returns?"

Felix shrugs, "Some, I think, although most wouldn't be. It won't make much difference in a way, as the ones taken to the village were always on the Requipacem list as well. It was what they paid for."

Riu looks at the girls and grins. "I have a plan," he says. "We take a few people to the village, especially the babies and children. It is better for them in the village anyway. The old people stay here, and are looked after here," he glances at Felix, "There is a clinic?" Felix nods and Riu continues, "We leave the others here, to die in their own time, when God takes the breath of life away from them. Every month, we will give the captain the right papers and the right valuables."

He looks at Felix, who shrugs. "It won't make much difference to us. Most of the time, the last person was given Requipacem just before the new boat arrived. We tried to do it quicker and have more free time, but the workers don't like too much free time. They complain when there isn't any work to do, so it's better to keep them busy." He stares at his sandals, "Why would you keep those people alive? They are hard work, many complain the whole time they're here and they can be dirty when they're weak and unwell."

Riu smiles at him. "We will explain that soon, but today, we need to get the practical things sorted out. The captain or any other workers of the boat must never see the people around when they land. Is it possible to build another clinic further away, or out of view, so people can be hidden?"

Felix nods, "We all like building," he admits, "it's why our, my, house is so nice and this place is big. We can build living places further away, where people can live by themselves, like the huts in the village Amara talked about. Some might live for a long time and not need too much care. We might need more workers, as some need a lot of care soon after arriving."

Riu looks at the girls, "We might have to get more young people trained," he grins, "and send them down here to help."

Once the details have been worked out, at least for the moment, Felix shows the young people around the place. It's spacious and light, and beautifully decorated. A few rooms are quite large, and Macia

CHAPTER 40

turns to Riu. "Should we make the little ones go here every day, and do their lessons, where it's clean and light?"

Riu thinks about it, and he smiles, "It would save us building another hut, as our space is limited and so are our workers. Maybe it would be better for them, and it's good to have a walk as well."

He looks at Felix, who shrugs. "We don't mind, as long as there is no extra work for my staff, and as long as it isn't the day the boat arrives." The others can easily agree to that, and Caecilia starts looking at the building with different eyes, seeing how the beautiful rooms can complement the village.

"Maybe we could even have a Meeting House, or Room," she says softly, and Riu raises an eyebrow. "It's where we come together one day a week to read the Book, hear the Book explained and expounded and we worship God together," she says and his face lights up.

"That would be a wonderful thing," he thinks for a moment, "it might not have too many older people for a while, but my people would be interested to learn more." Macia can feel her heart beating faster as she can see the village transformed, and the entire feel of Downstream changed. "Those who have come to die will instead be reached with the Breath of Life," Riu continues in a whisper, his eyes glistening with tears.

"Won't people be angry?" Caecilia bites her lip, but Riu shrugs.

"Nobody will make them come to the meeting, and they won't be forced to read the Book," he says. He looks at Felix, "There is no way they can contact Elabi and complain? I wouldn't want to see you out of your job."

Felix shakes his head, too fast? "No, we will make sure they can't do anything to put this place at risk," he says, and he glances over his shoulder. "My workers might not like it, but as I said before, they don't ask questions. I don't want to change what I have, as it's a good life for me, even though Amara is no longer here." He looks away, and Macia feels her heart stir when she sees the tears in his eyes. He clearly loved her mother. The image of Brutus' twisted, angry face in the hospital makes her shudder. Did he ever love her mother? Maybe before she left with Halit he might have done.

They leave the clinic and find Siate outside, watching the peaceful setting. "It's pretty here," she smiles, "it's a shame it is such a sad place." They agree that some of the Levato will hang around, without Felix or the workers knowing. They don't trust Felix, and anything might happen in the next few days. "We can stay around in small groups," Siate agrees, "and once things are set up in the village, we can change the setup."

The village has changed by the time they get back. There are more young people for starters, and work has started on new huts. The outside wall of the village has been extended to make space, and Macia is glad to see Halit smiling. "We have been working on our housing first," he explains. "That way, we will be in the village, so we can start our different jobs. We had a meeting," Macia is sure he has grown taller in the last few hours, "and we have decided on who will have which jobs. At least for now," he adds quickly, "as some might want to change once they have tried the job they chose."

Riu grins and touches Halit's shoulder. "Great job," he says, "and it is good to see the village more lively. We'll be busy for the next few weeks, I think, getting used to all of it, as well as the new people arriving and new clinic setup." He quickly explains to Halit what happened in the afternoon.

Halit frowns when he hears about Felix. "I don't think I will trust him," he says, glaring at his sandals, "after all he has done, and the lies he and my mother used. I can't believe she did that," he says slowly, his face warming up. "And I believed her, so now I don't know what else I shouldn't have believed."

"It will become clearer over time," Caecilia says, and Halit shrugs.

CHAPTER 40

"Sometimes truth is hard to see, but time spaces things out, so it can be separated," Caecilia explains, and Halit grunts.

The girls decide to visit Gax after dinner, to fill him in. "I'm glad you came," he says, his voice quiet, "the young lad that helped me today was very quiet, and I didn't know what to talk about."

Macia and Caecilia tell him about Downstream and Felix. They explain the new scheme and how the clinic will be used as a school as well as a Meeting House, their faces flushed and eyes shining. "What will you do with the older people?" he asks, "they might not want to attend, and will they make things difficult? What if they want Requipacem? What will Felix do then? And Riu won't be able to stop him." His hands slide across the blanket, side to side, and wringing the cloth between shaking fingers, he says, "Who will lead the Meeting? We need to get back as soon as we can so the Mission School can send people to help. We can't do it all. I don't even know when Resurrection Day is, I have lost count of the days, and what will we say to the people?" His voice rises with each sentence, and a lone tear hangs off his nose, making Macia want to wipe him.

Caecilia takes his shaking hand, "We have to trust God," she says softly, "just keep asking God to do things His way, and like Riu says, ask for His Breath of life to come and fill us."

Gax frowns, "It's hardly ever that easy," he says, "we still have to serve and do all that needs doing. The Mission School takes a long time to train people, and even then, it's hard. Riu has had no training, hasn't even had the whole Book and hasn't had much education. They will need a lot more help, and how are we getting them that help with me stuck in this room?"

Caecilia's smile stays in place and she touches his hand again. "We will get there, God will help Riu and us, and the right people will be sent." She glances at Macia who smooths out her frown as fast as possible, and Caecilia says, "We read that chapter the other day in the

Book, about being written on the palm of God's hand. Riu is, and we are, and God won't erase any of us; He always thinks of us."

Macia looks away, feeling her eyes burning. When they read those words, she had somehow known her mother wouldn't welcome her back with open arms. Still, she had hoped she would at least acknowledge Macia and maybe even say how hard it had been to leave her girls behind. Something to lessen the pain Macia had carried for so long. Would the Breath of life be able to take that pain away? She smiles through the tears, knowing exactly what Riu would say to that. Her head agrees; she isn't sure how long till her heart will follow.

Soon, the girls have to leave Gax for the night, as the old woman comes in to check on him. "The helpers were fine when they came and introduced themselves this afternoon," she says when Macia asks. "They will need a lot of support and training," she tuts, "but over time, they will do well. It is good to have help, as I didn't go Downstream for nothing," she says, and Macia feels sad for the bitterness in her voice.

"We will have to help Gax," Caecilia says over breakfast, "as he will need to get stronger and able to move around. He wants to go back, but if he stays in bed too long, he could get complications, and he needs the fresh air." She glances through the open doorway, "He will need encouragement as well, as he has been feeling unwell."

Macia glances at Riu, who looks serious. "I'm sad he's feeling like that," he says, "we will need to ask God to breathe new life into Gax as well, so he will feel differently." Macia nods but keeps her thoughts to herself.

Caecilia looks at Macia and frowns a little. "He has lost a lot and been through much as well," she says.

Macia looks down at her plate. "He isn't the only one," she says, trying to keep her voice slow and relaxed, "but he still knows more than anyone about the Book and living for God. He must recover

CHAPTER 40

quickly. Being able to help others will make him feel better as well."

Caecilia's frown deepens. "He's sure to be praying for us, and there isn't much more he can do," she says, her face turning a little flushed. "He's come all this way, and…" She hesitates, she was going to mention the power of the Stream, but knows how that will be received by the others. "Nothing has gone the way he was expecting, so we need to look at it that way," she says in the end.

Macia gets up, arms crossed. She frowns at Caecilia. "I know it's my fault, or at least it feels that way. I was desperate to see my mother, and managed to persuade Gax to come along. But nothing has worked out the way we expected. You constantly make excuses for him, and…"

She stops, she can hear the anger in her voice, her eyes sting and she doesn't want to say more than she should. Maybe she has said too much already.

Caecilia gives a small sob. "I didn't want to go," she says, her voice wobbling. "I just didn't want to stay behind by myself. Maybe that is why it all went wrong, because I didn't have faith in the mission or didn't pray aright. And I do feel for Gax. And I…" She hesitates and in a soft voice continues, "I felt you had made him come and it made me resent the trip and…and you. And Gax, for going along."

Macia looks at her friend, tears flowing. "I'm sorry," she whispers, "I am sorry. I was wrong, although…although I still think God blessed us and good came out of it. I am sorry," she repeats and the girls hug for a long time. "I was angry with Gax, but mostly with myself because I knew I was the one who caused all this. The mission and everything, I mean," she says and Caecilia smiles through her tears, giving Macia another tight squeeze.

Macia dries her tears and sits down again. "I just pray that Gax will feel the blessing from now on," she says, "and that he will see the good that has come out of all the evil."

Siate smiles, "It'll be good for him when he sees the changes you have brought, and how the Book is affecting people. When he sees the Breath of Life at work in the village and maybe even in the clinic, it will revive Gax as well. It must be hard for him; like you say, nothing has gone according to plan."

Looking at her friends around her, Macia suddenly wonders what day it is. And how long they have till the first meeting. What will they do about songs? Macia and Caecilia don't know many off by heart. Maybe Gax can write a few out on some of their special paper? Can he write a message as well, or can they even carry him to the clinic? Has Felix some kind of transport? Otherwise, how do they get all those babies to the village? Macia's mind is racing ahead, and she sips some water, enjoying the voices of her friends around her, knowing it's not up to her alone.

Chapter 41

Macia looks around the village. She can't believe the changes that have taken place in the last weeks. The village is lively, with voices and laughter and the sound of children playing. She smiles at two little girls running past, dragging a wooden toy made by Riu. She turns at the sound of voices and watches Caecilia and Gax walk towards her. "How is the new leg?" She smiles at Gax, even though she can't remember when he last smiled back. "You're walking faster than yesterday, I'm sure," she continues, but her bright voice sounds too loud, even to herself.

"It still hurts, but they say it might get better," Gax says, "and although the leg is heavy, once it's on, it doesn't feel too bad. I nearly fell, but Caecilia held onto my stick so we were alright," and a little smile does appear, aimed at Caecilia, who nods.

"It's so much better, unlike my arms," she laughs and Macia pulls a face, rubbing her arms in response. "I can row longer than before, and I nearly made it the full length of the beach before I needed a rest," she adds, and Macia grins.

"Soon, you'll be able to do the beach as many times as you want," she laughs, "although my arms are happy with one stretch of beach at the moment. We might have help from tides and currents, I suppose, although that could work both ways. The boat is easy to manage, which helps. It's the endless paddling that makes it hard work."

"Once my leg no longer hurts, I will be able to help with the rowing as well," Gax adds, "but we might have to leave before the pain has gone. We should start thinking of going soon, as more help is needed than we can give."

Macia smiles but says nothing. Caecilia and Gax soon carry on with their walk around the village and Macia walks home. Their hut has been enlarged, having extra rooms added, so Riu, Siate and another girl from the Levato can stay in one hut. As she is sorting out various belongings and written notes, she sighs. She has been training every day to row the boat further, longer and faster, to get back to Mataiox, but her heart is not in it.

In her head, she can see her beautiful silver pen, and smooth, white paper. "Dearest friend," she starts and hesitates. "Dear friend, or even very dear friend," she doesn't want to think about what has changed, "so many things have changed in the village, as I wrote to you before. The village has changed. Many of the old people have gone, even the old woman." She squeezes her eyes shut, remembering the painful loss of the woman, who had enjoyed her last few days more than her entire life, it seemed.

"There are a few old people and we had three new ones a couple of days ago. Together with a bunch of babies." She smiles through her tears, remembering the rather chaotic few days that followed their arrival. "The young people are kept busy, the children have been to school more than a week and we have had three Resurrection Day meetings."

She frowns. The meetings aren't as easy as she had hoped. Gax is the one who knows the most, but he doesn't want to be in the front, because of his leg. Riu has read out the notes each time, after spending a long time preparing. Macia enjoys helping him, and she smiles, "So dear friend, in a way, I love it more when Riu reads the notes, as we get to read it together first, we discuss it and even change it, and then

CHAPTER 41

we pray together and read some parts of the Book together to make sure the talk will be right." She realises it's the best part of the week for her.

"Weeks are busy and it's hard to get time to sit and spend time with friends," she continues, the silver pen in her mind flying across the paper in even strokes. "Looking at the talk with Riu feels important enough to drop other things, so it's been a blessing. We often go down to the clinic together as well, as I practise my rowing and Riu checks Felix is doing well."

Felix has been a bit of a surprise, at least so far. "Felix has built several beautiful little lodges down in the jungle near the bay," she writes, "and they have people living in them already."

She sighs, the letter is not anywhere near finished, but it's dinner time. She waves at Halit, who is chatting to friends and collects the dinner for all of them. "I saw Gax walking around the village," Siate smiles at Macia and Caecilia. "I'm glad he is improving. The leg looks good, you're good with wood, Riu," she inclines her head towards Riu who shrugs. "I hope it will help Gax to feel better as well," Siate continues, "as he looked so sad the last few times I saw him. He must feel lonely in the clinic, and with the leg, he might get around more."

Macia nods, trying to smile and struggling to swallow her food. She isn't sure the wooden leg will improve Gax's mood. "He's been busy sorting out notes for the Book as well as writing the talks for the Meetings," she says, "and that will help to fill his days and make him feel part of the village."

"It's not the same though," Caecilia says softly, "It was only today, walking around longer, he saw how much had changed, and I think it helped him to see what he has been a part of; that he has contributed to all that, like the water system for the clinic, so little ones don't have to carry water anymore."

"Dear friend," Macia writes, leaning against a palm tree overlooking the blue water, "two more meetings have passed since Gax walked around the village for the first time. He has even been down to the clinic, and managed to upset Felix." She pulls a face, should she write this down, even if just in her head? Maybe this is more a matter for prayer, she decides, and moves on with the letter instead. "I don't know about leaving. What am I going to do in Mataiox? Do my training, I suppose, but I'm learning things here as well. I love working with Riu. And with Siate," she adds quickly, "and to see the babies growing, and the young children able to read the first few verses we gave them from the Book, that's been so special."

Macia's eyes fill with tears, "I don't think I want to leave, dear friend," she whispers out loud, then looks over both shoulders in turn, shocked by her own words. But it's true, she doesn't want to go and leave Riu. Or the village.

Just then, she spots Riu coming up the path, straight towards her. He smiles as he sees her, his eyes lighting up. "You look serious," he says, and his eyes lose some of their light, "I hope you are feeling well? Soon, you will be leaving," he swallows and looks across the blue bay as well, towards the distance, where the wide bay turns into a river, ready to carry the three young people away from the village, the jungle and the clinic. "Are you ready?" he asks after a few quiet minutes, and Macia shakes her head, tears suddenly on her cheeks.

"I am not ready at all, I don't want to leave," she says, trying to catch the sob before it escapes, and Riu takes her hand in his warm, tanned hands. He doesn't say anything, simply looks at her. "I was thinking about it, a moment before you came along," she says, having to smile a little, "and I realised that I don't want to go. I love helping in the village and down here; I love working with you, being with you and the others," she adds quickly, "and the thought of having to return to Mataiox and never see you again…" Her voice trails off as tears come too fast to carry on speaking.

CHAPTER 41

Riu holds her close, his hand firm on her shoulder blade, the other one cradling her shoulder. "Don't cry, just breathe," he says softly. "Simply ask for the Breath of Life to fill you, and your mind and hear His voice telling you where He wants you to go. Maybe He wants you here, to carry on bringing life to us, or maybe there is a path He wants you to follow in Mataiox. He will breathe life into you, and give you all you need, for He will supply what you need, like we saw in the Meeting Room last time."

Macia nods against his shoulder and tries to take deeper breaths, and soon, she feels calmer. She stands up straighter, drying her face, embarrassed to see the large wet patch on Riu's shoulder. He follows her gaze and laughs softly. "It's good we're in the jungle," he teases, "for being wet on your shoulder could mean anything." He touches her wet face. "Feeling unsure about returning isn't a bad thing," he says, "it's good to talk to God about everything, as you might go the wrong path if you don't stop and think. I love having you here. You are special to me. To us," he chuckles at Macia's look, and shakes his head, "I mean it. You are special, and I…" He looks away and swallows several times. "Without you here, everything will be different," he whispers. "The Meetings, the preparation for the Meetings, the walks through the jungle, the care for the others, everything will change. I don't know what life will be like when you're gone. I can only imagine, and I don't want to think that far ahead. I know help might come, but it's not the help we want or need."

He turns abruptly, "I can't say more," he tries to smile, "as you need to listen to God, rather than use my feelings or emotions as a path to follow. He will shine on your path, it said so in that very long special poem in the Book," he grins, his face sunny once more. "Come, let's go and eat then see if the young people need help in the night."

Macia takes his hand, letting herself be pulled away from the tree. After one last look at the palm trees and the white sand, they set off towards the village.

Macia looks at her friends over dinner. Gax has been eating with them for the last few days, and Macia stares down at her plate. Mealtimes have changed. Gone are the light-hearted chatter and fun stories. Gax's input usually ends with his wish to be back home, to go up the river and see his parents. To get the medical help he needs, to get the village more help... Macia sighs, but catching Riu's eyes, she sits up straighter. "I have been thinking," she says, and adds, "praying as well, asking God to make things clear. And He has. I won't be going to Mataiox this time. I will be staying here, in the village."

She hesitates, and decides to carry on eating as if it's no big deal, but her hands shake as she watches Caecilia's face. "Stay here? But what about..." Caecilia's voice trails off and she smiles a little. "Actually, I'm not surprised," she says, "you have enjoyed the last few weeks, and you and Riu have done a great job. Everything has changed and I know other things will change as well. I will miss you," she says, her eyes suddenly filled with tears, her voice wobbly. "It will be so hard without you, and part of me hopes you'll change your mind."

Macia grins, her lips trembling, "I... thank you, I can't imagine changing my mind, but it's always possible," she says, trying to cheer up her friend. "I will be so sad when you're gone, but I need to stay here, I know, but I will miss you a lot. If only there was a way to write?"

Riu leans forward, "There is still a link between Colchuyni and Felix. He hasn't said anything, but letters can be sent through my mother to Felix. You will have to do it once a year though, although Gax might find a regular route via boat?" He grins at Gax, trying to pull him into the conversation.

"I can't believe you won't return with us; it's a long way to row," Gax says, ignoring Riu. "We will miss you in Mataiox, and what will I

CHAPTER 41

tell the Mission School and my parents? They might be worried for you. What if something happens? Who will sort out your room and your belongings? Others will have to do that as well." And he looks down at his leg, and sniffs.

Caecilia pats his hand and assures him she will look after Macia's belongings for as long as needed.

"The Breath of Life will sustain us, and we will rest in the palm of His hand," Riu says, his voice low and the words deliberate. "We will rest in Him, and follow His path through this life's jungle, and never be lost or in danger of falling." He stirs his food, "We have His Book, and it will be our guide, like a lamp in the darkest night. We have His breath, giving us life and everything we need. We will miss you, of course, but we will remember that you will be guided and protected by the same Hands."

The last week flies past and Macia is shocked to find herself on the white sand, watching Gax climb into the small boat, Caecilia smiling at him, helping him to balance. "We will write as soon as we can, and we will pray that another contact route can be set up. Linu might be able to do something via radio, who knows! Felix said it wasn't impossible. Write a letter as well, so it can be taken to us as soon as the mudflats are exposed." She sighs, grabbing Macia's hands, "I will miss you so much. I'm sad to leave you, but happy for you, for you're glowing and enjoying the challenge, and I can see that. Remember us," she says, her voice breaking, and Macia squeezes her hands.

"I will be praying for a safe journey," she smiles at her friends, "and I can't wait to read your letter. Also, I will continue to pray that we will see each other again as well."

Macia watches them rowing away, waving every few strokes until the boat is a little speck on the sunlit water. She still stands there, her toes digging into the warm sand, her fingers tightly linked with Riu's warm ones. She finally releases her breath when he whispers, "Are you ready for the next chapter in our lives? It could be a poem, like in my favourite part of the Book. We can sing His song together, and see His breath move through the village, the clinic, the jungle, and even Colchuyni. Let's drink from the streams of Living water, and see it transform everything."

Macia glances one more time at the blue waters, and she is sure she can feel the breeze entering her heart, giving her courage and strength, filling her with unspeakable joy as she walks away with Riu towards the jungle.

Acknowledgements

First of all, this book has taken a lot longer than I hoped. I blame it on Goldie, our young Labrador, and my children's evening activities…

It was such a pleasure to be back with Gax, Macia and Caecilia. I had been looking forward to visiting Downstream, and here we are! The journey with them has been wonderful, frustrating and surprising in equal measures, so I hope you have enjoyed it as well!

My thanks as always to Beverley Haagensen who works so hard to shape and mould my words into proper English. I'm so grateful for your prayers, suggestions and support throughout, my wonderful friend!

Special thanks for all things ferret go to Catherine L Owen, who showed us her ferrets during special Zoom chats, and inspired me to add them into a book. Any misunderstandings of ferrets is on me, and I assure you, no ferrets were harmed in the writing of this story.

Thank you to Richard and my four wonderful children as well. I have enjoyed finding time to sit and write, and I'm grateful for the opportunities and allowances you have all made!

And most of all I'm grateful to God who saves, breathing His Life into our souls, bringing us from darkness into His light. Writing about faith gives me so much joy and is such a blessing. I'm so pleased to share this blessing with others, praying for those that read my books and as always, I would love to hear from you! Feel free to email me at vicarious.ome@gmail.com or visit my website at https://www.vicarioushome.com

www.ingramcontent.com/pod-product-compliance
Lightning Source LLC
Chambersburg PA
CBHW030253100526
44590CB00012B/392